Designing Web Graphics

Lynda Weinman

New Riders Publishing, Indianapolis, Indiana

Designing Web Graphics

By Lynda Weinman

Published by:
New Riders Publishing
201 West 103rd Street
Indianapolis, IN 46290 USA

Printed in the United States of America   2 3 4 5 6 7 8 9 0

CIP data available upon request

Warning and Disclaimer

This book is designed to provide information about designing Web graphics. Every effort has been made to make this book as complete and as accurate as possible, but no warranty or fitness is implied.

The information is provided on an "as is" basis. The author(s) and New Riders Publishing shall have neither liability nor responsibility to any person or entity with respect to any loss or damages arising from the information contained in this book or from the use of the disks or programs that may accompany it.

Publisher	*Don Fowley*
Publishing Manager	*David Dwyer*
Marketing Manager	*Ray Robinson*
Managing Editor	*Tad Ringo*

This book was produced digitally by Macmillan Computer Publishing and manufactured using 100% computer-to-plate technology (filmless process), by Shepard Poorman Communications Corporation, Indianapolis, Indiana.

Development Editor
John Kane

Production Editor
Laura Frey

Associate Marketing Manager
Tamara Apple

Acquisitions Coordinator
Stacey Beheler

Publisher's Assistant
Karen Opal

Cover Designer
Karen Ruggles

Book Designer
Sandra Schroeder

Manufacturing Coordinator
Paul Gilchrist

Production Manager
Kelly Dobbs

Production Team Supervisor
Laurie Casey

Graphics Image Specialists
Clint Lahnen
Laura Robbins
Craig Small
Todd Wente

Production Analysts
Jason Hand
Bobbi Satterfield

Production Team
Troy A. Barnes
Kim Cofer
Joe Millay
Erika Millen
Beth Rago
Gina Rexrode
Erich J. Richter
Christine Tyner
Karen Walsh

Indexer
Gina Brown

About the Author

Lynda Weinman teaches Motion Graphics, Interactive Media Design, Digital Imaging, and Web Design at Art Center College of Design in Pasadena. She writes for a number of trade magazines and journals on similar subjects. Her animation work on television, feature films, and music videos using desktop computer tools has earned her national recognition. In her alleged spare time, she draws cats with her six-year old daughter, Jamie.

Trademark Acknowledgments

All terms mentioned in this book that are known to be trademarks or service marks have been appropriately capitalized. New Riders Publishing cannot attest to the accuracy of this information. Use of a term in this book should not be regarded as affecting the validity of any trademark or service mark. QuickTime and the QuickTime Logo are trademarks used under license.

Acknowledgments

A very special thanks to the incredible Bruce Heavin, who made images, files, tests, and Web pages for this book. He painted the awesome book cover art, too.

My primary support system—Mary Thorpe, Joy Silverman, and Ali Karp—who offered monumental helpfulness, intelligence, talent, and motherly advice!

David Dwyer, the best publishing manager a gurrrl could want.

Susan Grode, the best attorney a gurrrl could want.

My various editors at *The Net*, *Digital Video*, *MacUser*, *New Media*, *Macromedia Users Journal*, and *Step-by-Step Graphics* who put up with my insistence that I only write about Web graphics until this book was finished.

My students and associates at Art Center who had to constantly listen to me moan about how tired I was from staying up the night before to meet my book deadlines.

My friends who learned to stop bugging me to call back or go out with them.

My six-year old daughter, Jamie, who put up admirably without having her mommy around as much as usual.

The rest of my family, who didn't see or hear from me for many months.

My dear friend and an exceptional computer artist Rand Worell, whose long, heroic battle with AIDS ended while I was writing this book. His memory will forever serve as an inspiration to me and all the other lives he touched.

Elmers, the sweetest kitty soul that ever was, who also passed while I was writing this book.

Douglas Kirkland, who took photographs of computer monitors in Chapter 2, when he could have been shooting a famous hunk, starlet, astronaut, or politician.

Mark Wheaton and Erik Holsinger for their invaluable help with the Toons and Tunes chapter.

David Theurer, author of DeBabelizer, for his help with several of the chapters.

Classic PIO Partners, for letting me use their great stock photo images from their Nostalgia CD-ROM.

Crystal Waters for emergency edit patrol and morale boosting.

John Kane and Laura Frey, whose "edits from hell" helped this book immeasurably.

Sandra Schroeder for doing an awesome job on the interior book design. Also, thank you to Gina Rexrode for laying out the book so beautifully.

Don Barnett for the great type design on the book jacket.

All the rest, who helped with advice, expertise, and support:

Dean Chamberlain, Linda Stone, Eddie Yip, Francoise Kirkland, Dave Tubbs, my incredible brother, Bill Weinman (look for his CGI book from New Riders, coming soon to bookstores near you), Jaime Levy, Marina Zurkow, Jeffry Dachis, Craig Kanarick, Brian Patrick Lee, Bart Nagle, Ann Monn, Chris Gwynne, Lior Saar, David Biedny, Marian Whitwell (Jamie's grandma) who took the infamous picture of Jamie's head, Philip Skeen, Gudren Frommez, George Maestri, Spencer Hunt, Joe Maller, Juan Gonzalez, Yoshinobo Takahas, Jeff Masud, Chris Casady, Susan Kitchens, Robin Berman, Art Holland, Eric Hardman, the Web design team at Disney, George Wright, Chauncey Cummings, Kathy Tafel, Shel Kimen, Scott Wimer, Sarah Hahn, Dominique Stillet, Khyal Braun, Joey Anuff, Rich Young, Debbie Lefkowitz, and Mark Thomas. And everyone who I forgot, please forgive me; once I get some sleep, my brain should work again!

New Riders Publishing

The staff of New Riders Publishing is committed to bringing you the very best in computer reference material. Each New Riders book is the result of months of work by authors and staff who research and refine the information contained within its covers.

As part of this commitment to you, the New Riders reader, New Riders invites your input. Please let us know if you enjoy this book, if you have trouble with the information and examples presented, or if you have a suggestion for the next edition.

Please note, though: New Riders staff cannot serve as a technical resource for Web graphics or for questions about software- or hardware-related problems. Please refer to the documentation that accompanies your Web browser or to the applications' Help systems.

If you have a question or comment about any New Riders book, there are several ways to contact New Riders Publishing. We will respond to as many readers as we can. Your name, address, or phone number will never become part of a mailing list or be used for any purpose other than to help us continue to bring you the best books possible. You can write us at the following address:

New Riders Publishing
Attn: Publisher
201 W. 103rd Street
Indianapolis, IN 46290

If you prefer, you can fax New Riders Publishing at (317) 581-4670.

You can also send electronic mail to New Riders at the following Internet address:

ddwyer@newriders.mcp.com

New Riders is an imprint of Macmillan Computer Publishing. To obtain a catalog or information, or to purchase any Macmillan Computer Publishing book, call (800) 428-5331.

Thank you for selecting *Designing Web Graphics*!

Contents at a Glance

Table of Contents

Introduction

Given all the incredible advancements in computer graphics today, it's hard to go backward and embrace techniques that seem primitive, outdated, and inferior. The Web might be considered by many the latest, most advanced technology in computing, but not to most artists. Even though graphics on the Web are what make it so popular and exciting, the tools and techniques used to create visuals are confusing and limited. Most graphic designers and computer artists using today's advanced imaging programs are going to be lost when it comes to authoring for the Web. This book is designed to help.

When I went to my favorite technical bookstore less than one year ago looking for a book on Web graphics it wasn't there. Back then, there were two books on HTML; a dozen the next time I looked, and now I wouldn't even venture to count how many books are out there about the Web, HTML, and the Internet. So, what *exactly* was in the book I couldn't find, and what possessed me to decide to write it upon discovery that it didn't exist?

As an artist, teacher, and writer, my first concern was to understand how to prepare artwork and media for the Web. Though it was also important to understand HTML, I found plenty of books and online sources to teach that. I looked at the Web the first time and wondered, why did some pictures have blue boxes while others didn't? How come some images started blocky and appeared to res-up into focus? How could I make non-rectangular art appear to float freely on a background? How did people put patterned backgrounds into their pages? What were the steps for preparing movies and audio? Most of the HTML books and Web page-based instructional materials I found didn't directly address these issues, or simply skimmed over them.

I've been teaching digital imaging, motion graphics, and interactive multimedia design for the past five years, and working professionally in related fields for the past 13. When I started college back in 1973 personal computers were not yet in existence. I started using computers in 1982 and have since taught myself most everything I know. I think this makes me a natural teacher, as I remember what it was like before I understood something, and try to reconstruct my learning process for others. I attempt to deliver my class materials with as non-technical and non-intimidating an approach as possible, and hope this same tone translates to my first book as well.

In multimedia, there are many roles, and you rarely find one person capable of filling all of them. I teach classes with the philosophy that my students will graduate to become art directors, visual content creators, and production artists for multimedia, video, film, and print. They will likely be teamed with programmers and technicians, and not expected to know the nuances and intricacies of writing interactive code, wiring a video studio, or running a linotronic imagesetting machine.

The same is true of the Web. It's important to understand the differences among the roles of programmer, information designer, and visual designer. All have great importance, but they are not necessarily going to be filled by the same person. Though this book is written with an artist's perspective in mind, I expect it will appeal to many Webmistresses and masters, HTML programmers, Web wordsmiths, and everyday folks who don't necessarily consider themselves artistically gifted. Because artists and programmers are going to occupy the same Web space, understanding each other's craft will always contribute to make the best possible content.

The Web's popularity is growing at a phenomenal rate. Last term, almost *half* of the undergraduate and graduate students I trained were asked to design Web pages as their first paying gig after graduating from art school. Graphic designers are no longer expected to only understand print mediums. If your client wants a Web site, they will most likely look first to you as the visual authority for their needs. If you don't know how to do Web publishing, they will look elsewhere, because having a Web site is quickly becoming as necessary as any other component in a visual identity system. In the future, a Web site address will be as common to many businesses as today's business card or custom designed letterhead.

Why the Web?

When I first looked at the Web I was somewhat appalled. Judging it from an aesthetic viewpoint only, it was a jungle. Though there's good work out there, it's still mostly a mess, and many ask "Why bother now, shouldn't we just wait until it gets better?" I had one designer friend say, "Wake me up in ten years when they get this all figured out!" There are many parallels to Web design and the early days of desktop publishing. Remember what happened to typography with the invention of the laser printer? Designers were horrified to see page layouts generated with bad spacing, poor font choices, mismanaged type sizes, and an uneducated sense of placement. Things have settled down since then, and with a little maturity the same will be true of the Web.

There are plenty of reasons to jump in now. First of all, there's never been a distribution medium like the Web. Where else could you reach a potential audience of millions of people without spending a fortune in time, money, and research to mail your work to them? It's platform-independent. The Web doesn't care if you're on a Mac, Windows, Sun, or SGI workstation. There are no geographical boundaries. Someone in Germany can look at my site as easily as someone who lives around the corner. It's democratic. The Web has no hierarchy. By looking at a site, you can't tell if the author is male, female, black, white, Asian, Hispanic, handicapped, rich, poor, old, or young. If you have a cool site, there's no one stopping more viewers from visiting yours than any number of boring well-funded corporate sites. Is this really an example of where the best designer wins? So far, yes. It represents freedom of expression in its most idealistic, raw form.

NOTE

I am not advocating that you do not learn HTML. In the world of programming languages, this is one of the simplest and easiest to learn. It is key to understanding what can and cannot be done, and there are plenty of hot shot sites out there designed by those who do understand how to code. Equally, some of the better sites are also created by artists who don't know a word of HTML.

I'm not saying, don't learn this. I'm just saying it is not necessary to know it in order to participate as an art director or Web site designer. There are also plenty of other, better sources for HTML instruction than this book. From my experience as an art college teacher, I know that many visually gifted people are intimidated by programming, and I think the Web needs more visually gifted contributors. I'm suggesting that you participate, whether you focus on learning the code or making the artwork or both. There's room for everyone.

Whatever skeptics might say, visuals are what have made the World Wide Web the fastest growing part of the Internet. Artists are going to define the look and feel of the place, and I doubt there's ever been another opportunity where individuals, not large ad agencies and corporations, have had a chance to influence a medium of this magnitude. This is the world unlike any of us ever dreamed—all connected across geographical and computer platform boundaries, all capable of being interactive spectators or active contributors. The old paradigm of commercially driven, spoon-fed entertainment and information is a thing of the past, and let's hope it stays that way. It's truly revolutionary.

The Web, like all graphical user interfaces, is easy to view and use, but more difficult to create for. It's one of those ironies life is full of; if it looks easy to use, it's generally hard to make. Multimedia is one of the most intense disciplines in computer graphics, as it combines many different mediums into one. As a result, this book is intended for designers who are already computer literate. Most of the software references relate to professional imaging tools, like Adobe Photoshop, Illustrator, and Fractal Painter. I've tried to stick to cross-platform tools and am writing the book on a PC and a Mac to make sure it can help artists on both sides. I do not make direct references to tools found on Unix-based computers, because I don't own one, but many of the principles described here will be helpful to artists working on those platforms as well.

This book is not another HTML book. I include HTML code only when it relates to supporting visual or external media. If you want to create your own Web site with no help from a programmer, you should buy an HTML book, or go to one of the many sites on the Web that offer HTML instruction for free. (Check out the CD-ROM for URLs and links to these sites.) This book is designed to help with the less obvious, but not less important, side of the equation—that of the visual content.

The World Wide Web is the first true multimedia medium for the masses. It's the wild west days of the Internet, where individuals can set the rules and standards, and there's plenty of uncharted territory around to homestead your own way. It is most clearly a craft in its infancy. Designing for the Web is like going backward in time; a throwback to graphics of the early days before 32-bit color and high resolution. I still maintain that an artist can make appealing visuals regardless of a tool's limit; that's why they call us artists. Though there are many frustrations and technical barriers to designing for the Web, the potential rewards, in my mind at least, far outweigh the limitations.

How This Book Works

This book has many chapters, but it's divided into two sections—Background Information and Lessons. The first section will give you an understanding of what environment you're dealing with: browsers, cross-platform compatibility, color palettes, file formats, and creating small image files. The second section will offer exercises and examples of working with hexadecimal color values, making patterns, aligning graphics, using transparency, making movies and sounds, and all kinds of other things.

Use the glossary when you come across a term or word you don't understand. I've done my best to make few assumptions and keep technical jargon to a minimum, but that doesn't mean I can or should entirely avoid Web-, computer-, and graphic-specific terminology.

Chapter 1—Browser Hell!

A look at the same page in all the major Web browsers, the ramifications of designing for a moving target, the notion of designing different versions of a site for different browsers, and a handy visual reference for which design features work where.

Chapter 2—Cross-Platform Hell!

This chapter discusses what happens when graphics are viewed on different computers, in different color spaces, with different monitor sizes, and what you can do about it.

Chapter 3—Making Low-Memory Graphics

Chapter 3 is a comparison of the two most supported still image file formats: GIFs and JPEGs. Visual reference of the same image saved at different JPEG compression rates, and GIFs saved at different bit-depths.

Chapter 4—Color Palette Hell!

This chapter covers understanding 8-bit and 24-bit graphics and which types of images work best at different bit-depths. Demonstrations are included on how to create 8-bit palettes for different types of browsers and images. Browser palette handling is described, and a browser-safe palette that will not dither in Netscape, Mosaic, or Internet Explorer is identified with instruction on how to use it on custom graphics.

Chapter 5—Fun with Hex

Learn how to change the color of backgrounds, body text, hypertext, visited link text, and active link text. Hexadecimal color charts of non-dithering browser colors, organized by value and hue, are provided. URLs to Web-based hex charts, and pages where you can convert Photoshop RGB readings to hex are included. Instruction on how to use shareware applications from the CD-ROM for converting RGB to hex is provided.

Chapter 6—Making Background Patterns

Step-by-step instruction on how to make seamless patterns using Photoshop. Valuable tips such as understanding what size to make pattern tiles and checking if your type is legible against the background you've designed are included. Help is offered for choosing which file format to save pattern tiles in.

Chapter 7—Making Irregularly Shaped Artwork Using Background Colors

This chapter provides a simple approach to making irregularly shaped graphics.

Chapter 8—Making Irregularly Shaped Artwork Using Transparency

Find out how to make transparent GIFs with clean edges. Examine the results of using aliasing versus anti-aliasing. This chapter also includes instruction for setting up files for transparency in Photoshop and Painter. Use shareware applications from the CD-ROM for setting Transparency and the official Photoshop Gif89a plug-in from Adobe.

Chapter 9—Typography for the Web-Impaired

This chapter describes how to change font sizes for HTML-based text. Learn how to use Photoshop and Illustrator to make image-based graphics that include type and use the proper HTML to include graphics on Web pages.

Chapter 10—Fun with Alignment

Understand how to make invisible placement objects to create more interesting page layouts. This chapter includes specifying the dimensions of an image to make type align to it. Understand and use HTML alignment tags to position graphics and text on Web pages.

Chapter 11—Horizontal Rules!

Learn how to change the shape, size, and alignment of HTML-based horizontal rules. Includes lessons on making custom horizontal and vertical rule art with Photoshop and Illustrator.

Chapter 12—Bullets-o-Rama

This chapter covers how to create custom bullets for lists using Photoshop and Illustrator. Look at the CD-ROM for some bullet ideas and libraries.

Chapter 13—Hot Spots

Make image maps and images that link to other graphics or pages. Includes instruction on using shareware image map utilities found on the CD-ROM.

Chapter 14—Table Manners

Chapter 14 shows you how to use tables to align type and create interesting page layouts.

Chapter 15—Dynamic Documents

This chapter covers making kinetic screens using animated GIFs, Server Push and Client Pull. Examples are included that use files and CGI scripts stored on the CD-ROM.

Chapter 16—Toons and Tunes

Learn how to prepare sound and media files. File format comparisons, compression guidelines, file-naming protocols, and information on streaming data (real-time audio) is also included.

Chapter 17—Pre-Visualizing Web Pages

Use Photoshop layers to mock-up a Web page. This chapter covers how to simulate pattern fills, blocks of text, and accurately place images.

Chapter 18—HTML Templates for Designers

This chapter provides examples of how to use our templates for making Web pages in minutes.

Appendix A—HTML for Visual Designers

This appendix is a quick instructional guide with tips and troubleshooting techniques for loading graphics to servers, checking pages from your hard drive, and working with proper file naming protocols. It is a compendium of commonly used HTML commands to do things graphic designers want to do, such as setting background colors, text sizing, image placement, and so on. All of these commands will be dealt with in detail in other chapters; this will serve as a quick and handy reference.

Appendix B—Glossary of Web Terms

This provides definitions of all technical words used in the book.

The *Designing Web Graphics* CD-ROM

The companion CD-ROM has helper applications that would take hours to download from FTP sites all over the Web. I've tried to put everything in one place; all the tools, guides, HTML, and online resources needed to understand how to design for the Web that I could gather are either in this book or on the CD-ROM. You'll also find companion tutorial files to some of the chapters, as well as clip-art and demo software.

If you don't have a CD-ROM player, most of the exercises and URLs are printed in the book.

Notes and Tips

Designing Web Graphics features special sidebars—Notes and Tips—which are set apart from the normal text by icons. These passages have been given special treatment so that you can instantly recognize their significance and easily find them for future reference.

> **NOTE**
> Notes include extra information you should find useful. A Note may describe special situations that can arise as you work on the Web, and may tell you what steps to take when such situations arise.

> **TIP**
> Tips provide quick instructions for your design or Web work. A Tip might show you how to speed up a procedure, or how to perform one of many time-saving and system-enhancing techniques.

What You Will Need

Starting out doing an unfamiliar task, such as Web design, one's natural first concern is: "What do I need to get started?" As you can see by the content on the Web today, all kinds of participants using all kinds of software and platforms have come together with varying degrees of successful results. The truth is, you need to think about content before worrying about tools to make a successful Web site. Once you've gotten a solid idea and plan, working with limited tools is much easier.

I am sharing my personal viewpoints about which tools work better and what hardware and software is optimum to do Web design. Having used computers since 1982, I have a different attitude from many folks starting today. I know what's possible with primitive tools, and sometimes scarcity is the best Mother of Invention. The only thing that really stands between primitive tools and good Web design is human creativity and skill (and patience!).

We find ourselves at an odd juncture in Web design today. We have powerful computers and powerful software, and we're working within limits that more primitive tools and software might be better suited for. Because there's no turning back—I certainly don't want to give up Photoshop or my Power Mac, and neither do you—I've made suggestions that are geared toward professional people like myself. If you don't have access to high-powered computers and expensive software, don't let my suggestions discourage you.

HTML Editor

One of the first questions I am always asked by Web designer newbies is, "What HTML editor should I use?" I typically say, "None." HTML editors (word processors that have HTML tags built-in, like <a href=""></a> for example) are only helpful if you understand HTML in the first place. What good is having an automated HTML tag handy if you don't know where to put it or what it does?

A new breed of WYSIWYG (What You See Is What You Get, pronounced wiz-zywig) HTML editors are also on the horizon. They will hide HTML tags from your unsuspecting eyes and let you type in bold, set tabs, place images, and do many things that page layout programs allow, with a Web-savvy twist. They will create an HTML document for you, without you having to know a word of it!

WYSIWYG editors have great promise. I am sure I will want to use one for *certain* things. If you are a casual dabbler in Web-page creation, they might serve your purposes fully. I think they actually will support the majority of users very well.

For professional Web designers, my guess is it will still be handy to understand HTML at its code level. When new features are announced (and they are, on a regular basis), a dedicated HTML editor is not going to understand the new tags. If you're practicing some of the more advanced techniques described in this book, such as working with tables for images, push and pull, or trying to pre-visualize how components look together before you commit to them, my guess is none of these editors will help.

If you are going to design artwork for Web sites, I believe it's still an important exercise to work with writing your own HTML code before you buy or obtain an editor. As these editors mature, I reserve the right to change my opinion!

Personally, I work with a standard word processor and type all my HTML code from scratch. I find that HTML editors bog me down, as I'm generally trying new things, checking them, modifying them, and so on. I have the luxury of enough RAM to let me have my browser and word processor open at the same time, and go between them regularly at breakneck pace!

Learning HTML

HTML (HyperText Markup Language) is the type of code required to publish graphics, text and files on the Web. If you've never used a programming language before, HTML can be intimidating.

A great way to teach yourself HTML is to use the view source command

found in most Web browsers. This command is usually found on a top menu and shouldn't be hard to locate. Viewing the source will show you the HTML source code of anybody's Web page, allowing you to reverse-engineer what they've done. This is one of the best and easiest ways to teach yourself HTML. Figure I.1 shows my home page, and the HTML source code used to generate my page follows.

Figure I.1

Here's what my personal page looks like on the Web.

If you were to use View Source on my page, here's the HTML source code you'd see.

```
<HTML>
<HEAD><center><TITLE>Lynda's Homegurrlpage</TITLE>
<BODY background= "ltspiralpat.gif" text="002E42" link="330066" vlink="330066">
</HEAD>
<p>
<center><img src="newlogo.gif">
</BODY>
<br><P>
<center><img src="man.gif">
<br><P>
<hr size=8 width=8>
<P>
<strong>News 'o Mine</strong>
<P>
The <strong>BIG</strong> news is I'm writing a book on <strong>Web
Design</strong> <br>for <strong>New Riders Publishers</strong>. Help me out, if
you want!  <br>Send <strong><A
HREF="mailto:MoShun@aol.com">me</A> </strong>links of pages you like, or
questions you wanna get answered.<br><p>
</BODY>
</HTML>
```

Software

This book assumes that you already work with imaging software. Adobe's Photoshop is an industry standard among design professionals. Photoshop is available for Macs, PCs, Unix, and Sun Workstations.

Photoshop is just a tool. It's a damn fine one, but in the hands of a great artist it will produce great art and in the hands of a mediocre artist it will produce mediocre art. It is not a replacement for human creativity, skill, or understanding.

I've seen great sites that were created in shareware imaging programs, or imaging software that was a lot less complex and expensive than Photoshop. It would be great to have time and space to address every software package that offered useful tools for Web design, but it's not possible.

Therefore, this book assumes that you own Photoshop and have an understanding of the basic principles of how to use Photoshop. If you don't, skip those parts, or see if you can understand them and figure out how to do the same exercise in your imaging program. Or, get Photoshop! Most people who get Photoshop are quite happy about it. It's a joy to work with software that can do as many things as this remarkable product.

The truth is, almost 100 percent of all well-designed sites use Photoshop to some degree. Photoshop books are ubiquitous in computer sections of bookstores. I recommend you invest in one or more if you're going to be a serious Web designer.

I've tried to stick to software packages in this book that are cross-platform between Macs and PCs.

Here's a list of software that's discussed in the book:

- **Photoshop 3.0.** Imaging software for creating graphics and photographic image processing.

- **Premiere 4.0.** Movie and sound software for creating movie and audio files.

- **Painter 3.1.** Imaging software for graphics and photographic image processing.

- **Illustrator 5.1 for Macs, Illustrator 4.0 for Windows.** Excellent type and illustration tools.

- **Netscape Navigator 1.1N and 2.0.** Recommended browser for testing your Web pages.

We also have tons of helper applications and utilities on the CD-ROM. You will find cross-platform tools that cover the following features:

- Transparent GIFs

- Progressive JPEGs

- Server Push

- Hexadecimal Calculations

- Pattern-Making

- Typography

- Browsers and Plug-ins

- Palettes and CLUTs

- File Conversion

- Quicktime Flattening

- Codecs

Hardware

The ideal set-up for a Web design studio would be to own a Mac, PC, Sun, and SGI, have a full video and sound studio, and own all the imaging, video, sound, and authoring software in the universe. No one will be quite so lucky, but that gives you an idea of how limitless the possibilities are for equipment acquisitions!

So, here are some very general guidelines. Macs and PCs are going to have the widest range of Web-design tools. Most of your Web audience will be on Macs or PCs. So, if you're lucky enough to work on a higher-end platform, you might consider getting one of these lower-end platforms to author Web pages on for several reasons. One, most of your audience will be on a Mac or PC, and this will give you a reality checkpoint. Two, there are more Web authoring tools on Macs and PCs than on other computer platforms.

If you are like most of us, you have limited budgets and time. This system will offer great versatility to the novice or professional Web designer:

Color Mac or PC

20 MB of RAM or more

24-bit color card

16-bit sound card

13" or bigger monitor

1 gigabyte hard drive

CD-ROM 2x speed or faster

My personal setup is much more opulent. Understand that I've been doing digital design for 11 years and make my living this way. Plus, I do a lot of video work on the same system, so it's a little more embellished than what you'd necessarily need for your average Web design studio.

Power PC 7100/80	Pentium 110 MHz
Internal 2x CD-ROM	Internal 4x CD-ROM
24-bit 17" monitor	15" monitor
40 MB RAM	16 MB RAM
Numerous Hard drives (over 3 gigs total)	1 gig internal Hard Drive
200 MB Removable Syquest Drive	24-bit color card
ISDN 3Com Impact Rate Converter	
Global Village Teleport Platinum 28.8 modem	US Robotics 28.8 modem

Everything Will Change

Like most first-time authors, this book was an intense undertaking and consumed most of my waking hours. It was especially difficult, I think, because the Web itself is always growing and evolving. It's hard to ever feel finished or complete when your subject matter is changing on an almost hourly basis.

I will share a little personal philosophy about this: I recently had someone who made his living through digital photography remark to me that he was not looking forward to the next version of his primary software application because he didn't want to have to learn it all over again. I told him that I felt exactly the opposite—when a new version of a favorite software program is released I cannot wait to tear into it and try every new feature until I've examined them all.

Software by nature is fluid. It will always change. That is its purpose! If it stayed the same, we would all complain. If the Web stays the same we shall all go mad! I want to see the Web get better. I want to see all software improve and provide tools for self-expression that are faster, easier, and cheaper for everyone.

If you plan to make your living doing anything in the digital arts, changing software is a fact you will not only have to accept, but embrace. It makes life rather interesting however, especially when you're trying to write a book about it!

As I was finishing this book, there were new announcements occurring on a daily basis. Netscape Navigator 2.0 was just announced, which promises to support many new partnerships. Microsoft's Web Explorer was looking to compete neck and neck with Netscape's feature set. Who knows, in this race to be better and bigger, what new announcement will be in effect tomorrow.

That's why having a Web-site-based companion to this book is critical. My home page, entitled "Lynda's Homegurrrl Page" can be found at http://www.lynda.com. I offer it to you as a resource to find new information and links to other interesting places.

Even with changing browsers, HTML, and future options that we cannot even imagine, there are certain principles that stay the same. The intent of this book was to focus on image preparation and design, not HTML. Making images small will be an issue for a long time to come. Working with limited palettes and tools is a reality that's here for the time being. Knowing how to create media, regardless of the platform or application, will be a part of Web design forever.

CHAPTER 1   Browser Hell!

Web browsers are the adversaries of all Web designers. What is a browser, and what does it do? It's software that reads Web pages and displays them for you. There are many different World Wide Web browsers, and no two are alike. Unfortunately, this means that different browsers interpret the visual content of a Web page differently. If you are a designer, this means you have the maddening task of designing a presentation that is subject to change according to which browser its being viewed from.

Why do browsers interpret the pages differently—shouldn't there be fixed standards? The browser interprets HTML (Hypertext Markup Language) code, which is the type of programming required to author Web pages. HTML uses "tags" for including links, graphics, and other media on a Web page.

HTML was created as an attempt to be a universally accepted, cross-platform standard language for displaying information, text, and visuals on the Web. Standards usually involve a standards committee, and committees often take a long time to agree on what they will officially support. HTML of the old days allowed for one-color text, text that was left-justified with paragraph breaks, left-justified images, and little else. This understandably created frustration among designers and Web browser developers, who wanted to see the Web evolve faster than the time it took outside committees to make formal decisions.

Entrepreneurial developers (primarily Netscape) took matters into their own hands and made Web browsers that supported more options, without the blessings or participation of the HTML standards committee. New HTML code was developed that was supported only on proprietary browser systems, starting with Netscape and followed by others. This created outrage among some, and an outpouring of support from others who created an avalanche of Web pages that included these new, unofficial HTML features.

As designers, it is not surprising that we want as many design features for the Web as we have access to in our desktop programs. HTML today lets us do a lot more than it used to, and we are grateful for every small morsel of design flexibility newly thrown our way. The downside is that some of these new design options have created a more confusing Web design environment. HTML has gone from being a universally accepted, cross-platform language to an every-browser-for-its-own kind of free-for-all.

Deciding Which Browser to Create Your Site For

What can a conscientious Web designer do about Browser Hell? You have some decisions to make. Do you go for the lowest common denominator and forget about layout, colors, font sizes, backgrounds, and all the other advanced features this book discusses? Or, do you push design to its fullest and force your viewers to use a specific browser, at the risk of excluding some? This personal decision will certainly depend on the content of your Web site. Some Web sites are appropriate in dull text only, or with limited graphics, whereas others are not. You and/or your client get to choose.

One solution that more and more Web designers are embracing is to set up multiple Web pages on sites that are maximized for which browser they are being viewed from. This involves creating duplicate sets of pages that are optimized for advanced browsers and limited browsers, so Web pages look like they were intended to when viewed under differing browser conditions.

Browser Comparison

I've been curious to see a visual browser comparison for some time. It's one thing to *hear* that pages look different on different browsers, but it is better to *see* how different they are. Pictures at times can say much more than words. It should be noted that browser versions change—usually for the better! After this chart is published, it is guaranteed to go out of date, as browser versions often change and improve. If you are designing for a specific browser, be sure to check to see if the chart here represents the latest version. I've included the browser version numbers next to each browser name for this purpose. If you want to search for current browser software, there are great search engines (programs that search through databases) on the Web. Try the following:

- **Browser Watch**
  http://www.ski.mskcc.org/browserwatch/browsers.html

- **Yahoo, WWW, browsers**
  http://www.yahoo.com/Computers_and_Internet/Internet/World_Wide_Web/Browsers/

- **Infoseek Search, browsers**
  http://www2.infoseek.com/Titles?qt=browser

- **Lycos Search**
  http://query3.lycos.cs.cmu.edu/cgi-bin/pursuit?query=browse

Browser Stats

To get an idea of which browsers are being used by whom, check out the various statistical Web sites listed here. There's no consensus to these findings, and some have more updated versions of the stats than others.

- **Browser Watch**: http://www.ski.mskcc.org/browserwatch

- **Browser Stats from Yahoo's Random Link:**
  http://www.cen.uiuc.edu/~ejk/bryl.html

- **Craig Knudsen's Stats:**
  http://www.btg.com/~cknudsen/stats/current.html

- **Jayfar's Web Survey:** http://www.netaxs.com/~jayfar/

> **NOTE**
>
> If you read the stats on browsers, there's no telling who has it straight. I've seen reports that vary this widely:
>
> Netscape ranges from 56–74 percent
>
> AOL ranges from 4–11 percent
>
> Mosaic ranges from 3.5–13.7 percent
>
> Internet Explorer ranges from 3.5–24.5 percent

Here are the types of Web design features the browser comparison test analyzed. This represents a list of Web page features and corresponding tags that you might or might not choose to include in your pages:

Align Test

- Centered Image/Text Alignment <center>

- Image Alignment <img src align>

- V-Space, H-Space Alignment <img src vspace hspace>

Color Test

- Colored backgrounds/text <body bgcolor text link vlink alink>

- Font size control <font size>

- Header type sizes <H1>

Pattern Text

- Pattern backgrounds <body background>

- Transparent GIFs file format support

- Border control <a href><img src border></a>

- JPEGs file format support

Tables and Horizontal Rule Test

- Tables <table> <tr> <td>

- Padded tables <table border>

- Horizontal rules <hr> <hr size> <hr width> <hr align> <noshade>

Table 1.1 is a chart depicting these categories and the different Mac browsers we tested. Table 1.2 is a chart depicting these categories and the different PC browsers we tested.

Table 1.1 Browser Comparison Chart for Macintosh Browsers					
	Netscape v.2.0 b1	Mosaic v.2.0.1	AOL v.2.6	eWorld v.1.0.1	MacWeb v.098a
Alignment					
Center Image/Text Alignment	yes	yes	yes	yes	no
Image Alignment	yes	yes	partial	partial	no
V-Space H-Space Alignment	yes	no	no	no	no
Colors/Text					
Colored Backgrounds/text	yes	no	yes	yes	no
Font Size Control	yes	no	no	no	no
Header Size Control	yes	yes	yes	yes	partial
Pattern					
Background Patterns	yes	no	yes	yes	no
Transparent GIF	yes	yes	yes	yes	no

	Netscape v.2.0 b1	Mosaic v.2.0.1	AOL v.2.6	eWorld v.1.0.1	MacWeb v.098a
Border Control	yes	no	no	no	no
JPEGs	yes	yes	yes	yes	no
Tables/Horizontal Rules					
Tables	yes	yes	no	no	no
Padded Tables	yes	no	no	no	no
Custom Horizontal Rules	yes	no	no	no	no

Table 1.2   Browser Comparison Chart for PC Browsers

	Netscape v.2.0 b1	Internet Explorer v.2.0 beta	Mosaic v.2.0	AOL v.2.5	NetCruiser v.2.0	Prodigy v.9.18.00
Alignment						
Center Image/Text Alignment	yes	yes	yes	no	yes	no
Image Alignment	yes	yes	no	yes	yes	partial
V-Space H-Space Alignment	yes	yes	no	no	no	no
Colors/Text						
Colored Backgrounds/ Text	yes	yes	yes	no	no	no
Font Size Control	yes	yes	yes	yes	no	yes
Header Size Control	yes	yes	yes	yes	no	yes
Pattern						
Background Patterns	yes	yes	yes	no	no	no
Transparent GIF	yes	yes	yes	yes	no	yes
Border Control	yes	yes	no	no	no	partial
JPEGs	yes	yes	yes	yes	no	no
Tables/Horizontal Rules						
Tables	yes	yes	yes	no	no	no
Padded Tables	yes	no	no	no	no	no
Custom Horizontal Rules	yes	yes	yes	no	no	no

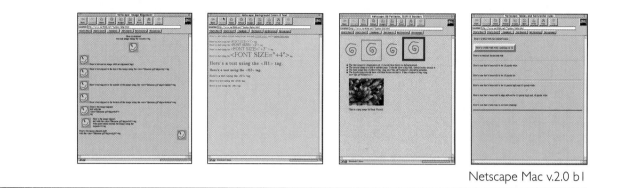

Netscape Mac v.2.0 b1

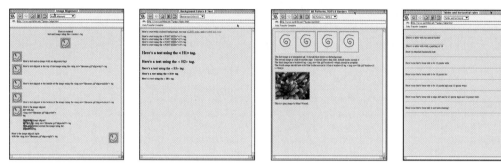

Mosaic Mac v.2.0.1

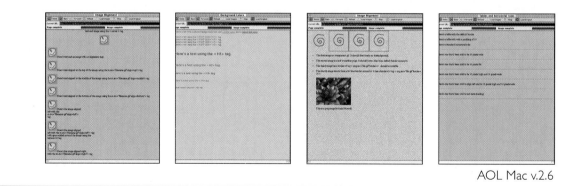

AOL Mac v.2.6

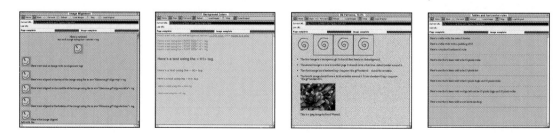

eWorld v.1.01

MacWeb v.098

NetScape Windows v.2.0 b1

Mosaic PC v.2.0

Internet Explorer v.2.0 beta

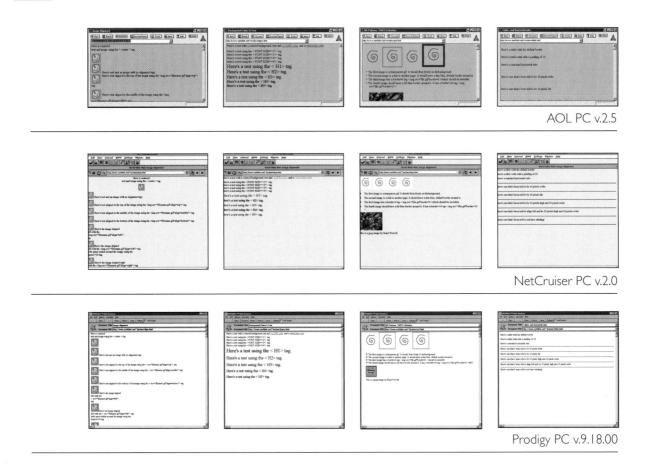

AOL PC v.2.5

NetCruiser PC v.2.0

Prodigy PC v.9.18.00

Understanding the HTML for the Browser Comparison Test

The browser test involves a series of four HTML documents that include features that designers might want to control on their Web pages. For each of the browsers analyzed here, I loaded the identical Web page to see how it displayed the same information.

If you are interested in learning how to do HTML coding, it's useful to study other people's source code. This is the way many people teach themselves HTML. You can backward engineer anyone's code by choosing a menu item within your browser called View Source.

This option will open a text editor automatically on your computer and show you the raw HTML code. I am providing the HTML scripts for the browser comparison tests, in case you want to study how I created them. They are printed here and also are on the CD-ROM in case you want to conduct your own browser comparison test on a browser that wasn't included in this chapter.

Text and Background Colors Page

This page was designed to show whether the browser supported colored backgrounds using hexadecimal callouts (see Chapter 5), and font and header sizing (see Chapter 9). Here's the code that was used to generate this page. No graphics were used. The file was written in a

standard word processor, and saved as a *text only* file with the extension
.html at the end of it.

```
<HTML>
<HEAD>
<TITLE>Background Colors & Text</TITLE>
<BODY BGCOLOR= "ccccff" TEXT ="ff0000" LINK ="017ed1" Vlink="a614e3">
</HEAD>
<BODY> Here's a test with a colored background, text and <a href="link">
a LINK color.</a> and a <a href="index.html">visited link color</a>
<p>
Here's a test using the <FONT SIZE=""+1">&#60 FONT SIZE=""+1"&#62
    </font> tag.<br>
Here's a test using the <FONT SIZE=""+2">&#60 FONT SIZE=""+2"&#62
    </font> tag.<br>
Here's a test using the <FONT SIZE=""+3">&#60 FONT SIZE=""+3"&#62
    </font> tag.<br>
Here's a test using the <FONT SIZE=""+4">&#60 FONT SIZE=""+4"&#62
    </font> tag.<br>
<H1> Here's a test using the &#60 H1&#62 tag.</H1>
<H2> Here's a test using the &#60 H2&#62 tag.</H2>
<H3> Here's a test using the &#60 H3&#62 tag.</H3>
<H4> Here's a test using the &#60 H4&#62 tag.</H4>
<H5> Here's a test using the &#60 H5&#62 tag.</H5>
</BODY>
</HTML>
```

BG Patterns, TGIFs, and Borders

This HTML page was generated to examine whether the browser supported
pattern tiles (see Chapter 6), transparent GIFs (see Chapter 8), border control
on image links (see Chapter 14), and JPEGs (see Chapter 3). Two graphics
were used. One was the pattern element, which was 100×100 pixels at 72
dpi, saved in Index Color mode as a Gif89a. It was saved with the file name
pat.gif. The other graphic was a JPEG image by 3D computer graphics wizard
Rand Worrell, and was saved in RGB 24-bit color at medium quality as a
JPEG and is titled rand.jpg. Here's the code that created the page:

```
<html>
<head>
<title>BG Patterns, TGIFS & Borders</title>
<Body background="purpat.gif"></head>
</body>
<img src="spiral.gif">
<a href="index.html"><img src="spiral.gif"></a>
<a href="index.html"><img src="spiral.gif"border=0></a>
<a href="index.html"><img src="spiral.gif"border=10></a><p>
<UL>
<P>
<P>
<LI>The first image is a transparent gif. It should float freely on the
background. <br><LI>The second image is a link to another page. It
should have a thin blue, default border around it.<br><LI>The third
image has a border=0 tag &#60 img src="file.gif"border=0 &#62which
```

```
should be invisible.<br><LI>The fourth image should have a fat blue bor-
der around it. It has a border=10 tag &#60 img src="file.gif"border=10
&#62</body>
<P>
<P>
<IMG SRC="rand.jpg">
<p>
This is a JPEG image by Rand Worrell.
</html>
```

Alignment

This HTML page was created to show whether the browser supported image alignment tags (see Chapter 10). One image was used over and over—the classic Bruce Heavin one-eyed smiley—which was saved in indexed colors as a Gif87a (CompuServe Gif). It was named smiley.gif. Here's the code that was used to generate this page:

```
<html>
<title>Image Alignment</title>
<body>
<center>Here is centered<br>text and image using the &#60 center &#62
tag <P>
<img src="smiley.gif"></center></body><p><p>
<img src="smiley.gif"> Here's text and an image with no alignment tags
<p>
<img src="smiley.gif" align=top> Here's text aligned to the top of the
image using the
&#60img src="filename.gif"align=top"&#62 tag
<p>
<img src="smiley.gif" align=middle> Here's text aligned to the middle of
the image using the
&#60img src="filename.gif"align=middle"&#62 tag
<p>
<img src="smiley.gif" align=bottom> Here's text aligned to the bottom of
the image using the
&#60img src="filename.gif"align=bottom"&#62 tag
<p>
<img src="smiley.gif" align=left> Here's the image aligned <br>left with
the<br>
&#60img src="filename.gif"align=left"&#62 <br>tag<br><br>
<p>
<img src="smiley.gif" align=left hspace=10>Here's the image aligned
<br>left with the
&#60img src="filename.gif"align=left"&#62 tag <br>with space added
  around the image using the <br>hspace=10 tag.
<p>
<img src="smiley.gif" align=right> Here's the image aligned right<br>
  with the
&#60img src="filename.gif"align=right"&#62 tag<br>
<p>
</html>
```

Tables and Horizontal Rules

This HTML page was designed to show whether the browser supported tables and custom horizontal rules. No graphics were used. The following is the code that generates this page:

```
<html>
<title>Tables and horizontal rules</title>
<p>
<p>
<table border>
<tr>
<td>Here's a table with the default border</td>
</tr>
</table>
<p>
<p>
<table border=10>
<tr>
<td>Here's a table with a padding of 10</td>
</tr>
</table>
</html>
<p>
<p>
Here's a standard horizontal rule:
<p>
<hr>
<p>
Here's one that's been told to be 10 pixels wide:
<p>
<hr width=10>
<p>
Here's one that's been told to be 10 pixels fat:
<p>
<hr size=10>
<P>
Here's one that's been told to be 10 pixels high and 10 pixels wide:
<p>
<hr size=10 width=10>
<P>
Here's one that's been told to align left and be 10 pixels high and 10
   pixels wide:
<p>
<hr align=left size=10 width=10>
<P>
Here's one that's been told to not have shading!
<p>
<hr no shade>
</html>
```

NOTE

As you learn more about the Web, you will begin to hear about HTML version numbers. HTML 1.0, HTML 2.0, HTML 3.0, and HTML+. As hard as you try to know what official HTML really is and who supports it, you will never succeed because it is, and always has been, in flux. Browsers change, HTML changes, and to top it off, browsers create their own HTML tags.

If you're confused, you are not alone. It's a difficult situation for everyone involved, but that's the price one pays for pioneering technology. For up-to-date HTML information, look to the following URLs.

HTML 3.0 Specs:

http://www.w3.org/hypertext/ WWW/MarkUp/MarkUp.html

HTML 2.0 Specs:

http://www.cs.tu-berlin.de/ ~jutta/ht/ draft-ietf-html-spec-01.html

HTML+ Specs:

http://www.w3.org/hypertext/ WWW/MArkUp/ HTMLPlus_1.html

Summary

Now you've seen for yourself how different browsers can be from one another. I believe it's always better to be informed than ignorant, so you've been duly warned about the existence of Browser Hell. You'll have to decide, based on what audience you're targeting, which browser to design for and which features to include on your pages. Here are some tips:

- Not all browsers are equal.

- You can't make one screen work for all browsers unless you limit the features you use to the lowest common denominator of the most limited browser.

- If you want to make graphic pages that cater to both the high- and low-end browsers, you would have to make duplicate pages that are laid out differently in order to optimize for different browser conditions.

- If you choose to create pages that only work well on one browser, put a disclaimer on your first page, such as "This page is Netscape-enhanced, or view with Netscape 1.1N and higher."

- A great way to learn HTML is to study other people's Web pages.

CHAPTER 2 | Cross-Platform Hell!

One of the coolest things about the World Wide Web is that it's cross-platform and people on Macs, PCs, Suns, and SGIs all get to communicate together in the same location for the first time in history.

If you're curious to know the percentage of systems used to access the Web, here's the breakdown:

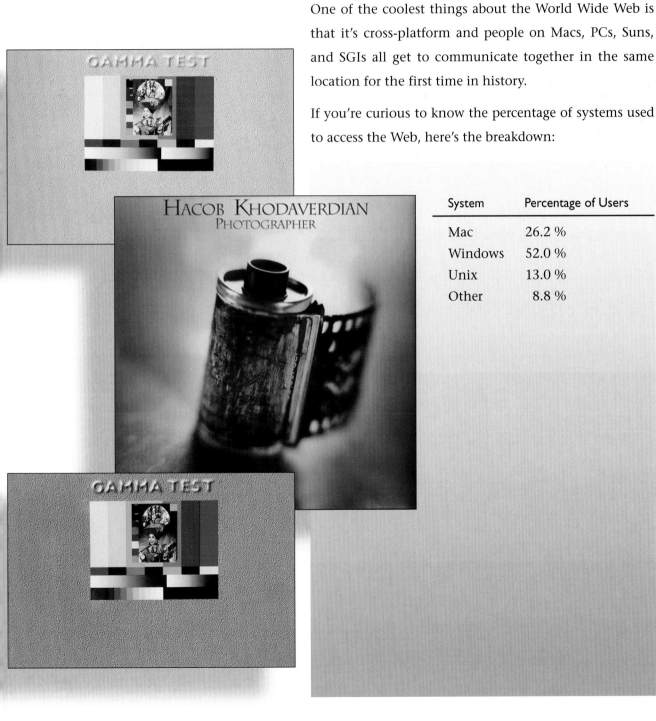

System	Percentage of Users
Mac	26.2 %
Windows	52.0 %
Unix	13.0 %
Other	8.8 %

Figure 2.1
24-bit original picture.

Figure 2.2
4-bit version of figure 2.1.

The unfortunate fact about cross-platform authoring is that viewers log on to the Web using different computers with different color spaces, color cards, monitor types, and monitor sizes. If you want to make yourself sad, spend hours making a beautiful full-color graphic (24-bit) as shown in figure 2.1 and then view it on someone's portable computer with a 4-bit color display, as shown in figure 2.2. It's not a pretty sight. This is typical of some of the things that can happen unexpectedly to artwork that you post to your Web site.

What can you do about such unplanned cross-platform discrepancies? This chapter helps you understand what can go wrong in cross-platform publishing, and what to do about it.

Cross-Platform Color Calibration Issues

Color calibration is a distressing problem to Web designers who expect the colors they've picked to look the same on everyone's system. Macs, PCs, SGIs, and Suns all have different color cards and monitors, and none of them are calibrated to each other. Figures 2.3 through 2.6 are samples of the same Web page, viewed on four different computer platforms:

Figure 2.3
Mac screen/Sony Multiscan 20se monitor.

Figure 2.4
PC screen/NEC Multisync 5FG monitor.

Figure 2.5
Sun screen/Sun Workstation Monitor.

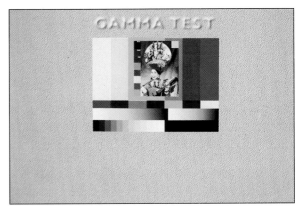

Figure 2.6
SGI screen/SGI Workstation Monitor.

Because you now see for yourself that you have no control over the calibration of systems that your work will be viewed on, what can you do to make good-looking graphics that look good everywhere? What becomes more important than the colors you pick, and what is stressed through-out this book is the *contrast* and *value* of a graphic. If you have achieved contrast and value balance, the brightness and darkness, or color differences, on various plat-forms are going to be less objectionable.

Figure 2.7

The original logo choosing my own colors.

Figure 2.8

Converting the logo to grayscale.

Figure 2.9

Lightening the purple.

Figure 2.10

Contrast and brightness values working grayscale.

Figure 2.11

The finished logo viewed in color, with contrast and brightness adjustments completed.

You can easily check contrast and value of a graphic by changing your monitor setting temporarily to grayscale. This converts all the color data to blacks, whites, and grays. This will yield much better feedback about brightness and contrast than a color display can. Colors are notoriously deceptive when judging brightness and darkness because variables, such as a florescent color or subtle hand tinting, are overpowering when judging value.

Here's a case study-in-point: Figures 2.7 through 2.10 show part of my home page. Figure 2.7 is the original logo, designed with colors that I liked. Figure 2.8 is the logo converted to grayscale. Notice that the purple paint beneath my Homegurrrl lettering is too dark. It competes with the blacks. In figure 2.9, I lightened the purple. Finally, figure 2.10 shows the difference in grayscale values that work much better. Figure 2.11 shows the finished logo with contrast and brightness adjustments completed.

Brightness Differences between Platforms

I've discovered, in general, that Mac monitors and color cards tend to make everything look lighter. This can be deceptive if you're authoring graphics on a Mac. I've included a gamma setting that can be downloaded from my site http://www.lynda.com, created by illustrator Bruce Heavin, to be used with Thomas Knoll's Control Panel utility "Gamma" that ships with every Mac. If you load this setting into the Gamma utility, it will closely simulates what your Mac graphics are going to look like on a PC.

Personally, when working on my Mac I try to make graphics a little lighter than I normally would, knowing that they'll display darker on PCs. When working on my PC, I do the opposite and make graphics slightly darker. There's no way to make it work perfectly everywhere, but knowing these general differences makes you an "informed" Web designer, so you can make educated guesses about overall color brightness. I always recommend that you view your graphics on as many platforms as possible and make necessary changes when needed based on informed feedback.

Summary

Cross-platform authoring is possible on the Web, but that doesn't mean it *looks* good. Take the following items into consideration, and you'll be able to make the best of a difficult design situation.

- Your pages will look different on different computer monitors and platforms.

- Check your pages on other platforms and make informed changes if necessary.

- Pay attention to the brightness and contrast of a graphic, and it will look best under poor monitor conditions.

CHAPTER 3 Making Low-Memory Graphics

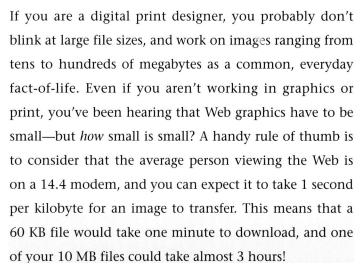

If you are a digital print designer, you probably don't blink at large file sizes, and work on images ranging from tens to hundreds of megabytes as a common, everyday fact-of-life. Even if you aren't working in graphics or print, you've been hearing that Web graphics have to be small—but *how* small is small? A handy rule of thumb is to consider that the average person viewing the Web is on a 14.4 modem, and you can expect it to take 1 second per kilobyte for an image to transfer. This means that a 60 KB file would take one minute to download, and one of your 10 MB files could take almost 3 hours!

So how do you translate your many-megabyte-sized file down to something small enough to fit on an average floppy disk? The two file formats of the Web, GIF and JPEG, both offer impressive compression schemes. Saving in these formats, as long as your images are under 640×480 pixels, at 72 dpi in RGB, will make fitting them on a floppy disk easy regardless of how complex your graphic is. Even though fitting a large graphic on a floppy may seem like a giant accomplishment if you're used to large files, this file size still won't cut it for the Web.

This chapter walks you through the stages of making smaller images; not in dimensions but in *file* size. You'll learn how to "read" the file size of a graphic, understand what the file format is doing to an image, and which file formats to use on which types of images. In the end, you should have a much better sense of to how to create the smallest possible images for Web delivery.

One thing to keep in mind while designing your graphics is that print quality is not expected on the Web, and a big difference exists between what looks good on paper and what looks good on screen. You will always need to work in RGB at 72 dpi for the Web. This is because 72 dpi is the resolution of computer screens. You are delivering your end result to computer screens, not high-resolution printers. CMYK and high resolution are reserved for print graphics only. You'll love this change once you get over the shock of it. In print, you never know what you'll get until it's printed; for online graphics what-you-see-IS-what-you-get. It'll probably be hard to go back to those huge, unwieldy print resolution files once you've experienced the luxury of working small.

Naming Conventions for JPEGs and GIFs

When saving a JPEG or GIF file for a Web page, always use the three letter extension of either .jpg or .gif at the end of your file name. Since most servers that store Web graphics are Unix-based, it is important to pay close attention to whether your files are named with upper- or lowercase titles. The HTML document must exactly match the upper- or lowercase structure of the file name. For example, if you have something saved as "image.jpg" on your server, and your HTML reads "image.JPG", the file will not load! For more information on storing graphics on servers, and file naming conventions, refer to Appendix A, "HTML for Visual Designers."

How to Know What Size Your File Really Is

A new Web vocabulary that will eventually include words like hexadecimal and transparent GIFs will now include kilobytes. We will be judging Web images by kilobytes, KB, or bytes from now on. For your information, a megabyte is composed of 1,000 kilobytes, and a gigabyte has 1,000,000 bytes! Files measuring in the megabytes and gigabytes will not be allowed on well-designed Web pages; they take too long to view! Because of this, you'll often get the directive from a client to keep page sizes within a certain file size limit. Or you might have an internal goal of not exceeding 30 KB per page. It's necessary to understand how to read the file size of a document if you're trying to make it fall within a certain target range of acceptability.

How can you tell how many kilobytes an image is? Most Photoshop users think the readout in the lower left corner of a document (see fig. 3.1) informs them about the file size. Not true! These numbers relate to the amount of RAM Photoshop is allocating to your image and its scratch disk virtual memory scheme.

You also might look to your hard drive for the file size. Figure 3.2 shows a file menu shot from the Mac. Notice that the file size numbers are all nicely rounded figures: 11k, 33k, and 132k. Your computer rounds up the size of a file to the next largest number depending on how large your hard drive partition is.

On a Mac, the only way to get information about the true byte size of a file is to do a Get Info command. First, highlight the file you want to check in the Finder, then go to the File menu, and choose Get Info. The dialog box shown in figure 3.3 appears showing you the actual file size.

On the PC, the file size shown in the menu is very close to the actual file size, with rounding to the next

lowest number occurring. Under DOS you can get a more accurate reading of the file size, but it is not much different from what you see in Windows.

Figure 3.1
The size reading at the bottom left corner of a Photoshop window is deceptive. It refers to how much RAM and disk space the Photoshop 3.0 file takes up, and has no relation to what the file size will be once saved in a Web image file format, like GIF or JPEG.

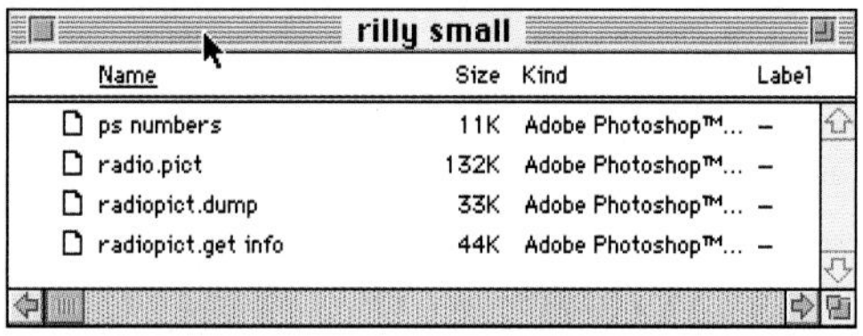

Name	Size	Kind	Label
ps numbers	11K	Adobe Photoshop™...	–
radio.pict	132K	Adobe Photoshop™...	–
radiopict.dump	33K	Adobe Photoshop™...	–
radiopict.get info	44K	Adobe Photoshop™...	–

Figure 3.2
A Mac file menu, showing rounded file sizes. The rounding relates to how the hard drive is partitioned, and does not show the true file size.

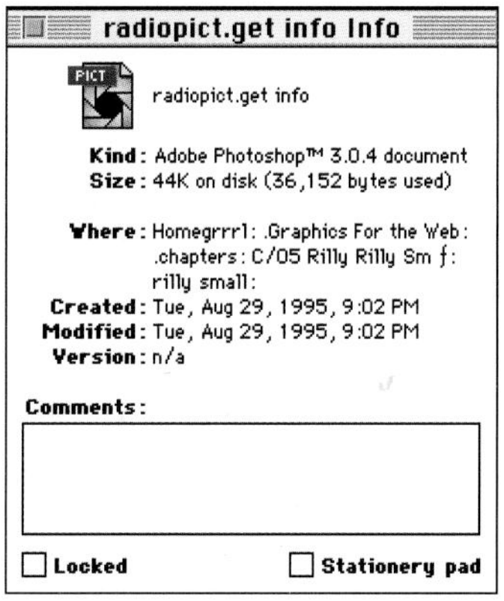

radiopict.get info Info

radiopict.get info

Kind: Adobe Photoshop™ 3.0.4 document
Size: 44K on disk (36,152 bytes used)

Where: Homegrrrl: .Graphics For the Web: .chapters: C/05 Rilly Rilly Sm ƒ: rilly small:

Created: Tue, Aug 29, 1995, 9:02 PM
Modified: Tue, Aug 29, 1995, 9:02 PM
Version: n/a

Comments:

☐ Locked   ☐ Stationery pad

Figure 3.3
The Get Info dialog box for the Mac, showing the disk size of 44k, and the true file size of 36k.

N O T E

Photoshop typically saves images with an icon. The icon is a small, visual representation of what the image looks like, which the file references. Photoshop icons take up a little extra room on your hard drive. This ultimately won't matter, because when you send the files to your server you'll transmit them as raw data, which will strip the icon off anyway. But if your goal is to get a more accurate reading of the true file size, you should set your preferences in Photoshop to not save an icon.

To set your preferences to not save the icon, choose File, Preferences, General. In the General dialog box, set the Image Previews to Ask When Saving as shown in figure 3.4.

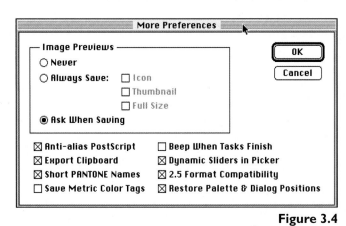

Figure 3.4

General Preferences dialog, where icons can be turned off.

Web File Formats

Compression is the key to making small graphics. Compression is not a necessary feature in other computer graphic file format specifications, which is why the file formats you'll find on the Web might be new to you. Web-based image file formats have to implement impressive compression schemes in order to transform large images to small file sizes. With compression, comes loss of quality. Some Web file formats use lossy compression techniques, meaning that there will be some loss of quality to the resulting images. Don't let that scare you though; there is no way these file formats could impose the required amount of compression needed for Web delivery and not sacrifice some quality. Remember once again, print quality is NOT expected on the Web. Two types of image file formats most commonly accepted by graphic Web browsers are JPEGs and GIFs. One difference between them is that JPEGs can be 24-bit (include up to 16.7 million colors) and GIFs must be 8-bit or less (256 colors maximum).

It's easy to convert to JPEGs and GIFs from other image file formats, such as PICT, TIFF, or EPS, if you have the proper software. In Photoshop, go to the Edit menu and select Save A Copy As. The long list of supported file formats includes CompuServe GIF and JPEG. Many other imaging programs support JPEGs and GIFs, or you can use several of the helper applications (a new term for small programs and utilities that help you with Web-based tasks) we include on the CD-ROM for the job. Look in the Mac or PC software folders depending on your platform.

This section examines the pros and cons of Web-based image file formats and gives you an understanding of how to choose which file format is appropriate for specific styles of artwork.

If you have a problem saving in GIF file format, make sure your graphic is 8-bit. Photoshop refers to this mode as Indexed Color. You cannot save a GIF until you convert your 24-bit document to 8-bit. Instructions for doing this are found below and in Chapter 4, "Color Palette Hell!" Choosing which palette to use is a complicated decision, and deserves its own chapter!

JPEGs

JPEG is pronounced, jay-peg. JPEG is a great file format for the Web because it can work with 24-bit (16.7+ million colors) images and still produce files that are small enough to meet online standards. It offers a lossy compression scheme that reduces image file sizes as much as 100:1.

JPEGs were created by the Joint Photographic Experts Group. It was developed specifically for photographic-type images and does a great job of compressing those types of images. It does not work well for graphic-based imagery, such as line drawings, illustrations, type design, and cartoons. Unlike other file formats, JPEG supports variable compression settings, which offers control over how much degradation and loss of quality an image has to suffer.

This section will introduce you to how JPEGs work and when and how to use them.

How JPEG Compression Works

JPEG images compress when they're saved in a graphics program, and then decompress when they're viewed by a Web browser. Herein lies a problem; even though JPEGs often can be smaller than GIFs, the decompression time sometimes takes longer than GIFs. Therefore, a smaller JPEG file with more colors might still take longer to download and decompress than a bigger GIF file with fewer colors.

Support for a new type of JPEG has just been introduced by Netscape Navigator 2.0, called a Progressive JPEG. A Progressive JPEG appears on the Web page in stages of quality, so the viewer sees the image before it comes fully into focus. This will fix the old problem of long JPEG decompression delays.

DeBabelizer has a plug-in for Progressive JPEG creation (contact http://www.equilibrium.com). I'm certain many other software developers will follow with Progressive JPEG file format options as soon as they can. For example, ProJPEGv1.0, a Mac-based Photoshop plug-in for progressive and baseline

www.

Figure 3.5
Example of photographic-type image.

Figure 3.6
Example of flat-style graphic.

Figure 3.7
Close-up on JPEG artifacts on a flat-style graphic.

JPEGs (compatible with other programs that support Photoshop 2.5.1 plug-ins), is now available for downloading from ftp://aris.com/boxtop and also from the ProJPEG home page at http://www.aris.com/boxtop/ProJPEG.

When to Use JPEGs

JPEGs are ideal for images that are photographic, organic in nature, and continuous-tone (see fig. 3.5). JPEG compression works better on images with small color changes—such as subtle lighting changes—than on images with lots of area of solid color like line art cartoons, flat-style illustrations (see fig. 3.6), and graphics with lettering or hard-edged shapes in them. You would never want to make black-and-white artwork into a JPEG file, for example. Anytime a JPEG file encounters a sharp edge, such as white pixels next to black pixels, it tends to introduce blur or ugly artifacts around the edges (see fig. 3.7).

JPEGs typically have more visible compression artifacts than GIFs. You can take an image through the different JPEG compression settings in Photoshop (low, med, high, max) and decide for yourself how much image degradation you're willing to accept (see figs. 3.8 through 3.11). Typically, a photographic or painterly, organic-style image will show very little image loss, even at low quality.

In Photoshop, I usually try the four different quality levels (maximum, high, medium, low) in the JPEG quality settings on a specific image to see how much compression it can withstand. Taking one image, I'll save it four times with four different quality settings. When finished, I'll open all four finished images to compare them for quality. By the way, don't *ever* save a JPEG over an existing JPEG. You'll add compression on top of compression and the results will be worse than if you start with a high-quality master image.

Steps to saving a JPEG in Photoshop:

1. Open the document.

2. Choose under File, Save A Copy, JPEG.

3. Select a compression setting (see fig. 3.12).

Figure 3.8
The low JPEG compression setting in Photoshop.

Figure 3.9
The medium JPEG compression setting in Photoshop.

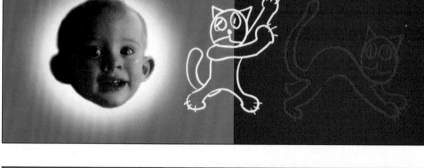

Figure 3.10
The high JPEG compression setting in Photoshop.

Figure 3.11
The max JPEG compression setting in Photoshop.

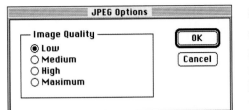

Figure 3.12

Selecting a compression setting for a JPEG in Photoshop.

GIFs

GIF is pronounced two ways. Some folks say it with a soft *g* as in jiffy; others with a hard *g*, as in gift. The official way is with a soft *g*, but so many people say it with a hard *g* that I've decided there is no correct way. I actually took a poll on *The Net Magazine's* Web site (http://www. thenet-usa.com/mag/design/design.html) where the hard g was last winning by a vote of 426 to 256. If most people pronounce it incorrectly, then perhaps it's time to change the pronunciation? GIF stands for **G**raphics **I**nterchange **F**ormat.

GIF files, by nature, can only contain 256 colors or less. GIFs use LZW compression (based on work done by Lempel-Ziv & Welch), which is a lossless method of reducing file size. Even though lossless compression offers higher quality than lossy compression, the resulting files might look worse than a 24-bit lossy compressed JPEG because GIFs have to be 8-bit.

GIFs are the source of some controversy these days, as the LZW patent is owned by Unisys, and they want to charge developers, like online services and browser developers, a fee for its use. This might be the demise of GIF on Web browsers, but so far no other image file format has taken its place

There are two types of GIFs: GIF87a's and GIF89a's. The first, GIF87a, is the standard, more common GIF file format. You'll rarely see these two types of GIFs called by their numeric names. GIF87a's are generally called plain old GIFs. Photoshop refers this file format as a CompuServe GIF. GIF89a's are a subset of the GIF87a file format. GIF89a adds the ability to tack on extra information to the file—such as transparency. GIF89a's are often called Transparent GIFs. Transparent GIFs have regions that are selected to mask out, and become invisible. Chapter 8 is devoted to understanding and creating transparent GIFs.

You will also hear about interlaced GIFs. Interlaced GIFs can be either GIF87a's or GIF89a's. Interlaced GIFs appear on a Web screen in chunks, starting at low resolution and resolving after several seconds to their finished form. This causes the graphic to appear sooner than if it had to download fully before being visible. Interlaced GIFs can be saved in either format, GIF87a or GIF89a, but most of the programs that support it do it under the

GIF89a guidelines. For more information creating interlaced GIFs, look to Chapter 8.

In order to save GIF89a files, you must find a program that supports the file format. Now that the Web has achieved its enormous popularity, almost all imaging programs support both types of GIFs. Photoshop has a plug-in called GIF89 Export, which is available from Adobe at http://www.adobe.com. Instructions for using it and other applications are found in Chapter 8.

How GIF Compression Works

GIF compression implements an interesting compression scheme.

Pixel transitions within a document are scanned and file size is added as color changes to pixels on a horizontal axis are identified. To demonstrate how a GIF file size changes, based on pixels, you could take a file with simple repeated vertical lines and save it. Then rotate the exact same image so that the lines run horizontally. Compress both to GIF files and then compare the file sizes. The horizontal image (see fig. 3.13) is 6.7k as shown in the Get Info dialog box (see fig. 3.14). The exact same image rotated so that the lines run vertically (see fig. 3.15) is 11.5k (see fig. 3.16) as shown in the Get Info dialog box.

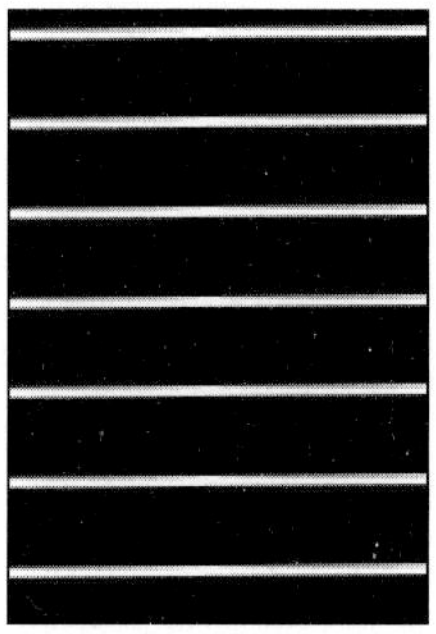

Figure 3.13
The horizontal image.

Figure 3.15
The vertical image.

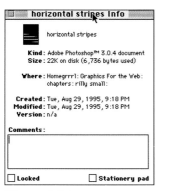

Figure 3.14
The Get Info dialog box shows the horizontal stripes image is 6.7k.

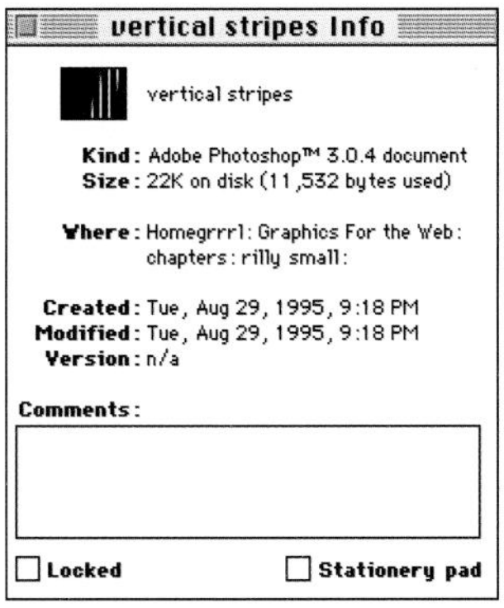

Figure 3.16
The Get Info dialog box shows the vertical stripes image is 11.5k.

This clearly demonstrates how GIF compression works. The GIF file format adds file size according to the number of times the pixels change in a document along the horizontal axis. To further emphasize this fact, let's add noise to the figure with the horizontal lines, as shown in figure 3.17. Because we have added more pixel changes across the horizontal axis, the file size increases dramatically from 11.5k to 56k as shown in figure 3.17. Therefore, when trying to make small-sized GIFs remember; it's not so much the size of GIF image in terms of dimensions or numbers of colors that count, it's how many times an image changes pixels on a horizontal axis.

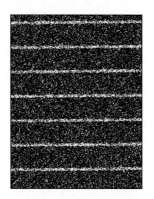

Figure 3.17
Adding noise to the horizontal image.

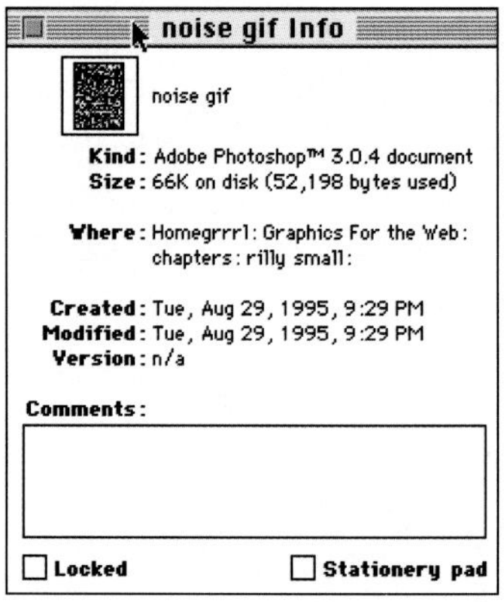

Figure 3.18
The Get Info dialog box shows the increase in file size from 11.5k to 56k.

Now that the way GIF handles compression has been explained, you can use this knowledge to your advantage. If you create illustrations with large areas of solid color, you can make huge images (in pixels) that are very small in file size. Here's an example (see fig. 3.19) of one of illustrator Bruce Heavin's tiles that is 700×1134 pixels, but only takes up 7.1k of space! This is because GIF compression works by counting how many pixels are changing. There is so much solid, flat color in this image that it almost doesn't matter how many pixels it measures up and down total.

Figure 3.19
A 700×1134 pixel GIF file that only totals 7.1k!

How to Use GIFs

In order to save an image as a GIF, you must first convert any file that is over 256 colors to 8-bit. Photoshop uses the term "Indexed Color Mode" for 8-bit graphics. If you're used to working in 24-bit, as I am, you might wonder why anyone with a choice would bother working in a file format that forces him or her to use 8-bit color. Though the 8-bit format can often result in an image that is far less pleasing than a millions-color original, there are some benefits that should not be dismissed lightly. Foremost is the fact that most viewers who are looking at the World Wide Web do not have 24-bit cards in their computers yet. The GIF 8-bit restriction might be a blessing in disguise, as it forces designers to make artwork that can be viewed by a wider audience.

Converting to 8-Bit Graphics

Saving an image to the GIF file format requires that it be stored in an 8-bit color depth first. In Photoshop, you would do the following:

1. Open your existing image.

2. Go to the Mode menu and select Indexed Color (see fig. 3.20).

3. Click OK to the Indexed Color dialog (see fig. 3.21).

4. Under the File menu, choose Save a Copy as CompuServe GIF (see fig. 3.22).

Figure 3.20

Changing the Mode in Photoshop to create an indexed 8-bit file.

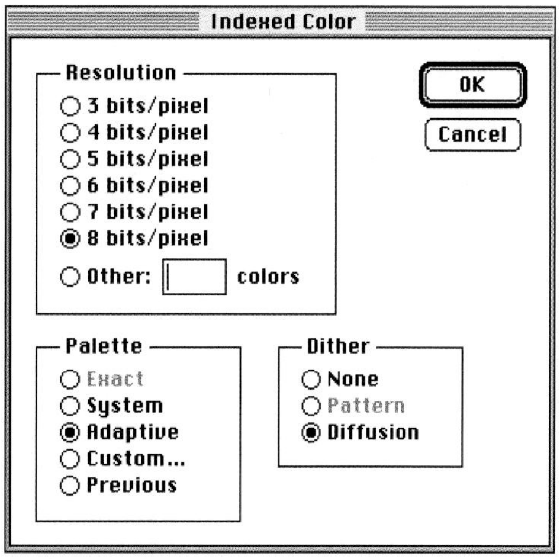

Figure 3.21

The Indexed Color dialog box.

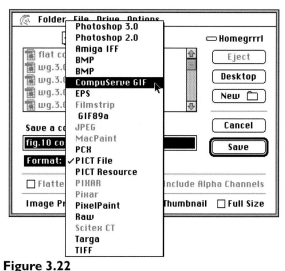

Figure 3.22

Save a copy as CompuServe GIF.

Figure 3.23
The original picture at 201k.

Figure 3.24
The dithered 256 color GIF at 72.5k.

Figure 3.25
No dither 256 color GIF at 44k. As you can
see, the image still looks pretty good, and
look at the file size savings!

This worked fine, but you can do better by simply clicking OK you get to the Indexed Color dialog, without trying any other settings. The rest of this section offers tips to make the best possible Indexed Color choices for the GIF file format.

GIF is an excellent compression scheme for flat graphics. It is not as efficient when compressing dithered graphics, because dithering introduces noise, which (refer to fig. 3.18) greatly increases file size. This is a shame, because 8-bit graphics are typically dithered by nature! (To learn more about dithering and 8-bit graphics, check out Chapter 4, "Color Palette Hell!") If you can get away without using the dither method for converting to 8-bit, your files will be significantly smaller. For example, figure 3.23 shows a radio image as a Pict file with a size of 201k. The same image converted to 256, 8-bit color, with dithering (see fig. 3.24) then compressed to a GIF file decreases the file size to 72.5k. By turning the dithering off during the conversion and then compressing the file to a GIF, the file size decreases even further to 44k (see fig. 3.25). For the smallest possible GIF files, turn the dithering option off in Photoshop when appropriate, before converting your images to 8-bit color as shown in the dialog box in figure 3.26.

These are just a few simple tips and tricks that will help you to produce efficient GIFs and keep your file sizes to a minimum. Check out the next chapter, "Color Palette Hell!," for more information on 8-bit color tables.

JPEG/GIF Comparison Chart

Next is a visual comparison chart of what happens to different types of images when saved in JPEG or GIF at different compression settings and bit-depths. I chose to compare images that represent the different styles of graphics that are used on the Web: flat graphics, photographs, soft-edges, aliased and anti-aliased, rainbow gradients, and grayscale gradients. These images were put through all the possible file formats, compression settings, and bit-depth color tables. This chart offers a great reference for what happens to different types of images using differing file formats and settings. Use this guide before you decide which format to use, and note how some of the types of images compress better than others.

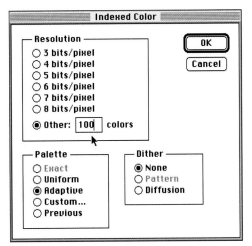

Figure 3.26

The Dither None box in Photoshop.

TIP

When indexing a color image to 8-bit color, you don't have to choose 256 colors, even if Photoshop plugs in that number automatically. Try typing smaller values into the Indexed Color dialog box as shown in figure 3.26 to see if the image can withstand less color. Most of the time you can get away with 128 colors, and often much less. What I'll do is type in a number, then if I don't like the results, I'll choose Undo and try it again with a new number.

JPEG Max
24.2K

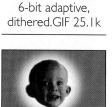

6-bit adaptive,
dithered.GIF 25.1k

7-bit adaptive, dithered
none.GIF 22.7k

JPEG Max
31.6k

6-bit adaptive,
dithered.GIF 10.3k

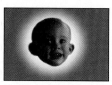

JPEG High
18.0k

5-bit adaptive,
dithered.GIF 21.8k

6-bit adaptive, dithered
none.GIF 18.2k

JPEG High
26.0k

5-bit adaptive,
dithered.GIF 10.3k

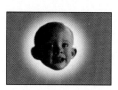

JPEG Med
12.7k

4-bit adaptive,
dithered.GIF 16.7k

5-bit adaptive, dithered
none.GIF 14.6k

JPEG Med
22.5k

4-bit adaptive,
dithered.GIF 10.2k

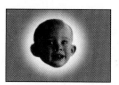

JPEG Low
11.4k

3-bit adaptive,
dithered.GIF 14.0k

4-bit adaptive, dithered
none.GIF 10.3k

JPEG Low
20.3k

3-bit adaptive,
dithered.GIF 10.0k

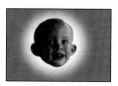

8-bit adaptive,
dithered.GIF 34.0k

2-bit adaptive,
dithered.GIF 14.2k

3-bit adaptive, dithered
none.GIF 7.7k

8-bit adaptive,
dithered.GIF 10.3k

2-bit adaptive,
dithered.GIF 19.5k

7-bit adaptive,
dithered.GIF 29.4k

8-bit adaptive, dithered
none.GIF 27.3k

2-bit adaptive, dithered
none.GIF 6.2k

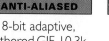

7-bit adaptive,
dithered.GIF 10.3k

8-bit adaptive, dithered
none.GIF 10.3k

7-bit adaptive, dithered none.GIF 10.3k	JPEG Max 22.7k	6-bit adaptive, dithered.GIF 38.8k	7-bit adaptive, dithered none.GIF 18.3k	JPEG Max 33.3k
6-bit adaptive, dithered none.GIF 10.3k	JPEG High 18.3k	5-bit adaptive, dithered.GIF 34.6k	6-bit adaptive, dithered none.GIF 13.5k	JPEG High 25.3k
5-bit adaptive, dithered none.GIF 10.3k	JPEG Med 13.1k	4-bit adaptive, dithered.GIF 28.1k	5-bit adaptive, dithered none.GIF 11.0k	JPEG Med 20.5k
4-bit adaptive, dithered none.GIF 10.3k	JPEG Low 12.4k	3-bit adaptive, dithered.GIF 23.0k	4-bit adaptive, dithered none.GIF 8.9k	JPEG Low 18.1k
3-bit adaptive, dithered none.GIF 10.0k	8-bit adaptive, dithered.GIF 50.7k	2-bit adaptive, dithered.GIF 17k	3-bit adaptive, dithered none.GIF 7.8k	8-bit adaptive, dithered.GIF 43.6k
2-bit adaptive, dithered none.GIF 9.3k	7-bit adaptive, dithered.GIF 44.0k	8-bit adaptive, dithered none.GIF 24.2k	2-bit adaptive, dithered none.GIF 7.5k	7-bit adaptive, dithered.GIF 36.5k

6-bit adaptive,
dithered.GIF 30.3k

7-bit adaptive, dithered
none.GIF 33.8k

5-bit adaptive,
dithered.GIF 23.8k

6-bit adaptive, dithered
none.GIF 28.2k

4-bit adaptive,
dithered.GIF 19.3k

5-bit adaptive, dithered
none.GIF 22.1k

3-bit adaptive,
dithered.GIF 16.7k

4-bit adaptive, dithered
none.GIF 16.9k

2-bit adaptive,
dithered.GIF 13.9k

3-bit adaptive, dithered
none.GIF 13.6k

8-bit adaptive, dithered
none.GIF 39.8k

8-bit adaptive, dithered
none.GIF 10.4k

Summary

Making graphics and images that work on the Web requires that images have as small a file size as possible. Understanding how compression affects image size and what types of file formats are appropriate for images is key to responsible Web design.

- Check the Get Info box on your Mac or the DOS DIR command on your PC to see the actual bytes of an image size, not the hard disk directory's inaccurate report.

- Use GIF and JPEG compression to reduce image sizes for Web publishing.

- JPEGs are good for photographs, grayscale files, continuous tone artwork, computer graphics with realistic lighting, and scanned paintings.

- JPEGs take longer to download than GIFs.

- Many viewers on the Web do not have 24-bit displays. This will cause JPEGs to dither.

- GIFs are good for graphics, cartoons, line-art, and flat-illustrations.

- With GIFs, try to use less than 256 colors, and whenever possible, don't dither!

CHAPTER 4 Color Palette Hell!

Most people viewing the Web today are on systems that have 8-bit color cards. In order to plan for this when you prepare your graphics, you must first understand the difference between 8-bit and 24-bit graphics. 8-bit and 24-bit terminology was something I resisted learning when first introduced to computer graphics. It sounded so technical and inhuman and math-like! Whenever I cover color palettes and 8-bit color in my multimedia classes, I still watch most of my art students' eyes glaze over. In the abstract, color technology is an unappealing subject; but I hope you'll force your way through understanding it, as it is key to making good-looking Web graphics.

If you don't understand how 8-bit palettes work; when to use them and when not to, your Web design will suffer. This chapter teaches you about which kind of images should be 8-bit and which shouldn't, and how to properly set the bit-depth of graphics so they'll look best within most Web browser systems.

24-bit original.   *photo by Marianna Dres*

Understanding Bit-Depth

Whenever you hear about "bit-depth," it is describing how many colors an image includes. Here's a simple chart that breaks it down:

Bits	Colors
24-bit	16.7+ million colors
16-bit	65.5 thousand colors
15-bit	32.8 thousand colors
8-bit	256 colors
7-bit	128 colors
6-bit	64 colors
5-bit	32 colors
4-bit	16 colors
3-bit	8 colors
2-bit	4 colors
1-bit	2 colors

What happens to an image in 8-bit depth and lower? Here's an example of one image, changed from 24-bit to lower bit-depths. You'll see the quality get lower as the bit-depth decreases.

8-bit

7-bit

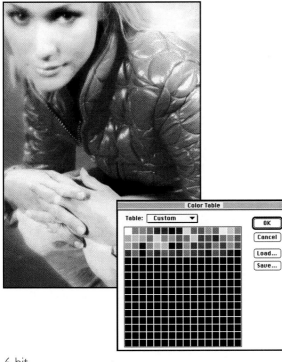

6-bit

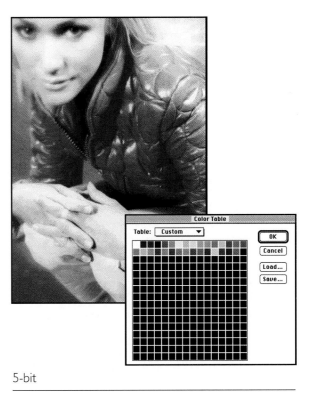

5-bit

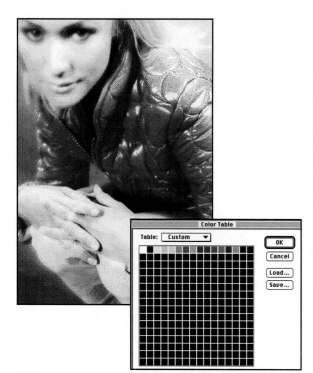

4-bit

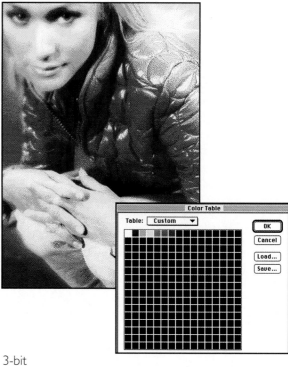

3-bit

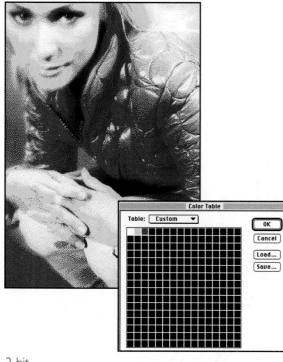

2-bit

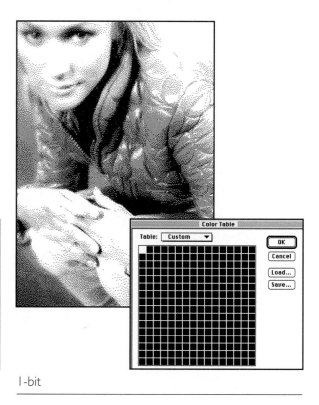

1-bit

As you can see, 8-bit graphic images are limited to 256 colors, and lower bit-depth graphics have even less. If a computer system only has an 8-bit color card, it cannot view more than 256 colors at once. When people with 256 color systems look at the Web, they cannot see images in 24-bit, even if they want to. If you have true-color (24-bit) graphics on your site, their 256 color display is going to downgrade your artwork to 8-bit or lower; they can't prevent it and neither can you.

Figure 4.1

You can choose a Mac monitor setting in grayscale, 256 colors, or 24-bit (millions) color.

Monitor Settings

As a Web site designer, it is your responsibility to ensure that your graphics look as good as they can on as many people's systems as possible. The majority of digital graphic designers (myself included) have 24-bit display cards and monitors, meaning our computers can display up to 16.7 million colors. If you are able to view that many colors at once, the problems this chapter describes will not be visible. Your monitor can show an unlimited number of Web graphics and never alter a pixel. *You* won't run into any display problems, but your audience *will*. The trouble is, most of your audience does not have 24-bit color, and you may not like the way your artwork looks on their systems.

How can you tell what color your monitor is set to?

On Macs, go to the Apple menu, choose Control Panels, Monitors, and assign the settings there accordingly (see fig. 4.1).

On PCs with Windows 3.*x*, double-click on the Windows Setup icon in the Main group of Program Manager to display your Windows Setup dialog box. From here you can find out which display setting has been set.

On Windows 95, click on the Start button, then choose Settings, Control Panel. Double-click on Display and click on the Settings tab. Look at the Color Palette setting and it will tell you how many colors you are set to (see fig. 4.2).

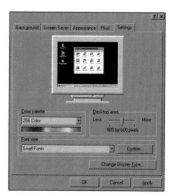

Figure 4.2

Choosing a Windows 95 monitor setting.

Figure 4.3
A 24-bit image displayed on a 256-color monitor.
Notice the "dithering."

Figure 4.4
A close-up of the "dithering."

Figure 4.5
An original 24-bit image displayed on a 24-bit monitor.

This will also let you see how many colors your color card makes available to you. If you don't have a 16-bit or 24-bit color card, your system will only give you the option of grayscale or 256 colors.

Dithering Away

When a computer display only has 256 colors to work with (such as the case when it has an 8-bit color card), and encounters a millions of colors (24-bit) document, it reduces the color information automatically and chooses to replace the millions of colors with its own fixed 256-color table (see fig. 4.3). This creates "dithering," which is the computer's best attempt to emulate what your original document looked like. *Dithering* is a process whereby the computer chooses two or more different colors from the palette of 256 colors and positions them next to each other to create the illusion of colors it can't display outside of the 256. Figure 4.4 shows a close up of the dithering caused by a 24-bit image being displayed on a 256-color monitor. Figure 4.5 shows the original 24-bit image displayed on a 24-bit monitor.

Studies have shown that the majority of people browsing the Web have 8-bit color cards, meaning they see the Web through dithered-colored glasses. Sometimes, dithering is not objectionable, and sometimes it is. Generally, dithering is more acceptable on photographic, continuous-tone images (see fig. 4.6), than it is on line art, flat-colored illustration-based artwork (see fig. 4.7). We shall examine how to prepare the best possible images for both types of artwork.

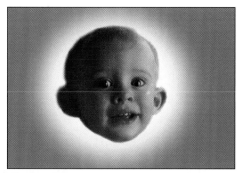

Figure 4.6
A photographic, continuous-tone image.

Figure 4.7
A line-art, flat-colored illustration.

How Web Browsers Deal with 8-Bit Graphics and Displays

With an 8-bit color monitor setting, a Mac system views a graphic in its own system 8-bit palette, a PC system in its own 8-bit palette, and guess what? Web browsers have their own custom way of displaying 8-bit graphics too. Ugh.

Most browsers have built-in checkers to know if a user's machine has a 24-bit or 8-bit color card. Most browsers (with the known exception of America Online which displays in 8-bit even if you are on a 24-bit color-equipped machine) will only dither images when running on a system with a 256-color display. Under-standing the way browsers deal with palettes will help you determine the proper course of action.

Web Browser 8-Bit Palette Management

When most browsers, including Netscape Navigator and Microsoft's Internet Explorer, detect an 8-bit display system they convert all the artwork they encounter to their own palette, regardless of what palette the artwork was originally saved in. For Photographs and continuous tone artwork, this is not a big problem (see fig. 4.8). For flat-color and line-art based illustration though, it can look very bad (see fig. 4.9). If you want to design specifically for these browsers, you should use the exact colors they used in their fixed palette, and then you won't get unwanted dithering in your flat-color presentations (see fig. 4.10). You might say to yourself, "this doesn't affect me. I just work with photographs on my site." This might be true, but chances are you still use occasional solid colored backgrounds or graphic tiled patterns, or logos, which all fall into the category of artwork that has a lot of flat color. The only way to ensure that flat-color artwork doesn't dither on a fixed-palette is to compose the artwork from those exact colors the fixed palette recognizes.

Figure 4.8
Converting the palette of a photograph or continuous tone artwork is not a big problem.

Figure 4.9
For flat-color and line-based art, converting the palette can make the graphic look bad.

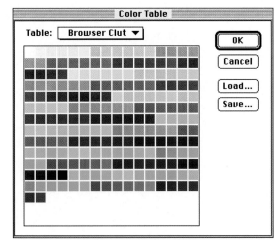

How do you know what colors exist in their fixed palette? This is not widely publicized information, but after extensive research (and enlisting the help of many others who are thanked in the acknowledgment section of this book), the fixed browser palette has been identified and included on the CD-ROM. From now on, it will be identified as the "Browser CLUT palette." CLUT stands for Color Lookup Table, which is another term for a limited bit-depth palette, such as 8-bit and below. If you don't have access to a CD-ROM player and would like to download this file from the Web, you'll find it on my personal site: http://www.lynda.com.

The Browser CLUT palette takes into account that Netscape Navigator has a slightly different fixed palette for Mac and Windows versions of their browsers (see fig. 4.11). The Mac browser uses the Mac System palette (see fig. 4.12), a pre-set 256-color table that ships with every copy of Photoshop. The Windows version of Netscape uses the Windows palette (see fig. 4.13), another, slightly different pre-set color table of 256 fixed colors. Because Microsoft's Internet Explorer was only available for PCs when this book was written, it uses the Windows 95 palette exclusively. Still, if you create artwork that you post to the Web, even if you personally use Internet Explorer, there will still be people on Mac systems viewing your pages.

Figure 4.10
In order to prevent bad-looking art, use the browser's fixed palette for color choices.

Figure 4.11
The Browser CLUT palette.

The good news is, the fixed-browser Mac and Windows palettes have 216 colors out of 256 that are identical on either platform. We have included a color lookup table of this shared 216 color palette on the CD-ROM. It is referred to in this book as the "Browser CLUT palette." In fixed-palette environments, such as Netscape Navigator and Internet Explorer, if you use this palette your images will not be re-color mapped or dithered unexpectedly. Instructions for loading and using the Browser CLUT palette follow.

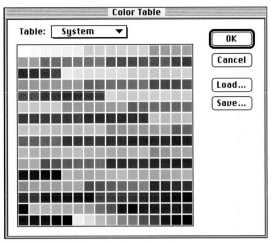

Figure 4.12
The Mac system palette.

Creating 8-Bit Artwork

When working with low-memory graphics, which is required when posting graphics to the Web, dealing with 8-bit artwork is an unpleasant, but necessary fact of life. The goal is to be in control of your own dithering and not have outside forces, such as a Web browser or someone's monitor display card, do things to your artwork that you didn't intend. The key to this is to learn how to control the dithering of your artwork, so you can avoid unnecessary loss of quality to your images.

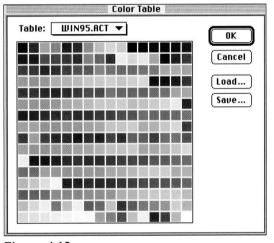

Figure 4.13
The Win95 system palette.

Most likely, you've never made 8-bit or lower artwork within these types of constraints before. The key to making good-looking Web graphics is to understand how to optimize the best palette for the type of images your site uses.

We will look to our trusty Photoshop toolkit for techniques that will help

you with the job ahead. Photoshop offers great flexibility with 8-bit color palette management tasks, and that's exactly what we'll need to deal with the tricky job of making artwork that fits to all the constraints imposed by differing browsers and the Web. If you work with a different imaging program, perhaps you can figure workarounds within that software environment. You may now understand why so many professionals use Photoshop; along with being a sophisticated high-end imaging program it also offers unparalleled control over 8-bit color management tasks.

There is no one universal way to prepare Web graphics. Artwork types, such as flat-illustration, cartoons, photographs, paintings, scans, and computer graphics all pose different problems, which each have different solutions. Next, let's examine each type of artwork style, and how to properly prepare them for 8-bit palettes and Web browsers.

Illustration-Based Artwork

If you are an illustrator, choosing color before you start an illustration is something you're already accustomed to. You're used to starting with a color palette, picking the colors you want, and creating artwork from scratch. Typically, the color palette is of your choosing, such as custom colors you've mixed or choosing from the entire 24-bit color picker at your disposal at whim.

In order to make browser color-safe illustrations, that work on the Web and do not dither, you would need to use colors from the Browser CLUT palette. Here's how:

1. In Photoshop, open the Show Swatches palette. Use the upper right hand arrow to find Load Swatches (see fig. 4.14). Load the file found on the CD-ROM called "Browser CLUT."

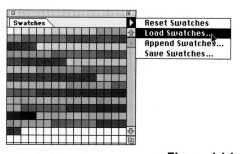

Figure 4.14
The Load Swatches command in the Show Swatches palette.

2. The Browser CLUT palette will appear below the regular system palette in the Color Swatches palette. Use the eyedropper tool to select colors from this palette (see fig. 4.15).

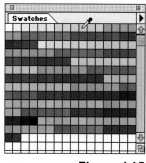

Figure 4.15
Selecting colors with the eyedropper from the Browser CLUT palette.

Converting Photographs or Continuous-Tone Artwork to Indexed Color

When you work with existing digital photographs or scans, you have a different situation entirely. These types of images always dither in 8-bit, whether you use a Browser CLUT palette or not. That's because this type of imagery uses more colors than flat artwork to represent all its subtleties, gradations, and lighting attributes. When artwork of this nature is viewed in 8-bit it will always dither, regardless of which 8-bit palette is applied.

For this reason, it's not worth the effort to force these types of images to the Browser CLUT palette. Avoiding the dithering that browsers impose is not an issue, since the 8-bit image will be dithered whether the browser does it or not. Browser dithering is not significantly different than if you define the 8-bit palette yourself.

You really don't need to convert this type of imagery to 8-bit at all. If you leave it in 24-bit, the browser will automatically choose a dithering scheme for it when it's viewed on in an 8-bit Web setting. By leaving it in 24-bit to begin with, you have the added advantage of allowing viewers with 24-bit systems to see the photograph or continuous artwork at the highest quality possible.

Adaptive Palettes

You might still need to convert photographs to 8-bit, especially if you plan to save them in the Gif format, which by definition is an 8-bit file format. If you decide to convert photographic or continuous-tone artwork to 8-bit first, it's better to create an "adaptive palette" rather than use the Browser CLUT palette we've supplied on the CD-ROM. An adaptive palette in Photoshop is the same thing as an "optimized palette" in other programs. The principle is that the 8-bit palette is derived from the best possible 256 colors or less based on what your image looks like. An adaptive palette "intelligently" picks a group of colors that best represents the image it's referencing. An adaptive 9-bit palette could be 256 shades of red, or it could be a rainbow of all the colors, depending on the image it was referencing.

Creating an Adaptative 8-Bit Palette

To create an adaptive 8-bit palette in Photoshop, you would follow these steps:

1. Open the image you want to change.

2. Change the mode from RGB to Index Color.

3. In the Indexed Color dialog box, choose Adaptive (see fig. 4.16).

Figure 4.17 shows the finished result of using the adaptive 8-bit color palette.

Batch Processing Options

What about when you are dealing with lots of images on a page? As you can see with each of the previous examples, creating good-looking 8-bit art is quite a chore! You couldn't possibly spend this amount of time on each image if you were, say, working on an online catalog.

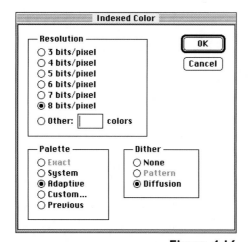

Figure 4.16

Choose Adaptive color from the Indexed Color dialog box.

Figure 4.17

The finished result.

There are alternatives to loading all of your images separately into Photoshop and indexing them as custom colors, such as our Browser CLUT, or an adaptive palette. Let's say you have lots of images, and the idea of repeating these steps in Photoshop makes you feel like this job would better suit a robot than a human being. If you're on a Mac, you might want to purchase DeBabelizer (a Windows version is promised, but not available yet).

Unfortunately, at the time this chapter was written, there were no good PC-based batch processing programs to recommend. DeBabelizer program batch processes Photoshop routines, such as converting all these files to Index Color using a common CLUT without having to load each one to Photoshop itself. Even better, DeBabelizer has a Super Palette routine, where it will take a folder of images, analyze each file in the folder, and arrive at a palette of 256 colors that are the most commonly repeated colors in all those files. If you have access to a Mac and need to process large volumes of images for your Web site, DeBabelizer is an invaluable tool.

If you can't use DeBabelizer, you might consider buying a macro program that is capable of "batch processing" a series of images. Batch processing files is a great way to increase your productivity, but it will still be important to test your files before you process large quantities of images. Productivity goes down the tube when you have to repeat the process because settings weren't what you really wanted.

When to Create 24-Bit Art

Some Web artists choose to disregard the 8-bit palette issue altogether. They have made a conscious decision to cater to a 24-bit graphics crowd. This is a valid choice if you've defined your audience and knowingly chosen to exclude those who aren't in it. Most designers and computer artists, for instance, have 24-bit displays.

If you were posting your design portfolio to the Web, for example, to try to find design work, you could assume that most art directors would have 24-bit displays. (If you were to be really savvy, you might have both a 24-bit version and an 8-bit version of your site to show the art directors that you knew how to design for the 8-bit audience, *too*.)

Working with images under 24-bit is foreign to most print-based computer designers, because print graphics don't have the same limitations that Web-based screen-presentation graphics do. The outcome of print graphics is that everyone who looks at the final result sees the exact same thing in printed form. To make the best possible product, graphic designers strive to work in the highest color settings (24-bit) and highest resolution possible.

The end product of a Web page is the exact opposite; it's dependent on what the end-users' systems allow them to see. Because the Web audience is on differing platforms, computer monitors, color systems with various calibration settings, there would seem to be no way to control what they ultimately see. Working on low-resolution graphics with limited colors offers better results for the Web designer, which is contrary to the way most digital print artists have been trained to work.

This book discusses changing bit-depth and creating 8-bit palettes in detail, because it's commonly required when preparing a large percentage of your Web graphic images. Even if you plan to work intentionally in 24-bit, you will have occasion where you need to understand how

> **NOTE**
>
> Batch processing is a term used to describe the handling of multiple files. For our purposes, we would "batch process" a group of images to an optimized 8-bit palette. Batch processing offers the ability to automate repetitive computer processes, and is extremely useful in Web, multimedia, and video production.

to prepare 8-bit artwork. The GIF file-format which is quite popular for many Web graphics is, by definition, an 8-bit file type. Any time an image is saved in 8-bit, you have to define a palette for it. Defining the palette that will work properly for Web browsers is a subject you will be hard-pressed to find much information on (until now, of course!).

There are going to be times where it is not necessary to dither your artwork or work in 8-bit. Artwork that is continuous tone, such as photographs and detailed computer generated 3D images, is a primary candidate for storing in 24-bit. The JPEG file format creates 24-bit images which are quite small and well-suited for Web design. Actually any photographic-style image that exceeds 256 colors in original form is going to look best as a 24-bit image; there is no denying that.

Working in 8-bit is something you do when working with flat-color, illustration-style artwork as a courtesy to those who don't have 24-bit displays. It will improve image quality for those type of images, whereas it will not improve image quality for photographic-style images. My guess is within the next five years, the balance will shift and the majority of the Web-based audience will be on 24-bit color equipped computers. This chapter should be moot by then, and I'm sure no one will mind!

Summary

How can you design effectively for different browser and 8-bit color card conditions? Preview your art in different color spaces and decide for yourself. If you have a 24-bit color card, change the bit depth to 256 colors, or 16 colors just to see the results. The safest bet would be to create graphics with limited colors; even less than 256 (see instructions on how to do this in Chapter 3). Different graphics lend themselves to this rule better than others, so limiting the colors often is handled on a case-by-case basis. But don't assume that everyone is on the same computer you are, or the results could be disappointing. Here are some rules to follow:

- If you have a 24-bit display you are not going to see the problems with palettes that viewers looking at the Web with 256-color cards are going to encounter. Even so, you should still know how to prepare art as if you are in 8-bit, because someone looking at your page will be seeing it that way.

- You'll get better results if you convert your flat-color illustration-based images to 8-bit, rather than let the browser do it for you.

- If you want to make sure the browser doesn't dither your flat-color illustration-based 8-bit images, use colors from the Browser CLUT palette we included on the CD-ROM.

- For photographs, or continuous tone-type images, you should use an Adaptive palette (Optimized palette) if you need to save the images in 8-bit. The Browser CLUT palette will not improve image quality or dithering on this type of imagery.

- It's best to leave photographs, or continuous tone-type images in 24-bit, if you can. These types of graphics will dither in an 8-bit environment whether they are saved first as 8-bit or 24-bit.

- Always switch your monitor setting to 256 and open your Web graphics in a browser before you deliver pages with GIFs (which by definition, have to be 8-bit) to your final server. Instructions on how to open files in a browser locally from a hard-disk are in Appendix A. This helps you preview any problems with your images and correct them if necessary.

CHAPTER 5 Fun with Hex

CCFFFF
R:204
G:255
B:255

009999
R:000
G:153
B:153

9933FF
R:153
G:051
B:255

I'm happy to say that until the Web came along, I lived life blissfully without uttering a word about hexadecimal code to anyone. Now that I'm devoting an entire chapter to the subject, I hope you'll understand that this was not my idea. I think working with hexadecimal math is a nuisance and wish it wasn't a part of Web design. Unfortunately, no one asked me!

Hexadecimal math code is often used by software programs and programmers, but has always been invisible to casual computer users. Seasoned digital artists are already accustomed to defining color choices through RGB or CMYK values. We are shielded from paying much attention to RGB and CMYK numerics because programs like Photoshop allow us to select color by appearance, not by mathematical values.

Hex on U

ifferent colored solid backgrounds, or change the
ave to write the RGB color in hex for HTML to
er the net that show you color swatches and their
s translation yourself, so as not to

Working with color on the Web is not nearly as intuitive as specifying color in Photoshop, and other imaging programs. If you want to use colors—as in colored text, colored links, colored backgrounds, and colored borders—describing them by their hexadecimal values is the only way HTML lets you do it. (Colored backgrounds can also be added by loading an image into the background of your page (see Chapter 7), but if you want solid colors, using hexadecimal code is the most efficient way because the colors will download faster.)

Let's say I wanted a white background on a Web page. In Photoshop, the RGB values of white are R:255 G:255 B:255. Using HTML on the Web, I would need to convert those RGB values to the hexadecimal values of white: FFFFFF. See figure 5.1 for an example of 4 colors with their RGB and hex values printed on each square. If you're scratching your head just now, wondering why and how, don't worry. This chapter is here to help!

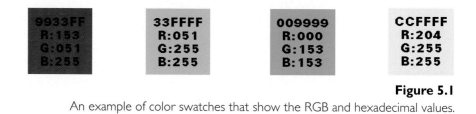

Figure 5.1
An example of color swatches that show the RGB and hexadecimal values.

Calculating hexadecimal numbers involves working with base sixteen mathematics which, before the Web came along, is something most artists did not have any need to understand. Luckily, there are ways for math-impaired people like me to cheat, and I'll gladly share each and every way I know of later in this chapter.

Hexadecimal-Based HTML Codes

To understand how hexadecimal math relates to color design on the Web, let's first look at some sample HTML that includes hexadecimal code. Here are the codes for doing the following (the # sign represents where the hexadecimal value should go):

■ Coloring the background of your page:

```
<body bgcolor="#">
```

■ Coloring your text:

```
<text="#">
```

■ Coloring your links:

```
<link="#">
```

■ Coloring your active links:
```
<alink="#">
```

■ Coloring your active links (when the mouse is down):
```
<link="#">
```

■ Coloring your visited links:
```
<vlink="#">
```

■ Coloring borders of image links (you can't put an HTML border around an image that is not a link):
```
<a href="http://www.domain.com">
<img src="animage.gif"border="#"></a>
```

■ See figure 5.2 for the results of the following code:
```
<html>
<body bgcolor="00000" text ="9933FF" link ="33FFFF"
alink="CCFFFF" vlink="009999">
<a href="http://www.domain.com"><img src="man.gif"></a><p>
Here's some background text, with a <a
href="http://www.domain1.com>link</a>,<br> a <a
href="http://www.domain2.com>visited link</a>, and an <a
href="http://www.domain3.com>active link.</a>.
</body>
</html>
```

Figure 5.2
A finished page that used hex to specify colors.

TIP

Just in you case you want to know more about how hexa-decimal arithmetic works, I wrote a page about it on my site: http://www.lynda.com/hexonu.html, which is reprinted here for your convenience (see fig. 5.3). Even though I know how to do hexadecimal math by hand using the method described on my page, I would NEVER waste my time doing so. That's what they invented hex calculators for.

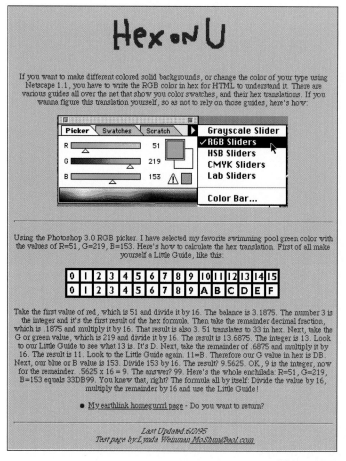

Figure 5.3

Lynda's Homegurrrl Web site's recipe for hexadecimal mathematics.

Netscape 2.0 has added some new tags for controlling the color of fonts. Before these tags, you could change the color of type, but it was a global change and affected the entire document. Now you can control the color of individual words or letters, and add multiple font colors to one page.

The code accepts hexadecimal values and looks like this: <font color=#>. Figure 5.4 is an example of a page and its source code.

```
<html>
<head><title>colortest</title>
</head>
<body bgcolor=ffffff>
<font color=6633CC>Hello!<p>
<font color=666633>Hello!<p>
<font color=ff3333>Hello!<p>
<font color=ccccff>Hello!<p>
<font color=33cc33>Hello!<p>
<font color=cc66cc>Hello!<p>
<font color=ffcccc>Hello!<p>
</body>
<html>
```

An alternative to hex (though a rather inflexible one), has been added that you can request the name of the color, such as: black, olive, teal, red, blue, maroon, navy, gray, lime, fuchsia, white, green, purple, yellow, and aqua instead of its hexadecimal equivalent. Unfortunately, it's limited to the preceding colors only, and Netscape 2.0 beta1 couldn't display all of them properly. Here's the code and the result (see fig. 5.5). How about RGB values, folks? Now THAT would be an improved solution!

```
<html>
<head><title>colortest2</title>
</head>
<body bgcolor=ffffff>
<font color=black>Hello!<p>
<font color=olive>Hello!<p>
<font color=teal>Hello!<p>
<font color=red>Hello!<p>
<font color=blue>Hello!<p>
<font color=maroon>Hello!<p>
<font color=navy>Hello!<p>
<font color=gray>Hello!<p>
<font color=lime>Hello!<p>
<font color=fuschia>Hello!<p>
<font color=white>Hello!<p>
<font color=green>Hello!<p>
<font color=purple>Hello!<p>
<font color=yellow>Hello!<p>
<font color=aqua>Hello!<p>
</body>
<html>
```

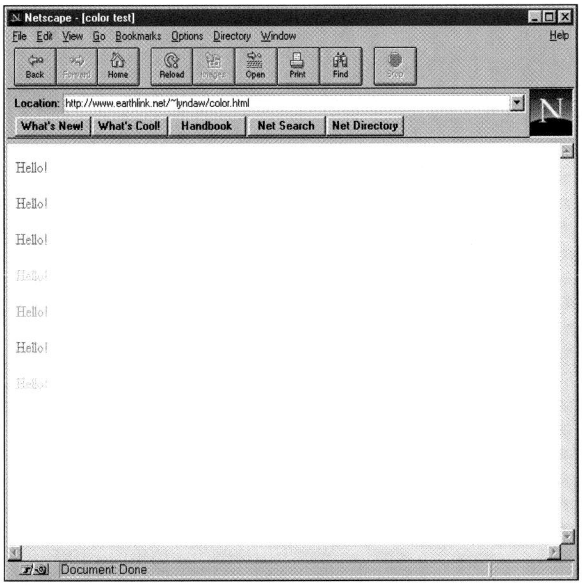

Figure 5.4

The finished words on a Web page in multiple colors using hex.

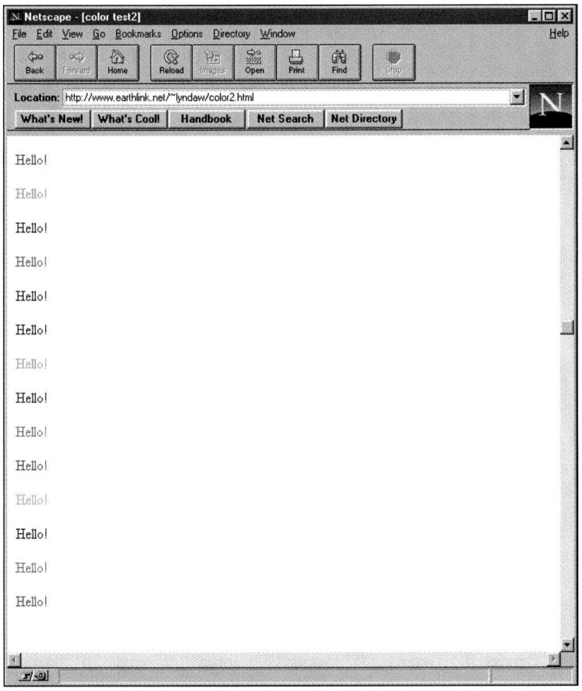

Figure 5.5

The finished words on a Web page in multiple colors using color names instead of hex.

Hexadecimal Resources

Many resources for converting RGB to a hex number exist on the Web. There are two different options: Hex Charts, which typically show color swatches and their hex values, and Hex Converters. Hex converters allow a user to type in RGB numbers, and offer the hexadecimal conversion in return. Both options will be covered in the following sections.

Working with Browser Safe Hexadecimal Colors

Designing with color on the Web requires that we specify RGB values with their hexadecimal equivalents. Having a chart that shows the conversion between RGB and Hex can be a useful design tool, such as the printed one here. The charts included in this chapter (see figs. 5.6 and 5.7) use the Browser Safe Palette, discussed in Chapter 4. These charts use the 216 colors that do not dither in a fixed-palette browser, and show you the hexadecimal numbers associated with each color.

Be aware, that you are looking at a "printed book." Colors in print (CMYK) vary dramatically from colors on computer screens (RGB). For a more accurate reading of what this chart will look like online, you should view it from the computer. It is on my Web site, located at http://www.lynda.com, or on the Designing Web Graphics CD-ROM.

The Browser Safe color palette (organized by hue). Each swatch lists its hexadecimal value and RGB components.

1	2	3	4	5	6	7	8	9	10	11	12	13	14	15	16
990033 R:153 G:000 B:051	FF3366 R:255 G:051 B:102	CC0033 R:204 G:000 B:051	FF0033 R:255 G:000 B:051	FF9999 R:255 G:153 B:153	CC3366 R:204 G:051 B:102	FFCCFF R:255 G:204 B:255	CC6699 R:204 G:102 B:153	993366 R:153 G:051 B:102	660033 R:102 G:000 B:051	CC3399 R:204 G:051 B:153	FF99CC R:255 G:153 B:204	FF66CC R:255 G:102 B:204	FF99FF R:255 G:153 B:255	FF6699 R:255 G:102 B:153	CC0066 R:204 G:000 B:102
FF0066 R:255 G:000 B:102	FF3399 R:255 G:051 B:153	FF0099 R:255 G:000 B:153	FF33CC R:255 G:051 B:204	FF00CC R:255 G:000 B:204	FF66FF R:255 G:102 B:255	FF33FF R:255 G:051 B:255	FF00FF R:255 G:000 B:255	CC0099 R:204 G:000 B:153	990066 R:153 G:000 B:102	CC66CC R:204 G:102 B:204	CC33CC R:204 G:051 B:204	CC99FF R:204 G:153 B:255	CC66FF R:204 G:102 B:255	CC33FF R:204 G:051 B:255	993399 R:153 G:051 B:153
CC00CC R:204 G:000 B:204	CC00FF R:204 G:000 B:255	9900CC R:153 G:000 B:204	9900FF R:153 G:000 B:255	CC99CC R:204 G:153 B:204	996699 R:153 G:102 B:153	663366 R:102 G:051 B:102	660066 R:102 G:000 B:102	9933CC R:153 G:051 B:204	660099 R:102 G:000 B:153	9000FF R:153 G:000 B:255	9933FF R:153 G:051 B:255	9966CC R:153 G:102 B:204	330033 R:051 G:000 B:051	663399 R:102 G:051 B:153	6633CC R:102 G:051 B:204
	9966FF R:153 G:102 B:255	330066 R:051 G:000 B:102		6633FF R:102 G:051 B:255	CCCCFF R:204 G:204 B:255	9999FF R:153 G:153 B:255	9999CC R:153 G:153 B:204	6666CC R:102 G:102 B:204	6666FF R:102 G:102 B:255	666699 R:102 G:102 B:153	333366 R:051 G:051 B:102	333399 R:051 G:051 B:153			
3333FF R:051 G:051 B:255	3333CC R:051 G:051 B:204	0066FF R:000 G:102 B:255	0033FF R:000 G:051 B:255	3366FF R:051 G:102 B:255	3366CC R:051 G:102 B:204	000066 R:000 G:000 B:102	000033 R:000 G:000 B:051		000099 R:000 G:000 B:153	0033CC R:000 G:051 B:204		336699 R:051 G:102 B:153	0066CC R:000 G:102 B:204	99CCFF R:153 G:204 B:255	6699FF R:102 G:153 B:255
003366 R:000 G:051 B:102	6699CC R:102 G:153 B:204	006699 R:000 G:102 B:153	3399CC R:051 G:153 B:204	0099CC R:000 G:153 B:204	66CCFF R:102 G:204 B:255	3399FF R:051 G:153 B:255	003399 R:000 G:051 B:153	0099FF R:000 G:153 B:255	33CCFF R:051 G:204 B:255	00CCFF R:000 G:204 B:255	99FFFF R:153 G:255 B:255	66FFFF R:102 G:255 B:255	33FFFF R:051 G:255 B:255	00FFFF R:000 G:255 B:255	00CCCC R:000 G:204 B:204
009999 R:000 G:153 B:153	669999 R:102 G:153 B:153	99CCCC R:153 G:204 B:204	CCFFFF R:204 G:255 B:255	33CCCC R:051 G:204 B:204	66CCCC R:102 G:204 B:204	339999 R:051 G:153 B:153	336666 R:051 G:102 B:102	006666 R:000 G:102 B:102	003333 R:000 G:051 B:051	00FFCC R:000 G:255 B:204	33FFCC R:051 G:255 B:204	33CC99 R:051 G:204 B:153	00CC99 R:000 G:204 B:153	66FFCC R:102 G:255 B:204	99FFCC R:153 G:255 B:204
00FF99 R:000 G:255 B:153	339966 R:051 G:153 B:102	006633 R:000 G:102 B:051	336633 R:051 G:102 B:051	669966 R:102 G:153 B:102	66CC66 R:102 G:204 B:102	99FF99 R:153 G:255 B:153	66FF66 R:102 G:255 B:102	339933 R:051 G:153 B:051	99CC99 R:153 G:204 B:153	66FF99 R:102 G:255 B:153	33FF99 R:051 G:255 B:153	33CC66 R:051 G:204 B:102	00CC66 R:000 G:204 B:102	66CC99 R:102 G:204 B:153	009966 R:000 G:153 B:102
009933 R:000 G:153 B:051	33FF66 R:051 G:255 B:102	00FF66 R:000 G:255 B:102	CCFFCC R:204 G:255 B:204	CCFF99 R:204 G:255 B:153	99FF66 R:153 G:255 B:102	99FF33 R:153 G:255 B:051	00FF33 R:000 G:255 B:051	33FF33 R:051 G:255 B:051	00CC33 R:000 G:204 B:051	33CC33 R:051 G:204 B:051	66FF33 R:102 G:255 B:051	00FF00 R:000 G:255 B:000	66CC33 R:102 G:204 B:051	006600 R:000 G:102 B:000	003300 R:000 G:051 B:000
009900 R:000 G:153 B:000	33FF00 R:051 G:255 B:000	66FF00 R:102 G:255 B:000	99FF00 R:153 G:255 B:000	66CC00 R:102 G:204 B:000	00CC00 R:000 G:204 B:000	33CC00 R:051 G:204 B:000	339900 R:051 G:153 B:000	99CC66 R:153 G:204 B:102	669900 R:102 G:153 B:000	99CC33 R:153 G:204 B:051	336600 R:051 G:102 B:000	669900 R:102 G:153 B:000	99CC00 R:153 G:204 B:000	CCFF66 R:204 G:255 B:102	CCFF33 R:204 G:255 B:051
CCFF00 R:204 G:255 B:000	999900 R:153 G:153 B:000	CCCC00 R:204 G:204 B:000	CCCC33 R:204 G:204 B:051	333300 R:051 G:051 B:000	666600 R:102 G:102 B:000	999933 R:153 G:153 B:051	CCCC66 R:204 G:204 B:102	666633 R:102 G:102 B:051	999966 R:153 G:153 B:102	CCCC99 R:204 G:204 B:153	FFFFCC R:255 G:255 B:204	FFFF99 R:255 G:255 B:153	FFFF66 R:255 G:255 B:102	FFFF33 R:255 G:255 B:051	FFFF00 R:255 G:255 B:000
FFCC00 R:255 G:204 B:000	FFCC66 R:255 G:204 B:102	FFCC33 R:255 G:204 B:051	CC9933 R:204 G:153 B:051	996600 R:153 G:102 B:000	CC9900 R:204 G:153 B:000	FF9900 R:255 G:153 B:000	CC6600 R:204 G:102 B:000	993300 R:153 G:051 B:000	CC6633 R:204 G:102 B:051	663300 R:102 G:051 B:000	FF9966 R:255 G:153 B:102	FF6633 R:255 G:102 B:051	FF9933 R:255 G:153 B:051	FF6600 R:255 G:102 B:000	CC3300 R:204 G:051 B:000
996633 R:153 G:102 B:051	330000 R:051 G:000 B:000	663333 R:102 G:051 B:051	996666 R:153 G:102 B:102	CC9999 R:204 G:153 B:153	993333 R:153 G:051 B:051	CC6666 R:204 G:102 B:102	FFCCCC R:255 G:204 B:204	FF3333 R:255 G:051 B:051	CC3333 R:204 G:051 B:051	FF6666 R:255 G:102 B:102	660000 R:102 G:000 B:000	990000 R:153 G:000 B:000	CC0000 R:204 G:000 B:000	FF0000 R:255 G:000 B:000	FF3300 R:255 G:051 B:000
CC9966 R:204 G:153 B:102	FFCC99 R:255 G:204 B:153	FFFFFF R:255 G:255 B:255	CCCCCC R:204 G:204 B:204	999999 R:153 G:153 B:153	666666 R:102 G:102 B:102	333333 R:051 G:051 B:051	000000 R:000 G:000 B:000								

Figure 5.6

The Browser Safe color palette organized by hue. It's useful to work with a palette that has all the colors organized by color, as you might want to see what color choices are available within a specific hue.

Browser Safe color palette (organized by value):

FFFFFF R:255 G:255 B:255	FFFFCC R:255 G:255 B:204	FFFF99 R:255 G:255 B:153	FFFF66 R:255 G:255 B:102	FFFF33 R:255 G:255 B:051	FFFF00 R:255 G:255 B:000	CCFFFF R:204 G:255 B:255	CCFFCC R:204 G:255 B:204
CCFF99 R:204 G:255 B:153	CCFF66 R:204 G:255 B:102	CCFF33 R:204 G:255 B:051	CCFF00 R:204 G:255 B:000	99FFFF R:153 G:255 B:255	99FFCC R:153 G:255 B:204	99FF99 R:153 G:255 B:153	66FFFF R:102 G:255 B:255
99FF66 R:153 G:255 B:102	99FF33 R:153 G:255 B:051	66FFCC R:102 G:255 B:204	FFCCFF R:255 G:204 B:255	99FF00 R:153 G:255 B:000	33FFFF R:051 G:255 B:255	FFCCCC R:255 G:204 B:204	33FFCC R:051 G:255 B:204
00FFFF R:000 G:255 B:255	66FF99 R:102 G:255 B:153	FFCC99 R:255 G:204 B:153	66FF66 R:102 G:255 B:102	66FF33 R:102 G:255 B:051	00FFCC R:000 G:255 B:204	66FF00 R:102 G:255 B:000	33FF99 R:051 G:255 B:153
FFCC66 R:255 G:204 B:102	FFCC33 R:255 G:204 B:051	CCCCFF R:204 G:204 B:255	33FF66 R:051 G:255 B:102	33FF33 R:051 G:255 B:051	00FF99 R:000 G:255 B:153	FFCC00 R:255 G:204 B:000	33FF00 R:051 G:255 B:000
00FF66 R:000 G:255 B:102	00FF33 R:000 G:255 B:051	00FF00 R:000 G:255 B:000	CCCCCC R:204 G:204 B:204	CCCC99 R:204 G:204 B:153	99CCFF R:153 G:204 B:255	CCCC66 R:204 G:204 B:102	CCCC00 R:204 G:204 B:000
CCCC33 R:204 G:204 B:051	99CCCC R:153 G:204 B:204	FF99FF R:255 G:153 B:255	99CC99 R:153 G:204 B:153	66CCFF R:102 G:204 B:255	FF99CC R:255 G:153 B:204	99CC66 R:153 G:204 B:102	66CCCC R:102 G:204 B:204
99CC33 R:153 G:204 B:051	00CCFF R:000 G:204 B:255	33CCFF R:051 G:204 B:255	99CC00 R:153 G:204 B:000	FF9999 R:255 G:153 B:153	66CC99 R:102 G:204 B:153	FF9966 R:255 G:153 B:102	66CC66 R:102 G:204 B:102
33CCCC R:051 G:204 B:204	CC99FF R:204 G:153 B:255	00CCCC R:000 G:204 B:204	FF9933 R:255 G:153 B:051	FF9900 R:255 G:153 B:000	66CC33 R:102 G:204 B:051	66CC00 R:102 G:204 B:000	33CC99 R:051 G:204 B:153
00CC99 R:000 G:204 B:153	CC99CC R:204 G:153 B:204	33CC66 R:051 G:204 B:102	00CC66 R:000 G:204 B:102	CC9999 R:204 G:153 B:153	FF66FF R:255 G:102 B:255	33CC33 R:051 G:204 B:051	33CC00 R:051 G:204 B:000
CC9966 R:204 G:153 B:102	00CC33 R:000 G:204 B:051	9999FF R:153 G:153 B:255	00CC00 R:000 G:204 B:000	CC9933 R:204 G:153 B:051	CC9900 R:204 G:153 B:000	FF66CC R:255 G:102 B:204	9999CC R:153 G:153 B:204
FF6699 R:255 G:102 B:153	999999 R:153 G:153 B:153	6699FF R:102 G:153 B:255	FF6666 R:255 G:102 B:102	CC66FF R:204 G:102 B:255	999966 R:153 G:153 B:102	6699CC R:102 G:153 B:204	999933 R:153 G:153 B:051
FF6633 R:255 G:102 B:051	FF6600 R:255 G:102 B:000	FF33FF R:255 G:051 B:255	3399FF R:051 G:153 B:255	999900 R:153 G:153 B:000	669999 R:102 G:153 B:153	CC66CC R:204 G:102 B:204	0099FF R:000 G:153 B:255
FF33CC R:255 G:051 B:204	3399CC R:051 G:153 B:204	CC6699 R:204 G:102 B:153	669966 R:102 G:153 B:102	FF00FF R:255 G:000 B:255	339999 R:051 G:153 B:153	669933 R:102 G:153 B:051	669900 R:102 G:153 B:000
FF3399 R:255 G:051 B:153	0099CC R:000 G:153 B:204	9966FF R:153 G:102 B:255	CC6666 R:204 G:102 B:102	009999 R:000 G:153 B:153	CC6633 R:204 G:102 B:051	CC6600 R:204 G:102 B:000	339966 R:051 G:153 B:102
FF00CC R:255 G:000 B:204	FF3366 R:255 G:051 B:102	009966 R:000 G:153 B:102	CC33FF R:204 G:051 B:255	FF3333 R:255 G:051 B:051	339933 R:051 G:153 B:051	009933 R:000 G:153 B:051	9966CC R:153 G:102 B:204
FF3300 R:255 G:051 B:000	FF0099 R:255 G:000 B:153	339900 R:051 G:153 B:000	009900 R:000 G:153 B:000	6666FF R:102 G:102 B:255	CC33CC R:204 G:051 B:204	FF0066 R:255 G:000 B:102	996699 R:153 G:102 B:153
FF0033 R:255 G:000 B:051	FF0000 R:255 G:000 B:000	CC00FF R:204 G:000 B:255	CC3399 R:204 G:051 B:153	996666 R:153 G:102 B:102	6666CC R:102 G:102 B:204	996633 R:153 G:102 B:051	996600 R:153 G:102 B:000
3366FF R:051 G:102 B:255	CC3366 R:204 G:051 B:102	CC00CC R:204 G:000 B:204	9933FF R:153 G:051 B:255	0066FF R:000 G:102 B:255	666699 R:102 G:102 B:153	CC3333 R:204 G:051 B:051	CC3300 R:204 G:051 B:000
3366CC R:051 G:102 B:204	CC0099 R:204 G:000 B:153	9933CC R:153 G:051 B:204	666666 R:102 G:102 B:102	666633 R:102 G:102 B:051	0066CC R:000 G:102 B:204	9900FF R:153 G:000 B:255	666600 R:102 G:102 B:000
CC0066 R:204 G:000 B:102	336699 R:051 G:102 B:153	993399 R:153 G:051 B:153	CC0033 R:204 G:000 B:051	6633FF R:102 G:051 B:255	336666 R:051 G:102 B:102	006699 R:000 G:102 B:153	CC0000 R:204 G:000 B:000
993366 R:153 G:051 B:102	9900CC R:153 G:000 B:204	336633 R:051 G:102 B:051	006666 R:000 G:102 B:102	336600 R:051 G:102 B:000	6633CC R:102 G:051 B:204	3333FF R:051 G:051 B:255	006633 R:000 G:102 B:051
993333 R:153 G:051 B:051	993300 R:153 G:051 B:000	6600FF R:102 G:000 B:255	990099 R:153 G:000 B:153	006600 R:000 G:102 B:000	0033FF R:000 G:051 B:255	663399 R:102 G:051 B:153	990066 R:153 G:000 B:102
3333CC R:051 G:051 B:204	663366 R:102 G:051 B:102	6600CC R:102 G:000 B:204	660099 R:102 G:000 B:153	0033CC R:000 G:051 B:204	990000 R:153 G:000 B:000	330099 R:051 G:000 B:153	663333 R:102 G:051 B:051
663300 R:102 G:051 B:000	660099 R:102 G:000 B:153	0000FF R:000 G:000 B:255	333399 R:051 G:051 B:153	3300CC R:051 G:000 B:204	003399 R:000 G:051 B:153	333366 R:051 G:051 B:102	660066 R:102 G:000 B:102
333333 R:051 G:051 B:051	003366 R:000 G:051 B:102	0000CC R:000 G:000 B:204	333300 R:051 G:051 B:000	660000 R:102 G:000 B:000	330000 R:051 G:000 B:000	000033 R:000 G:000 B:051	003333 R:000 G:051 B:051
003300 R:000 G:051 B:000	000099 R:000 G:000 B:153	330066 R:051 G:000 B:102	330033 R:051 G:000 B:051	000066 R:000 G:000 B:102	330000 R:051 G:000 B:000	000033 R:000 G:000 B:051	000000 R:000 G:000 B:000

Figure 5.7

The same Browser Safe color palette organized differently by value. It's also useful to view the colors organized by lights and darks.

Web Hex Converters

There are a number of sites on the Web that let you plug RGB values into them and then generate hex code for your values on-the-fly. This can be very convenient when you're working and want a quick visualization of what a certain color scheme will look like. Some sites even go so far as to accept RGB in and give you hex *and* HTML back (see fig. 5.8). Now you're talking! Here's an example of working with Inquisitor Mediarama's RGB-HEX Converter found at: http://www.echonyc.com/~xixax/Mediarama/hex.html (see fig. 5.9).

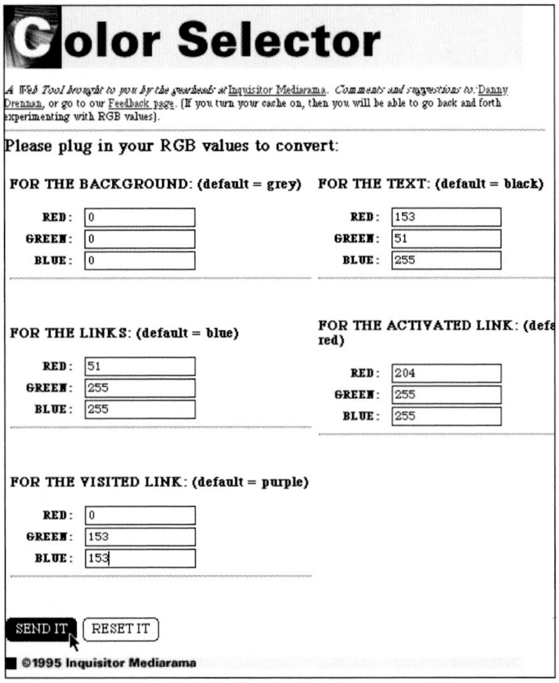

Figure 5.9

Voilà! An accurate previsualization of your page, plus the added bonus of having the HTML tag written out for you on the screen.

Hex Calculators

Lastly, there are hexadecimal calculators that let you enter RGB values and convert the math automatically. PCs ship with a hex calculator (see fig. 5.10), which usually is found in the Accessories group. Open the Calculator and then under View, select Scientific. This changes the standard calculator to a scientific calculator. Then, simply select the Hex option to start converting your RGB values. Mac owner's aren't so lucky, but we've included a shareware hex calculator on the CD-ROM (see fig. 5.11). Once you have calculated your hex number, you are ready to use it in your HTML code.

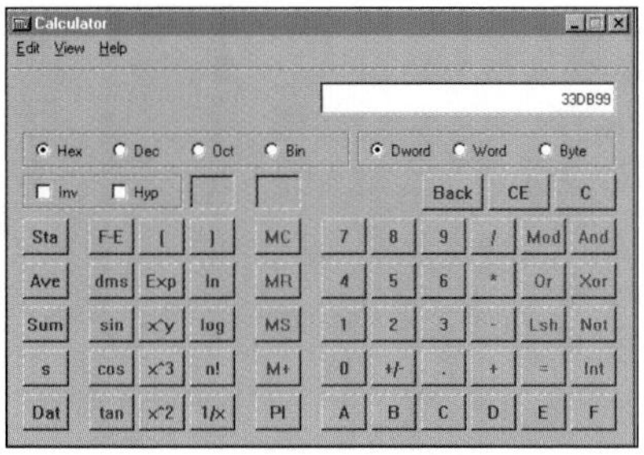

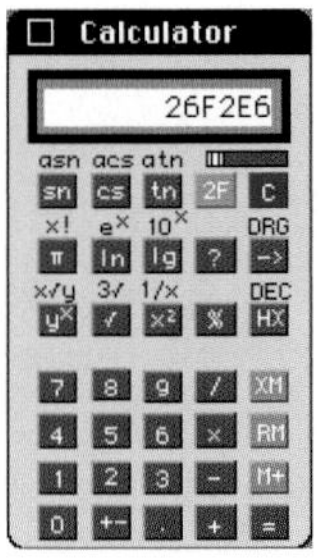

Figure 5.8

Enter the RGB values and press SEND IT.

Figure 5.10 and Figure 5.11

The scientific calculator (on left) that ships with Windows.

Calculator II+ (on right) by Joseph Cicinelli for the Mac.

A Case Study in Managing Hex Values

This section offers a case study of how I personally work with my pages to arrive at the hex numbers I like. Figure 5.12 shows my color picking arsenal.

I like to previsualize pages in Photoshop (see Chapter 18). I find it impossible to judge color unless I'm looking at it in context. Sometimes a small amount of color will look fine against another small amount of color, but if you change the ratio from small to large, the color doesn't look good any more. Here, I've set up a layered document that represents how my page is going to look. I've already tweaked the colors, and have decided on my choices for a background, the links, visited links, borders, and so on.

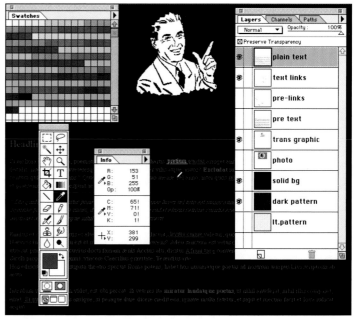

Figure 5.12

Here's an example of my color picking arsenal: Using the eyedropper tool and the Get Info palette, I'm able to select color values by appearance and easily read their RGB values. I always try to use the Web Browser palette that ships on the CD-ROM, and have it loaded here in the Swatches palette.

1. I choose colors from the Web Browser palette. As long as I am working with solid colors, I might as well choose ones that won't dither on other people's systems that only have 256 - color displays.

2. I fill each appropriate layer with colors that balance well for contrast and brightness.

3. Once I'm satisfied, I use the eyedropper tool to click on each color to locate its RGB value. I make sure the Info palette is open so I can read the values easily.

4. I convert the RGB numbers to hex, using my handy hex calculator, or switching to my online browser to use a Hex Converter. Next, I write down the hexadecimal numbers on paper, and switch programs to my word processor.

5. I write the HTML code, insert the hex values where I want them, and test the results in my Browser. More information can be found in Chapters 17, 18 and Appendix A on testing Web pages from your hard drive and loading them to a server.

HTML 3.0 and Hex

As if dealing with hex isn't bad enough, there is speculation that HTML 3.0 is not going to officially sanction or recognize hexadecimal tags for colored text, links, backgrounds, and borders. As much as I dislike the hassle of converting RGB to hex, I do treasure the capability to color my text and backgrounds if I want to. The capability to color backgrounds and text was initiated by Netscape, and as you can see by the browser comparison in Chapter 1, other browsers recognize the code even though it isn't formally a part of HTML. Perhaps the authors of future HTML versions have some other, better way of dealing with color in mind. If so, there's no word of it yet, leaving us with hex or nothing if we want color on our pages. Are we having fun yet?

Summary

Now that you've experienced the joys of hexadecimal mathematics, you too can have color on your pages! There are just a few things to remember:

- Use the proper HTML tags to make your hex values translate to colored text and/or backgrounds.

- If you're going to pick colors, pick those that won't dither on most browsers by using the chart from this book's CD-ROM or downloading it from http://www.lynda.com.

- You can use a hex calculator or an online service for RGB/Hex conversion.

- HTML 1.0, 2.0, and 3.0 do not officially sanction the use of hexadecimal tags for color, but many browsers support it anyway.

CHAPTER 6

Making Background Patterns

Making full-screen, wall-to-wall graphics on the Web would seem to be an impossible feat, given the slow modems and teenie weenie phone lines most of us have to squeeze connections through. Not to mention the fact that full-screen graphics can mean one thing to a compact portable computer Web user and another to someone with a 21" monitor! You might think it would take way too long to download an image that fills a viewer's browser screen, and that it would be irresponsible to prepare images of this size for Web graphics.

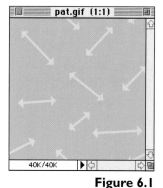

Figure 6.1

An example of a small tile source file.

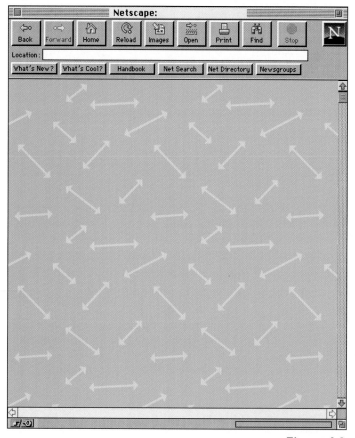

Figure 6.2

The same tile, repeated over the background of a Web page.

Patterned tiles are the answer (see figs. 6.1 and 6.2). This chapter covers an HTML tag called <body background>, which allows a single small image to be repeated endlessly so that it fills an entire Web page, regardless of size. These single small images will be referred to in this chapter as patterned tiles. They have the advantage of being small, so they load fast, and the ability to repeat over the size of whatever Web screen they appear on. Because a small graphic loads faster than a big one, this technique works well to cover a lot of real estate on a Web page without incurring a lot of overhead in downloading time.

We will examine the following aspects of patterned tile creation:

- How to make pattern-based images.
- How to make seamless patterns.
- How to know what size to make the source pattern image.
- What file format to save patterns in.
- How to write the HTML to place patterned tile images on a Web page.

Tiling Backgrounds

Netscape was the first browser to bring the <body background> tag to the Web. From the preliminary specs, it looks like HTML 3.0 will offer official support of this tag as well. Check the Browser Comparison test in Chapter 1 to see which browsers support pattern backgrounds and which don't.

The <body background> tag allows the browser to work with a small graphic and turn it into a full-screen graphic. It accomplishes this effect by taking a single image and repeating it, creating a tiling effect many times over, filling any size screen regardless of computer platform and browser area. The browser only needs to load a single source file for the pattern, and once it's downloaded it fills the entire Web page. This saves time, because the wait time is for a single small image, even though the result is that the entire screen fills with an image. This is a great solution for creating full-screen graphics for low-bandwidth delivery systems like the Web.

Bandwidth limitations aren't the only problem using patterned tiled backgrounds solve. One of the great frustrations most Web designers share is HTML's inability to allow for images to be layered. If you consider that layering is a main feature of programs like Photoshop, QuarkXpress, and Pagemaker, you'll understand why the absence of this capability is sorely missed.

The good news is that tiled backgrounds are the first step toward allowing for layered images. HTML allows text, links, and images to go on top of tiled backgrounds, making it an extremely useful and economical design element. The HTML code for this tiling effect is quite simple. The real challenge is making the art look good, and controlling whether the seams of each repeated image are obvious or invisible.

Determining Tiled Pattern Sizes

One of the first questions that comes to mind is, how big should the tiled image be? HTML puts no restrictions on the size of a source for a background tile. The image has to be in a square or rectangular, though, because that's the native shape of any computer file.

The size of the image is entirely up to you. You should realize that the size of a tile is going to dictate how many times it repeats. If a viewer's monitor is 640×480 pixels and your tile is 320×240, it will repeat 4 times. If it were 20×20 pixels, it would repeat 32 times. See figures 6.3 through 6.8 for examples of how tile size affects the end background pattern result.

Figure 6.3
A large-sized source tile.

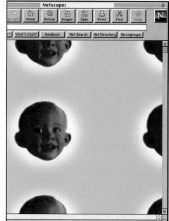

Figure 6.4
Results of largest source tile as a Web background.

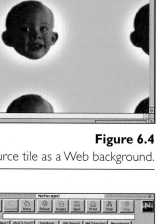

Figure 6.5
A medium-sized source tile.

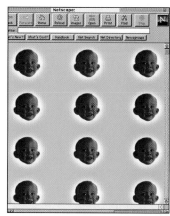

Figure 6.6
Results of medium-sized source tile as a Web background.

Figure 6.7
A small source tile.

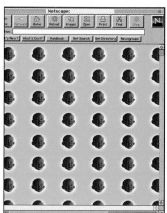

Figure 6.8
Results of smallest source tile as a Web background.

If your tile has images that repeat on each side, it will not show visible seams and the viewer will not know how many times it repeats. If the image has an obvious border around it (see fig. 6.9), the border will accentuate the fact that the image is being tiled (see fig. 6.10). The size of your tile is up to you and the effect you are striving for.

Be aware though, that file size restrictions must still be honored. If you make a tile that takes up a lot of memory, it will take the same amount of time to load as any other kind of huge graphic you put on the Web. If need be, refer back to Chapter 3, "Making Low-Memory Graphics," for tips on how to minimize file sizes and follow those same rules.

If you use an image source that has large dimensions, it will not repeat as often. If it is large enough, it will not repeat at all. The speed advantages of having a small image load once and automatically repeat without incurring any additional downloading time would not exist. On the other hand, if you could make a large image that did not take up a lot of memory, then loading it in as a background image instead of a regular graphic could have its merits. Sometimes the pixel size count of a document and the amount of memory they take up are not relational. Check out Bruce Heavin's 12 KB 800×600 pixel tile (see fig. 6.11) from The Net Magazine's Web site (http://www.thenet-usa.com/mag/mag.html).

Figure 6.9
Source tile with an obvious border.

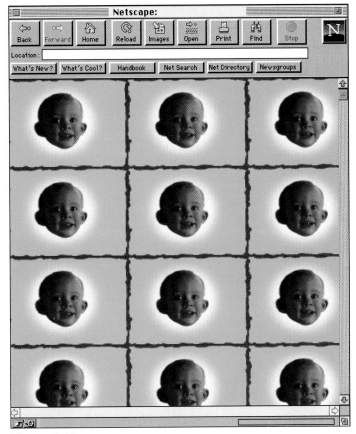

Figure 6.10
Results of the tile with an obvious border.

Figure 6.11

A large tile source (800×600 pixels) that only measures 11.6 KB!

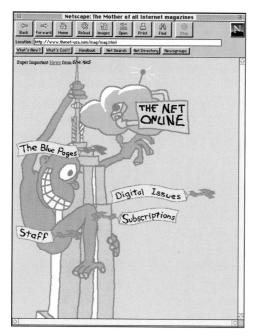

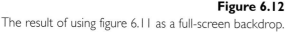

Figure 6.12

The result of using figure 6.11 as a full-screen backdrop.

Why would you use an image with large pixel dimensions as a tiled background, as it seems to defeat the point? Because it could go behind other images and text, making full-screen backdrop to other images on your page (see fig 6.12). HTML doesn't let you put text or images over regular images. The only way around this restriction is to use a background tiled graphic.

File Formats for Patterned Background Tiles

GIFs and JPEGs are the standard file formats for the Web, and tiled patterns are no exception. Just remember to follow the kilobyte rule. Every KB of file size represents 1 second of download time to your viewer. The full size of the background pattern gets added to the download! If you have a background that's 60 KB and two images that are 10 KB each, the total file size of your page will be 80 KB. You would have just added a minute of download time to your page! Therefore tiled backgrounds that take up a lot of memory are extra annoying to your audience during download.

Interlaced GIFs (discussed in Chapters 3 and 8) work for tiled backgrounds, but they have to res up, just like when you use them for a single image. Sometimes this just multiplies the annoyance factor to your viewers because they have to wait a little longer to see what else is on your page. Other times it looks like a cool, animated special effect. Be sure to test your pages before you post them, and use the interlacing option sparingly on backgrounds.

As usual, always save your file names in lower case and use the extensions .jpg or .gif to let the HTML code know what kind of image it has to load. I usually put the word *pat* somewhere in a pattern file name, just for my own reference. That way I know what I intended to use the file for when searching for it in a text list, such as my server directory!

Figure 6.13
The pat.gif document.

The Code, Please!

Here are HTML sample documents showing how to use patterns, images, and text. The files used are shown in figures 6.13 and 6.14.

It is very simple to include a patterned background in an HTML document (see fig. 6.15). Here's the bare minimum code required:

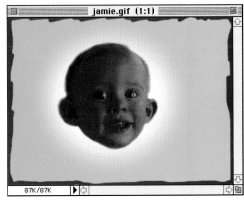

Figure 6.14
The jamie.gif document.

```
<html>
<body background="pat.gif">
</body>
</html>
```

Figure 6.15
A patterned background.

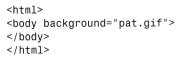

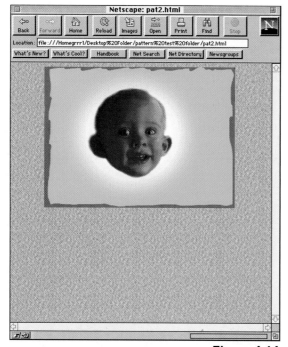

Figure 6.16

An image laid over a background.

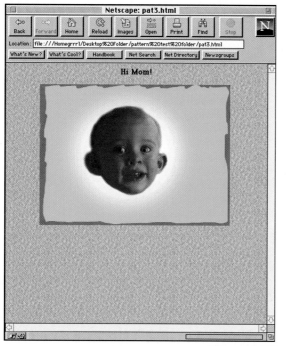

Figure 6.17

Text and an image over a background.

If you wanted to have an image lay over a background, as in figure 6.16, the code would look like this:

```
<html>
<body background="pat.gif">
<img src="jamie gif">
</body>
</html>
```

If you wanted text and an image to lay over a background (see fig. 6.17), the code would look like this:

```
<html>
<body background="pat.gif">
<center>
<b><fontsize=4>Hi Mom!</font><b>
<img src="graphic.gif">
<body>
</html>
```

Aesthetics of Backgrounds

Always pay attention to contrast and value (lights and darks) when creating background tiles. If you have a light background, use dark type. If you have a dark background use light type. If you aren't going to change your type colors (see Chapter 5 on hexadecimals), use a light background; about the same value as the default light grey you see as the background color of most browsers. The light background will insure that the default colors of black, blue, and purple text will read against your custom background.

When making art for pattern tiles, try to use either all dark values or all light values. If you have both darks and lights in a background neither light nor dark type will work consistently against them. This is a basic, simple rule to follow, and your site will avoid the pitfalls of poor background tile aesthetics. Using either all dark values, or all light values seems like common sense, but tour the Web a bit and you'll soon see rainbow colored backgrounds with unreadable black type everywhere.

Seams or No Seams, That Is the Question

The next sections take a look at two different ways to present your background tile on your Web page: with or without seams.

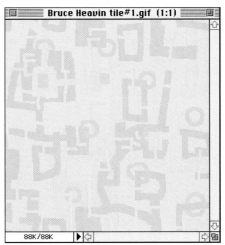

Figure 6.18
The source for a seamless tile.

Seams

When an image has obvious seams, it looks tiled on purpose. Some Web pages look great wallpapered with an obvious border. Andy Warhol shocked the art world in the 1960's and first earned his notoriety by making images of repeating soup cans on a single canvas. Video walls are often built on the power of images repeating in squares. There's nothing wrong with making patterns that have obvious borders and repeats, especially if that's what you had in mind. Making a tiled pattern with an obvious repeating border is fairly simple. Refer to figures 6.9 and 6.10 as examples.

No Seams, the Photoshop Way

When "seamless" patterns are described, it means the border of the pattern tile is impossible to locate (see figs. 6.18 and 6.19). There aren't any pros or cons to using seamless or seamed tiles; it's purely an aesthetic decision. Seamless tiles, however are much trickier to make.

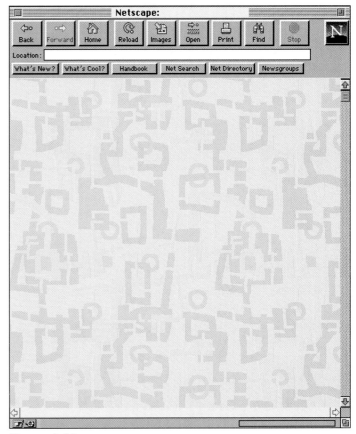

Figure 6.19
The boundaries of a successful seamless tile are impossible to see.

Here's a step by step example of how Bruce Heavin, using Photoshop, made smiley face wallpaper for *The Net Magazine*'s Web site:

1. Using Photoshop 3.0 on his Mac 840 AV, Bruce opened a new document at 300×300 pixels, 72 dpi, in RGB. He started drawing a group of smiley faces, and was careful to compose the art to one side. He always begins making seamless tiles this way, either favoring the left, right, top, or bottom of the file as shown in figure 6.20.

Figure 6.20
The beginning of a seamless tile. Note how the illustration is kept intentionally to one side.

2. Bruce used the Offset filter and entered a value that was less than half the size of the file. The point of this was to have the drawing he just made jump to a new position in the document so that he could start to see where gaps appeared. If he chose an even value, the edges he'd need to see wouldn't show up, because they would stay evenly positioned to where they are now. By making the offset value arbitrary, he was able to see where to draw next. By checking the wrap around button, he was able to have the background of the tile stay the same color (see fig. 6.21).

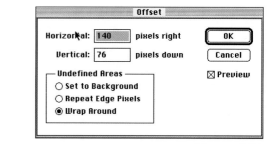

Figure 6.21
The offset filter is at 140/76, with wrap around checked so the image will move and not be erased.

3. Here's the result of his file shown in figure 6.21 with an offset of 140/76 entered into the filter. Now the edges can be seen that weren't apparent in the last view (see fig. 6.22).

4. Bruce continued to fill in the graphic, making sure his artwork had a rhythm to the spacing, but no glaring irregularities that would make the repeat of the pattern obvious (see fig. 6.22).

Figure 6.22
The results of the first offset. New edges are in view.

5. Here's the result of the same offset value of 140/76 repeated, offsetting what was already offset (see fig. 6.23). New "holes" in the repeating pattern are now visible.

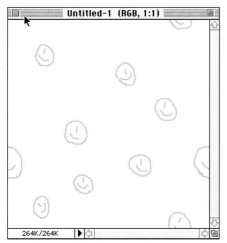

Figure 6.23
More holes appear and are filled.

6. Bruce filled in the holes that appeared in the new gaps (see fig. 6.24).

Figure 6.24
Bruce fills in more shapes.

7. One more offset showed Bruce if there were any problem areas in the pattern (see fig. 6.25).

8. Figure 6.26 shows the finished tile. Bruce always checks his pattern in Photoshop before sending the final version to the server. He creates a larger Photoshop file (640×480 at 72 dpi) to simulate the size of a standard Web page. Next, he chooses "Select All," "Define Pattern," and "Fill w/pattern" and tiles the image into the large document. If there are holes or problems, he goes back to the tile to repeat this entire process again until he's happy with the results. Figure 6.27 shows what the tile looks like on a Web page.

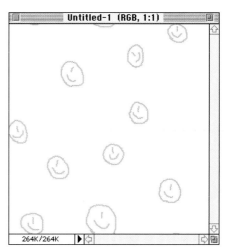

Figure 6.25
One last offset shows there are still a couple of holes in the spacing.

Figure 6.26
The final tile.

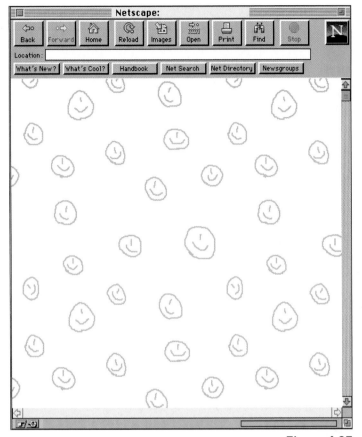

Figure 6.27

What the tile looks like on a Web page.

When Bruce saved the image, he chose Index Color, and converted the document from RGB to 8-bit so it could be saved in CompuServe GIF format.

No Seams, the Painter 3.1 Way

Fractal Design Painter 3.1 is an excellent environment to make seamless tiles in. If you open a new document and choose Tools, Patterns, Define Pattern before you draw, Painter will do an automatic offset filter process, similar to Photoshop's, but in real time. If you draw off a corner on one

side, your stroke will automatically appear on the other. It's like drawing with a mirroring tool. It's kind of hard to control, but very fun to experiment with. Here's the step-by-step process for the finished tile in figure 6.33:

1. Open a new document in Painter at 300×300 at 72 dpi.

2. Select a paper color (see fig. 6.28).

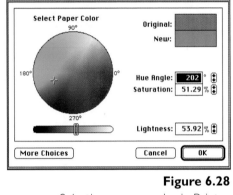

Figure 6.28

Selecting a paper color in Painter.

Go to the Art Materials palette and select a paper stock (see fig. 6.29). Under Effects, Surface Control, Apply Surface Texture, create the lighting effect you want to use to create a textured paper effect (see fig. 6.30).

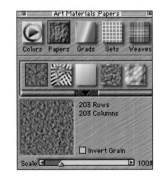

Figure 6.29

Working with paper textures in the Art Materials palette.

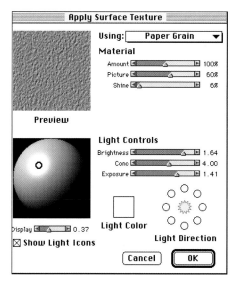

Figure 6.30
The Apply Surface Texture Filter dialog box.

Figure 6.32
Using the color picker from the Art Materials palette.

3. Go to Tools, Patterns, Define Pattern.

4. Choose a drawing tool. I've chosen to use the chalk tool (see fig. 6.31).

Figure 6.31
The Brushes palette, with Chalk selected.

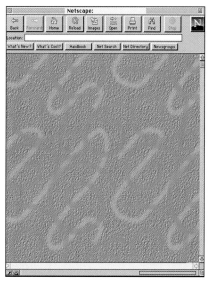

Figure 6.33
The finished GIF showing the mirrored image.

6. When you're happy with the results, save the pattern as a .jpg or a .gif.

7. Put the pattern on a Web page using the HTML you learned in the preceding sections.

5. Pick a color from the Art Materials, Colors palette (see fig. 6.32). Start to draw. Your brush strokes will automatically mirror and repeat on the opposite side, creating a seamless pattern (see fig. 6.33).

One of the great features in Painter is the ability to use and store paper textures that simulate traditional media—like watercolor stocks, canvases, and abstract, seamless paper textures. If you look at the paper texture palette (refer to fig. 6.29), you'll notice that the number of pixels used to define each texture is displayed next to the paper swatch. If you make a new document the same size as the swatch indicates, and apply Surface Texture, as described in Step 2, you'll be able to make your own tile of the paper texture. If you use paint tools over the paper texture, it will duplicate the tooth of the selected paper stock, making for some very cool possibilities for pattern tiles.

There's much more that can be done with Painter than I have room to show here. Look for books on Painter in the bookstore, and check out Fractal Design's Web site at: http://www.fractal.com for product announcements, upgrades, lots of tips, and a gallery of artwork created by Painter artists.

Figure 6.34

Home Economics major, Brandee Selck shares her home decorating ideas with an accommodating offering of quality wallpaper selections.

Summary

Using pattern tiles on a Web site is a great way to cheat the effect of filling the entire screen with a graphic. By using a small tile, you can save download time and still achieve an effect of having wall-to-wall image area. Patterns are also useful, because other graphics and text can be laid over them. Here are some tips to follow when working with patterns:

- The size of your original art for tiling dictates how many times the tiled pattern will repeat in browser windows on different computer screens.

- Keep file sizes of pattern source images small, as they add to the overall total page size and download time.

- Choose whether you want to see the seams of a tile or not. If you want to make seamless patterns, be sure to check the file as you're creating it using offset features in paint programs to check to see if repeated edges are showing.

- Remember to make sure type can be read over your background pattern tile. Keep the tile light, or dark, but lights and darks should not be mixed. Use light type over dark backgrounds and dark type over light backgrounds.

> **NOTE**
>
> Don't overlook online resources for background patterns clip art (see fig. 6.34). Netscape has some sites for patterns and instructions on adding background patterns to your Web pages.
>
> **Netscape's Pattern instruction:** http://www2.netscape.com/assist/net_sites/bg/
>
> **Netscape's pattern library page:** http://www.netscape.com/assist/net_sites/bg/backgrounds.html
>
> **IUMA's Home Decoration Ideas:** http://www.iuma.com/IUMA-2.0/pages/wallpaper/

CHAPTER 7

Making Irregularly Shaped Artwork Using Background Colors

Let's face it, too much art on the Web is in the shape of rectangles: buttons, pictures, splash screens, menu bars. It's no wonder, considering a computer image file is by nature automatically saved in a rectangle. You can't change that, and the Web can't change that. It's a problem without an obvious solution.

The trick is rather simple to explain. Let's say you have a circle and you want it to look like it's free floating even though it must be inside a rectangular shape. Make the background behind the circle the same color as your Web page. If you put the two together, there should be no obvious rectangular border. Sounds simple? It is.

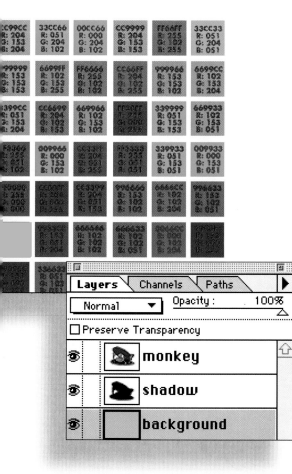

Figure 7.1

An example of a Web page where background color matching failed.

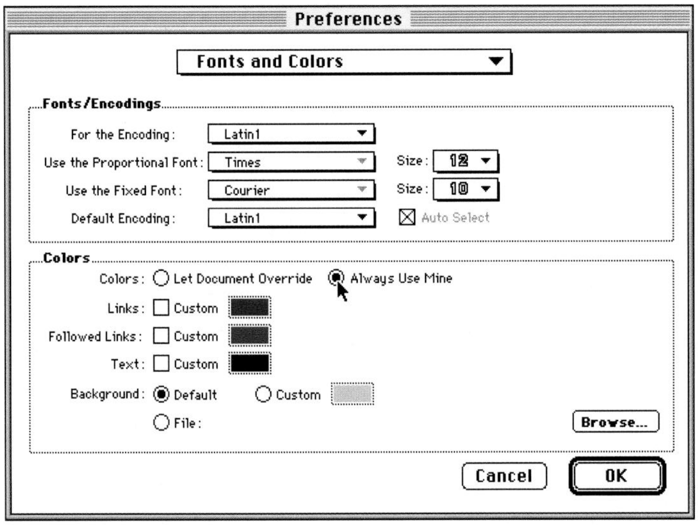

Figure 7.2

If the "Always Use Mine" preferences are checked in Netscape, none of the custom background or text colors you designed will show up!

There's a snag. As you can see by the browser comparison chart in Chapter 1, "Browser Hell," there is no standard background color for a Web page. Some browsers default to using grey, some white, and some off-white (see fig. 7.1). Not only that, but individual computer users can set their browser preferences to change the color of their Web pages and override the browser's default settings (see fig. 7.2).

This chapter teaches you how to set exact background colors (assuming your end viewer has not changed his or her preferences—for which there is *nothing* you can do), using two HTML-based techniques. One involves using hexadecimal code to set a specific background color, and the other requires setting up the HTML to use a solid pattern tile. Step-by-step examples will help you understand these two techniques, and how to make the irregularly shaped artwork go on top of the colored backgrounds. All of the tutorial files referred to in this chapter are included on the CD-ROM, if you'd like to use them. Or you can make your own art and follow along.

Creating Background Color the Hexadecimal Way

Because there's no way to rely on the browser for a fixed background color, we have to set our own. This first example demonstrates how to include irregularly shaped artwork using the <body bgcolor> tag.

1. See figure 7.3 for the sample art used in this step. It is named monkey.jpg. I intentionally gave it a drop shadow to demonstrate the effectiveness of this technique with hard-edged or soft-edged artwork.

2. Next, I wrote the following HTML. This code tells the background to be white, using the hexadecimal code FFFFFF, and inserts the monkey image on the same page:

```
<html>
<body bgcolor="FFFFFF">
<center><b><font size=4>
Where's the Monkey?
</font></b><p>
<img src="monkey.jpg">
</center>
</body>
</html>
```

As you can see, it worked (see fig. 7.4)! But what if you want some other background besides white? The following shows you how to create a lavender background for the monkey.

1. Open the file value.nr.gif from the CD-ROM (or look at the chart in Chapter 5 and pick a color from there). If you choose a color from the browser-safe palettes supplied with this book, your files will not dither in Netscape or Microsoft's Internet Explorer.

2. Choose the eyedropper tool and click on a color of choice (see fig. 7.5). For this example I chose a lavender color. Looking at the chart tells me that the hexadecimal color is 9966CC.

3. Using Photoshop's layers, I fill a background layer with the lavender color and Save a Copy using the JPEG file format in max. compression quality. It is named monkey2.jpg (see fig. 7.6).

Figure 7.3
Here's the monkey.jpg document. The monkey illustration was originally created by Bruce Heavin.

Figure 7.4
An example of the finished Web page.

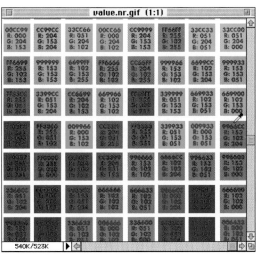

Figure 7.5
Using the eyedropper tool in Photoshop to select a color from the browser-safe hexadecimal chart arranged by value (available on the CD-ROM).

Figure 7.6

The file monkey2.gif that uses the hexadecimal color 9966CC for its background.

Figure 7.7

The finished Web page using the <body
bgcolor=9966CC> tag.

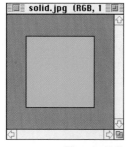

Figure 7.8

The solid colored background pattern,
called solid.jpg.

4. When I write the HTML code for this example, I
change the <body bgcolor> tag from white to the
lavender color by using the hex value 9966CC. I
also decide to change the color of the type to white,
for added variety. Here's the code:

```
<html>
<body bgcolor="9966CC" text="FFFFFF">
<center><b><font size=4>Where's the
Monkey?</font></b><p>
<img src="monkey2.jpg">
</center>
</body>
</html>
```

Creating Background Color Using Solid Patterns

At the moment, quite a few Browsers support hexadecimal related tags. (See Chapter 1 to check the Browser
Comparison chart.) Because there is some question
about whether HTML 3.0 will support hexadecimal-
related tags (see Chapter 5), you might choose to dictate
the background color using a different approach.

Another way to color the background of a Web page is to
use a solid color swatch within the background pattern
tag, <body background>. This tag is more commonly
used with artwork that has an image in it, such as a
marble texture. The <body background> tag takes
whatever art you tell it to use, and repeats the artwork
tiles so they fill the entire Web page. For instructions on
how to make image-filled types of pattern tiles, refer to
Chapter 6.

We are going to use the same technique that Chapter 6
described in detail, but our source image for the pattern
tile is going to be made out of a solid color (see fig. 7.8).
As it is repeated over the page, this tile will produce a
solid background, identical in appearance to what was
demonstrated using the hexadecimal method previously
mentioned.

Here's step-by-step instruction:

1. Choose a background color for your irregularly shaped image. This time I'm going to pick a turquoise color, for variety's sake. First I fill the background color of the monkey image. Then, using my Photoshop layered document (see fig. 7.9), I'll save it as monkey3.jpg. The finished monkey is shown in figure 7.10.

2. Next, I'll open a new empty file in Photoshop by going to the menu File, New. For this example, the new file will be 100×100 pixels, though size does not matter. It could be 1×1 pixel and still work. Because we're filling the background with a solid color, the number of times our background pattern repeats will not matter. When dealing with images in background tiles, the size is much more important (see Chapter 6). I fill this file with the solid turquoise color by going to the menu Edit, Fill, Background Color, Normal. I name this file solid.jpg.

3. Here is the HTML code that puts it all together in a Web page. Figure 7.11 shows the final page.

```
html>
<body background="solid.jpg">
<center><b><font
size=4>Where's the
 Monkey?</font></b><p>
<img src="monkey3.jpg">
</center>
</body>
</html>
```

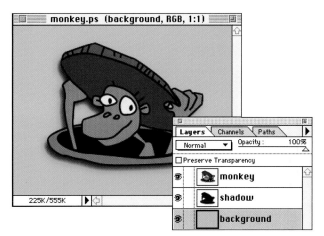

Figure 7.9

Changing the background color in a Photoshop layer.

Figure 7.10

The finished monkey3.gif.

Figure 7.11

The finished Web page using the <body background> tag.

TIP

You can use a combination of the <body bgcolor> tag and <body background> tag at the same time for extra insurance against browsers that might not support hexadecimal backgrounds or pattern backgrounds. This would be the sample HTML code:

```
<html>
<body bgcolor="FFFFFF"
 background=white.gif>
<img src="monkey.jpg"
</body>
</html>
```

JPEG or GIF?

It doesn't matter whether your images or tiled background patterns are saved in JPEG or GIF file format. Those decisions should be based on principles described in Chapter 3, "Making Low-Memory Graphics." I have chosen to use JPEG files in these examples because JPEGs are preferable for images with soft edges, such as figure 7.11 with its drop shadow.

Summary

Making irregularly shaped artwork is possible by carefully planning the background color of the image's background and ensuring that the background color of your Web page matches. Use either HTML technique, the <body bgcolor> tag or the <body background> tag, but make sure the browser you're using supports those tags. These tips are useful to follow:

■ Make irregularly shaped artwork over the same background color you use for your page. That will make it look like it's free-floating.

■ Use <body bgcolor> or <body background> tags to specify a background color; do not depend on the background color of the browser!

■ Remember that HTML 3.0 will not support the <body bgcolor> tag, but that many browsers recognize it anyway. Check the Browser Comparison chart found in Chapter 1 to see if the browser you're designing for recognizes hexadecimal-based background colors.

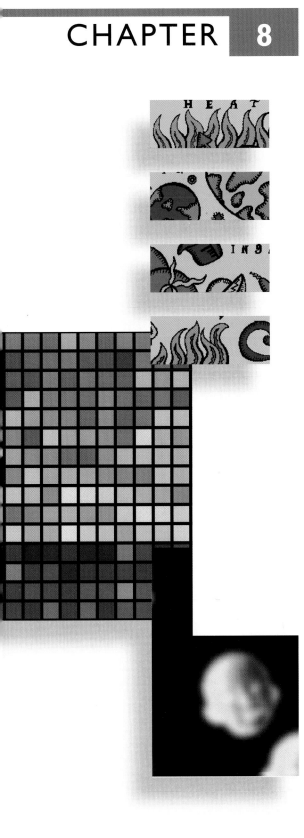

CHAPTER 8

Making Irregularly Shaped Artwork Using Transparency

Transparent GIFs

If Transparent GIFs (TGIFs) are an unfamiliar term to you, don't worry. I know of no other application for transparent GIFs other than the Web, so they're relatively new to everyone. Transparent GIFs are used to create the illusion of irregularly shaped computer files, by assigning one color in a graphic to be invisible (see figs. 8.1, 8.2, and 8.3). This process is often called masking.

Figure 8.1

The logo art from my personal Web site, with its original background color. The gray was assigned to be invisible in the transparent GIF file, as seen in figure 8.3.

Figure 8.2

The 1950s man art from my personal Web site, with its original background color. The gray was assigned to be invisible in the transparent GIF, as seen in figure 8.3.

Figure 8.3

The finished page, with all the transparent GIFs in effect.

Transparent GIFs, commonly referred to as Gif89a, are different from the standard Gif87a (see Chapter 3) in that they allow for transparency. Not all imaging programs let you save graphics in the Gif89a format, so details on how to use the various helper applications, online services, and programs that support it are included at the end of this chapter. Most of these programs also support saving files using interlacing. These files are often called interlaced GIFs. If you've surfed the Web much, you've probably seen interlaced GIFs everywhere (see fig. 8.4). They're the graphics that start out blocky and come into focus. The file format Gif89a supports interlacing or transparency, either together or separately. A transparent GIF does not have to be interlaced and an interlaced GIF does not have to be transparent. The file format allows you to assign both properties to one graphic: transparency and interlacing. It's a mouthful of words, but the principles are really quite simple.

Figure 8.4

A simulation of an interlaced GIF on a Web page. Note how the image starts chunky and comes into focus. This allows the viewer to see the graphic quickly and decide whether to wait for it to finish loading or move on to another page.

Transparency and interlacing are assigned when the file is saved. There are helper applications that convert ordinary graphics to Gif89a format, as well as Photoshop plug-ins. Using those software applications makes interlacing as simple as clicking an on or off button. Setting transparency is quite a bit more complex. When working with transparent GIFs, there are two things to keep in mind: first, how to make art properly for one color masking transparency, and second, how to use the programs that let you save the artwork in this file format.

Making Art

I only recommend using Transparent GIFs on Web pages that have pattern backgrounds (see Chapter 6, "Making Background Patterns"), as you can create the same effect against solid colors by using the techniques described in the previous chapter.

The key to producing effective transparent GIFs is ensuring your art is produced correctly. We need to begin by first going through a short primer on aliased versus anti-aliased artwork. What is anti-aliasing, you ask? Anti-aliasing is the process of blending around edges of a graphic to hide the jagged square pixels it is made of. If you zoom into an anti-aliased edge, it looks like figure 8.5.

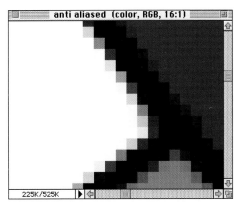

Figure 8.5
A close-up of anti-aliased artwork.

Many of the Transparent GIFs I see on the Web have ugly residual matte lines, usually in the form of white or black edges (see figs. 8.6 and 8.7). These matte lines can be traced back to the way in which the image was anti-aliased.

Figure 8.6
Artwork that was originally anti-aliased against white, leaving a white matte line when put on top of a black background.

Figure 8.7

Artwork that was originally anti-aliased against white, leaving a white matte line when put on top of a pattern background.

Figure 8.8

Artwork with aliased edges against a black background.

Most well-trained digital artists would never think to work without anti-aliasing, but for the best looking transparent GIFs that's exactly what you'll want to do. The anti-aliased blended edge is precisely what causes fringing problems once the graphic is converted to transparent GIFs. Because transparent GIFs only drop one color out of your image, you will see all the remaining colors along the blended edge of anti-aliased artwork, even when what you really want is for all of them to disappear. There is no way to avoid this, unless GIF file formats supported masking for more than one color. (Photoshop and PICT file formats, for example, let you mask with 256 levels of transparency, where transparent GIFs let you mask with only one.)

Figure 8.8 shows the image with aliased edges instead of anti-aliased edges. The ugly matte lines are gone.

Motto: The edge of your image should be aliased in order for a one-color mask to work efficiently. Sadly, drop shadows and glows cannot be aliased, so they are unsuitable subjects for this type of image file (you'll see how to deal with them later in this chapter). Therefore, do not use artwork with glows or drop shadows for transparent GIFs.

Aliased art actually looks far more acceptable on computer screens than in print or video. If you look at the desktop of your Mac or PC, you'll notice that none of the icons or type are anti-aliased. They wouldn't read right if they were! If you anti-alias small type it turns to mush (see fig. 8.9).

yucky mushy small type that's anti-aliased.

Figure 8.9

Anti-aliased type in a small point size.

Anti-aliasing was designed to hide the fact that computer graphics are made of square, jagged pixels. Computer screens are a pixel-based medium, so our compulsion to hide this fact in print and other media is not always appropriate for computer screen-based design, such as the Web and other multimedia delivery systems like CD-ROMs. Low-resolution Web graphics are much more forgiving with aliasing than their print graphic counterparts.

Photoshop Tips for Creating Aliased Images

In the following sections, we'll look at how to create artwork for transparent GIFs with aliased edges. Photoshop was designed as a sophisticated graphics editing program, and working there with aliased tools is foreign to most designers. Understanding which types of tools are appropriate for the job, and how to configure them so they don't anti-alias is key to mastering clean-edged TGIFs. There are a few different types of graphics we'll study: illustrations, scanned illustrations, and scanned photographs.

Creating Illustration-Based Artwork for Transparent GIFs

If you're an illustrator, you're used to making artwork from scratch. It's best to start with the correct tools for the job—and they'll most likely be tools you don't normally use. Most paint programs default to working with anti-aliased brushes and fill tools. To create aliased graphics in Photoshop, you want to use the pencil tool (see fig. 8.10) and the paint bucket tool to draw and fill shapes with.

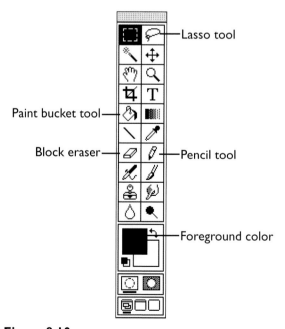

Lasso tool

Paint bucket tool

Block eraser — Pencil tool

Foreground color

TIP

When making aliased illustrations, use aliased tools. Make sure Anti-Aliased is *unchecked* in the Paint Bucket Options for aliased fills (see fig. 8.11) and use the Pencil tool for aliased brushes (see fig. 8.12).

Figure 8.10
The aliased tools within the Photoshop toolbar.

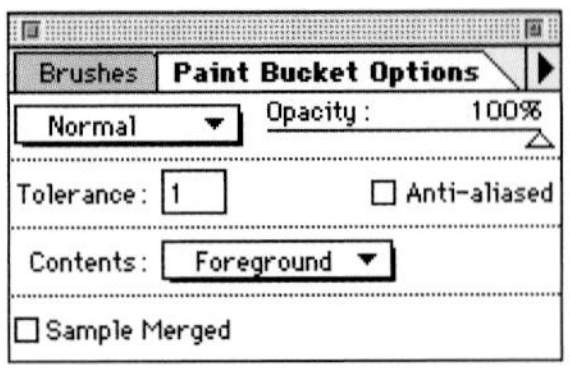

Figure 8.11
Uncheck anti-alias when using the Paint Bucket tool.

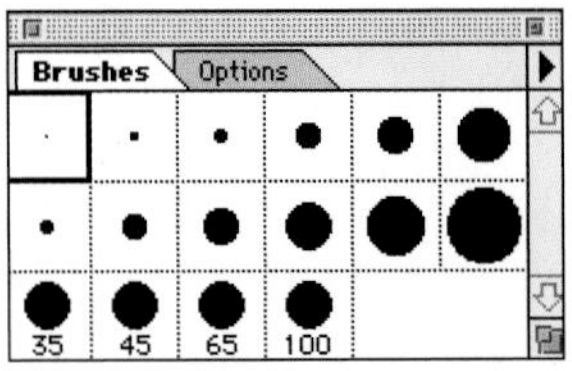

Figure 8.12
Aliased brushes used by the Pencil tool.

While creating your illustrations, be sure to fill the areas that are going to go transparent with a different color. Here's an examples of how Bruce Heavin's illustration was prepared properly for converting to a transparent GIF (see fig. 8.13).

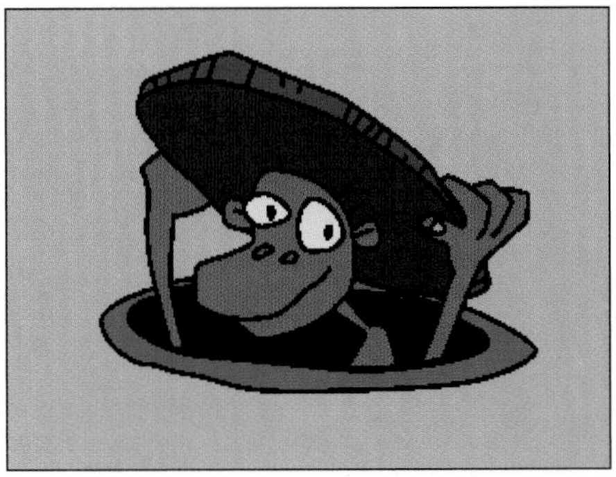

Figure 8.13
Bruce filled the background of this image with gray. Because the gray color did not exist elsewhere in the image, when it became assigned as the transparent color in the GIF, he got the results of cutting out the monkey in an irregular shape.

The techniques reviewed here, using aliased bucket and pencil tools, work great if you're creating flat illustration artwork directly in the computer, but what if you're not? The next section addresses other techniques for converting graphics to TGIF.

Turning Pre-Scanned Illustrations into Aliased Art

Sometimes, the source material supplied for Web page art has already been scanned and is pre-anti-aliased. This might be the case with a company logo, or something you're bringing in from a clip art book. When working with existing anti-aliased artwork, you can convert the image to being aliased by changing the Mode from RGB to Bitmap. Go to the top menu bar to Mode, Bitmap and set the Threshold setting to 50%. Changing to this mode strips all the anti-aliasing away from the image. You can convert back to RGB mode and access colors in the document, but the lines will remain aliased. There's an example of this Photoshop technique on my Windows 95 equipped PC using Yeryoung Park's wonderful original sketches for the HotHotHot site [http://www.hothothot.com]—check out the great use of aliased artwork on the site.

Here are the steps used to convert a scanned image to an anti-aliased image:

1. Open the original scan. In our example, we have Yeryoung Park's original pencil sketch for the HotHotHot site (see fig. 8.14).

2. Go to the menu item Mode and change it to Bitmap. Insert the settings that you see in figure 8.15. By using the Threshold 50% setting, it equalizes all the greys and makes a black-and-white aliased image.

3. Yeuryoung used the pencil and paint bucket (refer to fig. 8.10) tools to create aliased fills for the artwork (see fig. 8.16).

Figure 8.14

Yeryoung's original pencil sketch scanned into the computer in grayscale.

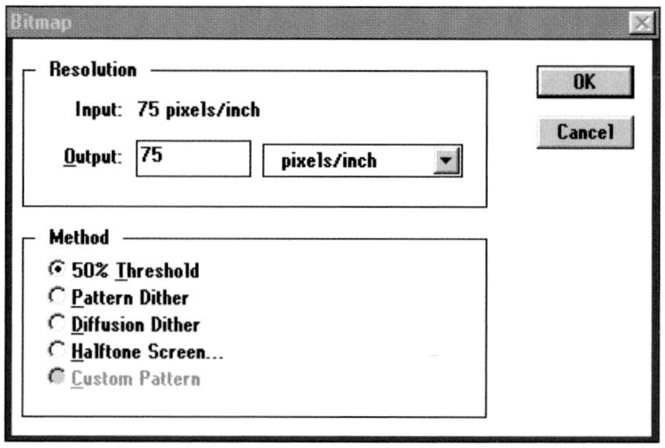

![Bitmap dialog box]

Figure 8.15

Converting the anti-aliased original to aliased artwork by changing the Mode to Bitmap and using a Threshold 50% setting.

Figure 8.16

The results of converting a greyscale anti-aliased image to a black-and-white aliased image.

Figure 8.17 shows the final results on Yeuryoung's Web page.

Figure 8.17
The gorgeous results, weighing in at under 4 KB!

Photographic Source Art for Transparent GIFs

Another common situation is where you have photographs or existing color illustrations with anti-aliased edges that you want to change to transparent GIFs. You don't have to change the interior of your graphic to be aliased, just the edges. For best results you can work large and use the magnifying glass tool to zoom way in to accurately erase the edge using the aliased "block" eraser tool. You also can use the lasso tool, and select the parts you want to delete. Just make sure the anti-aliased box is unchecked! The edge will look terrible in Photoshop, but will look much better on the web!

Here's a step-by-step demonstration of how I would put my daughter's cherub head on a Web page.

1. Scan the photo. Remember to use the correct scale for the Web—72 dpi, RGB color and small dimensions! Jamie's photo was scanned in at 72 dpi, 3 inches by 4 inches (see fig. 8.18).

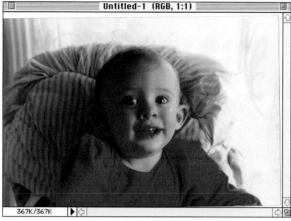

Figure 8.18

The original Jamie scan.

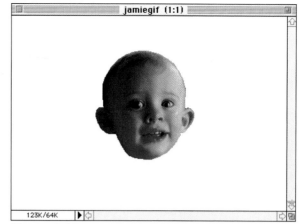

Figure 8.19

Jamie's head cut-out using the lasso tool set with anti-aliasing unchecked, inverting the selection and filling with white.

2. Select the lasso tool (with the Anti-Aliasing box *unchecked* in the Options window).

3. Trace around the shape of her little cherub head.

4. Click on white as the foreground color. Inverse the selection by going to the menu item Select, Inverse. Go to the menu Edit, Fill, Normal, Foreground, 100%. This should fill the outside with white (see fig. 8.19).

5. Save the image as a transparent GIF and put it on a Web page (see next two sections for instructions on how to do this).

Figure 8.20 shows the aliased head against a background. Notice the lack of matte lines.

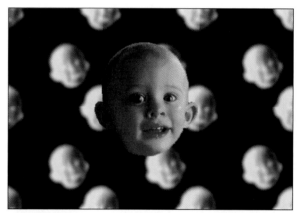

Figure 8.20

Here she is on a Web page with aliased edges. Look Ma, no matte lines.

The preceding examples show the correct method to prepare photo-based source material properly for TGIFs. The following examples show what can (and does!) go wrong with transparent GIFs. As you look at these examples, you should understand why they didn't work successfully, and know how to prepare artwork so this doesn't happen.

TIP

Holding down the option key on a Mac or the Alt key on a PC causes the lasso to behave like a rubber band, making it possible to carefully click around a shape and giving you much greater control.

Figure 8.21 shows what would have happened had I not chosen to cut Jamie out with aliased tools.

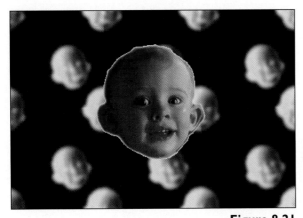

Figure 8.21

If the original cut-out had been done with anti-aliased tools, the resulting unwanted white-fringed edges would appear.

If you really want to get down and ugly, make a transparent GIF out of artwork that has a glow around it! Figure 8.22 shows Jamie with a glow around her head.

Figure 8.22

Talk about fat and glaring matte lines! Don't ever use artwork with a glow around it as a source for TGIFs.

Glows should always be pre-composited in Photoshop against the colored or patterned background they'll be on top of and posted as regular GIF images. Photoshop uses 256 levels of masking, as opposed to only one in the transparent GIF's file format. That's why glows look beautiful in Photoshop and the edges fall apart abruptly as transparent GIFs on the Web (see fig. 8.23).

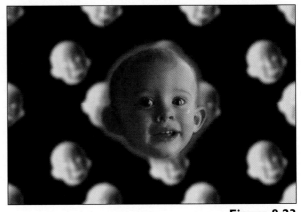

Figure 8.23

If the glow is created in Photoshop, and composited with the background there, it looks great.

NOTE

A lot of Web designers use anti-aliased edges and glows and drop shadows in their source art saved as transparent GIFs, but make sure they anti-alias the original graphic to the same color background as the background color of the Web page. The resulting TGIFs will not have unwanted edges, because the edge color matches the background color. This method works fine, but has no advantages over the techniques described in the preceding chapter. Making the graphic as a transparent GIF as opposed to a regular GIF or JPEG buys no extra quality, just creates a little extra unnecessary work.

Transparent GIFs and interlaced GIFs don't always work on Web browsers—even those that support the file format (see fig. 8.24). I don't know the reason for this, but sometimes the edges that were transparent on one moment's viewing are not the next time the same page is requested. When this happens in Netscape, clicking the Reload button generally refreshes the screen and makes it work again. Strange things happen to interlace GIFs at times too, like the edges never finish coming into focus and remain jagged and pixellated. If you use transparent or interlaced GIFs this seems to be an unfortunate fact of Web designer life for the moment.

NOTE

There's a way in DeBabelizer to shave the anti-aliased edges of an image:

- Open the image.

- Specify the background color via Palette, Options, Dithering & Background.

- Color, and then point the eyedropper at the background color.

- Choose Palette, Shave-Outline, Shave Edges or Shave Edges and Corners.

This will remove a 1 pixel wide border of pixels around any part of the image touching the background color. It was designed to remove bluescreen fringe.

DeBabelizer has another function designed specifically to avoid anti-aliasing: in Edit, Scale, there's a checkbox "Don't factor in background color.." which prevents anti-aliasing when scaling an image that's set against a solid background color. This can be very useful when working with images that have already been anti-aliased, and need to be saved as transparent GIFs.

Figure 8.24

Transparency when it's not working on my Web page.

Interlaced GIFs

In theory, the advantage to using interlacing (refer to fig. 8.4) is that it makes the graphic appear faster in lower resolution. This can help your viewers decide if they want to wait for the graphic or click onward and elsewhere. It also causes the HTML body text to appear faster on a page, before the graphic fully appears.

Making the graphic appear faster in lower resolution works great for images that are readable at chunky resolutions. Where I object to the usage of this technique is when it involves images that include menu text or table of contents information. From a design standpoint, it's frustrating to your audience if your interlaced GIF contains small text, as they have to wait for the entire image to appear before being able to read it. In my opinion, this defeats the purpose—if you have to wait a long time for the image to appear, why not make that known to the user from the onset and include a regular GIF or JPEG? An interlaced GIF might force your viewer to actually wait longer to read essential information than a simple non-interlaced GIF would. This waiting creates frustration, something you do not want *your* Web site to be the cause of.

How to Make Interlaced GIFs

Photoshop does not directly support the Gif89a format, so outside helper apps or plug-ins are needed. All of the following reviewed software

allows for saving interlaced or transparent GIFs or both. It's typically found as a clearly marked check box in all the software and is easy to find and use (see fig. 8.25).

Figure 8.25

Checking the Interlace box in the Photoshop plug-in from BoxTop. (http//www.aris.com//boxtop)

Transparent GIF Software

The next section is going to cover how to save files as transparent GIFs. The process varies depending on which software is being used, so I've included instruction for a lot of different packages that support TGIFs. Currently Gif89a's are not directly supported from within Photoshop, though Adobe has released a Gif89a plug-in available on our CD-ROM.

I predict that it's only a matter of time before transparent GIF is as common a file format as today's PICT, BMP, or EPS. The Web is far too important and popular for software packages to ignore supporting its file formats. The only reason why most software doesn't already support it is because GIF's popularity as a file format is too new. The World

Wide Web crept up on all of us, including software companies! A year from now, specialized software to save in transparent GIF format will not be necessary as it will be widely supported everywhere.

Meanwhile, there are lots of options for software, shareware, plug-ins, and online transparent GIF support. Some are cross-platform tools, others are platform-specific, and others reside online. Following is a list of some of the best available, with instructions for how to use them:

Macintosh

Mac Transparency software is fairly easy to use. If you're on a Mac, these are some choices for programs that save transparent GIFs.

Transparency

A popular Mac freeware application is Transparency, by Aaron Giles (giles@med.cornell.edu). It can be downloaded from ftp.uwtc.washington.edu/pub/Mac/Graphics/. It lacks bells and whistles, like some of the other programs mentioned here, but hey, the price is right!

To use, launch the program and open a GIF file. The file must already be saved as GIF to work. Hold your mouse down on the color you want to make into the invisible background and save the file. Figure 8.26 shows an example of a picture being edited with Transparency.

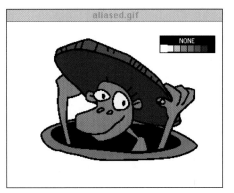

Figure 8.26

When you open a GIF with Transparency, the palette of the image is automatically displayed. Click on the single color you want to disappear and save the file as a Gif89a.

DeBabelizer

Many multimedia developers already sing the praises of DeBabelizer, and its Web support is no less impressive. One of the best features about this program is its capability to batch process. (See more on batch processing in Chapter 4, "Color Palette Hell!") This capability allows you to take a folder of images and convert them all at once to a specific palette, or make them all go transparent as Gif89as. It's a must-have tool for Web designers doing volume image processing (similar to what might be required when putting a mail-order catalog online).

Batch processing a series of GIFs in DeBabelizer is no easy task, due to its unusual interface. Here's what you'd do.

1. Put all the images you want to convert to transparent GIFs in one folder. If the images need to be converted to 8-bit first, include steps 3 and 4, otherwise skip, and progress from step 2 to step 5.

2. Choose the menu commands File, Batch, Save. Click on the New button in the Batch Save dialog box that appears. Locate the folder you want to batch, click on it and push the Append button. Then click save.

You now have the folder saved as a batch that can be group processed.

3. Choose File, Batch, Super Palette and click Do It. The program will make a custom, optimized palette (for more information on optimized palettes, see Chapter 4) of all the images in your folder.

4. Choose File, Batch Save, Do Script, Dither to Super Palette (see fig. 8.27). This converts all the images in your folder to the optimized palette.

5. Next, open one of the images from your folder that's been converted to this new palette and go to the Palette menu.

6. Choose Options, Dithering and Background Color. Check the Color Index radio button in the Dither Options & Background Color dialog box that appears (see fig. 8.28). Use the eyedropper to select the color you want to make transparent in your image.

Figure 8.27

Setting up a DeBabelizer script for Dither to SuperPalette.

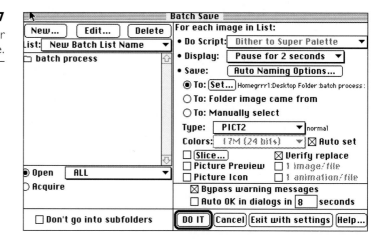

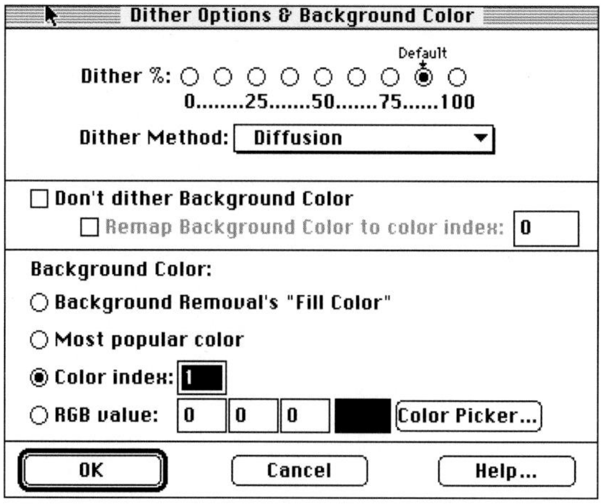

Figure 8.28

The Dither Options & Background Color dialog box.

7. Next, go to the File menu and Choose Batch, Save. Once this dialog is open, choose GIF89a as the file format. When you click the Do It button, it will convert the entire folder of images to transparent GIFs, dropping out which ever color you have identified as the background color.

Windows

The software for transparency on Windows is a tad less sophisticated than on the Mac. Most notably missing in most of the Windows software is the eyedropper and color picker tools used to locate the value of the color you wish to have drop out. These software tools are still a lot easier to use than some of the command-line DOS tools available, that we won't even discuss! Windows developers should take note of this and make some better color choice tools for those of us wanting to create transparent GIFs.

LView

Download LView from ftp:// gatekeeper.dec.com/pub/micro/ msdos/win3/desktop/lview31.zip. It's shareware; costs $30 to register, and is written by Leonardo Haddad Loureiro (mmedia@world.std.com). To use, open your image, and under Options choose Background color. The 256-color palette of that image opens (see fig. 8.29). Choose white, black, or a specific color for your transparent selection. Once you've made a selection, save as a Gif89a and you're done. You can also select Interlace from the Options menu if you want to interlace the file.

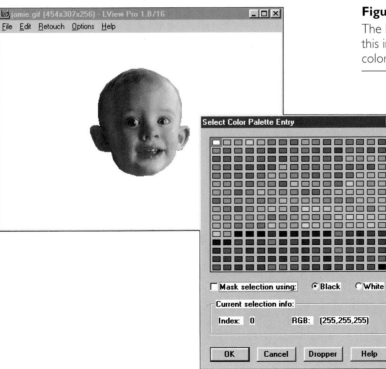

Figure 8.29

The LView interface with the color table for this image open to select a transparent color from.

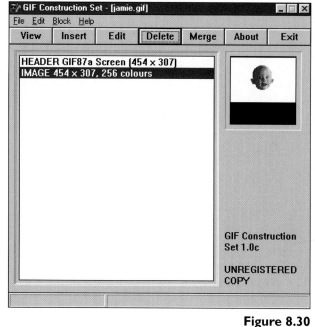

Figure 8.30

The Script window.

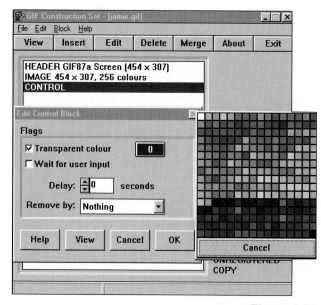

Figure 8.31

The Control command added to the Script window brings forth the palette to choose a transparent color from.

GIF Construction Set

The GIF Construction Set which is available from ftp.www.north.net /pub/alchemy, also makes transparent GIFs. If you open your GIF file, a script window appears (see fig. 8.30). Under the Insert menu, select Control. This adds a Control command to the script window (see fig. 8.31). Double click on the word Control in the script window and a new window appears. When the transparent colour (French Canadian company and spelling) check box is marked you can click on the colored square and the 256 palette of the image opens. From there, select the correct color, save as a Gif89a, and faits accomplis!

Paint Shop Pro

The very popular and reasonably priced Paint Shop Pro (version 3.11) is the latest paint software company to get with the TGIF program. You can download version 3.11 from ftp://ftp.winternet.com/users/jasc/ps p311.zip . The software can be used free for 30 days, then must be registered for $69.00. It does much more than saving GIFs—this is a full-bodied paint that's offered for a fraction of the price of Photoshop (with not as much power, of course).

Open the file and determine whether you want white, black, or another color to be transparent. If you want another color, go to the Colors menu and select Edit Palette. Click around to locate the number (1-255) of the color. Next, go to Edit, do a Save As, and choose GIF-CompuServe as the file format. From the submenu that appears, choose either an interlaced or non-interlaced 89a. To set the color, click on the Options button, select the Set the Transparency Value to radio button (see fig. 8.32), and enter the numeric value you found when you were in the edit palette mode. Where's the eyedropper tool when you need it?

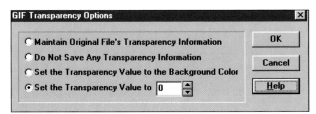

Figure 8.32

The GIF Transparency Options dialog box requests numeric values, instead of allowing designers to pick color from a palette or use an eyedropper.

Cross-Platform Tools

Cross-Platform tools are also available for saving TGIFs. Two excellent imaging programs, Adobe Photoshop and Fractal Painter, have TGIF options in updated software that's available over the Web.

Adobe Photoshop GIF89a Export Plug-In

Photoshop doesn't directly support transparent GIFs, but it does have a plugin that does the job well, located on its site at: http://www.adobe.com/Software.html. This plug-in works on Mac and Windows versions of Photoshop.

As might be expected, it's one of the most full-bodied transparent GIF tools on the market. Here's a step-by-step tour through some of its features using the jamie.scan image found on the *Designing Web Graphics CD-ROM* in the Chapter 18/Hex folder. (Feel free to use your own image, of course!)

1. Place the Gif89a Export plug-in in your plug-in folder. Make sure that Photoshop is closed. The plug-in will not be effective until the next time Photoshop is opened.

2. Open the jamie.scan document (found on the CD-ROM in this chapter's folder) or a document of your own.

3. Convert the file from RGB to Index Color. Go to Mode, select Index and leave it at its defaults. Or, you could practice some of the principles described in Chapter 3. Test the image in 100 colors, or 50 or whatever. You can decide how low to take the bit-depth and the lower you take it the smaller the file size will be.

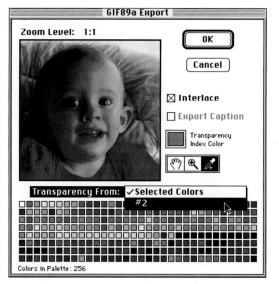

Figure 8.33

By holding down on the Selected Colors menu, I can base the transparency on channel #2, which was created in step 5.

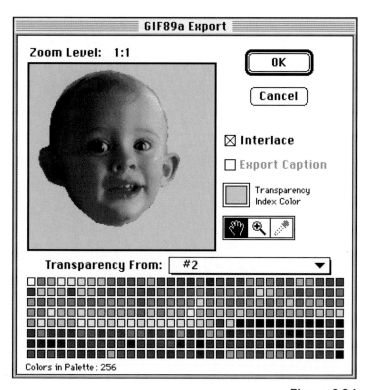

Figure 8.34

Here's the preview of where the image will be transparent.

4. Once the image is indexed, make a selection. Use the lasso tool in aliased mode, and hold the option key on a Mac or the Alt key on a PC to drag a selection around the shape of her head. Go to the Select menu, Inverse the selection and return to the Select menu to choose Save Selection.

5. Under File, select Export, Gif89a. The transparent color can be based on Selected Colors or #2. By saving a selection in step 4, I created a channel in the document, called channel #2. If I choose to use the #2 mask, I do not have to base the selection on color at all (see fig. 8.33).

6. The selection, based on channel #2 is previewed, allowing me to check it before I click OK to save the file (see fig. 8.34).

This plug-in worked great for a photo. Let's try using selection based on color for the next example. You will find Bruce Heavin's monkey.gif in the Chapter 8 folder on your CD-ROM.

1. Open the monkey.gif (see fig. 8.35) file from the CD-ROM. (It's already 8-bit, so no conversion is necessary.)

2. Under File, select Export, Gif89a. This time we will base the selection on Selected Colors. Using the eyedropper tool, I clicked on the areas I wanted to go transparent. This feature is very convenient, because the background and the eyes are white. By using

the eyedropper tool, I can select some of the whites to go transparent and not others (see fig. 8.36). The preview tells me what I need to see. When I'm finished selecting with the eyedropper, I click OK and am ready to save.

Fractal Painter 3.01

Painter 3.01 offers great support for transparent GIFs. This free upgrade lets you save an image as a GIF, either by selecting the background color or using one of its floater selections as a defined region for the mask. Open a document (any file format that Painter supports) and convert it to Index Color in the saving process.

Painter is a complicated program to use, and I unfortunately lack the space in this chapter to walk new users through its interface. For those readers who already use Painter, here are the steps for working with its transparent GIF features.

1. Using Painter's type frisket tool, and converting it to a Floater, you can identify a masking region for the transparent GIF.

> **NOTE**
>
> An upgrade to Painter 3.01 can be found at ftp.fractal.com/ pub/macintosh/update/ for Macs or ftp.fractal.com/pub/win/update/ for Window machines.
>
> Keep your eyes peeled on this site for the Painter 4.0 announcement. It promises to support more Web-related file formats, including making image maps. See Chapter 13, "Hot Spots," for more information on image maps.

Figure 8.35

The monkey.gif image. Note how the eyes and the background are both white.

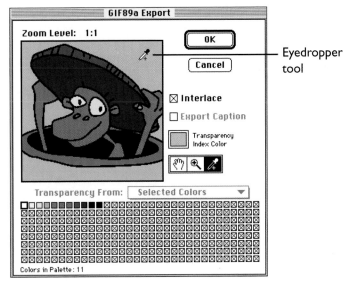

Eyedropper tool

Figure 8.36

Basing the selection on Selected Color, and using the eyedropper tool, it's possible to select some of the whites, but not all.

Save As GIF Options

Number of Colors:	Imaging Method:
○ 4 Colors	⦿ Quantize to Nearest Color
○ 8 Colors	○ Dither Colors
○ 16 Colors	
○ 32 Colors	Transparency:
⦿ 64 Colors	⊠ Output Transparency
○ 128 Colors	⦿ Background is WWW Gray
○ 256 Colors	○ Background is BG Color

Misc Options: Threshold ◁▦▦▦▤△▭▭▭▷ 25%
□ Interlace GIF File

[Preview Data] [Cancel] [OK]

Figure 8.37

When you get to the Output Transparency dialog, choose to preview before you say OK to check to see if the mask is working.

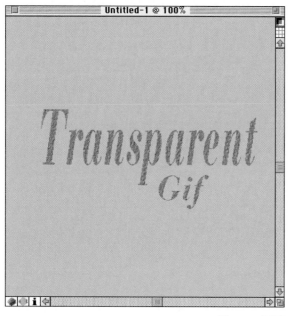

Figure 8.38

A preview of the image with the type mask in effect.

2. In the save as GIF Options, choose to Output transparency (see fig 8.37).

3. Output transparency does a great job of making a selection based on shape, rather than a background color. Figure 8.38 shows a preview of the image with the type mask in effect.

Online

For those who like to do their work *and* surf at the same time, you can make transparent GIFs online over the World Wide Web! There are several sites that convert a regular GIF into a transparent GIF while you wait. These sites look for a URL that includes a GIF image, and will convert the image to the GIF 89a format. Some sites let you choose black, white, or an RGB value to go transparent, and others let you click on the image to choose the spot.

To use the online transparency service, you'd have to give the URL of your image, not the URL of an HTML document. A correct URL would look like this:

http://www.myprovider.com/mysitename/imagetoconvert.gif

Remember, your artwork must be loaded on a server and be a valid URL (see fig. 8.39). For instructions on how to load your art to a server, check out the Appendix: HTML for Visual Designers.

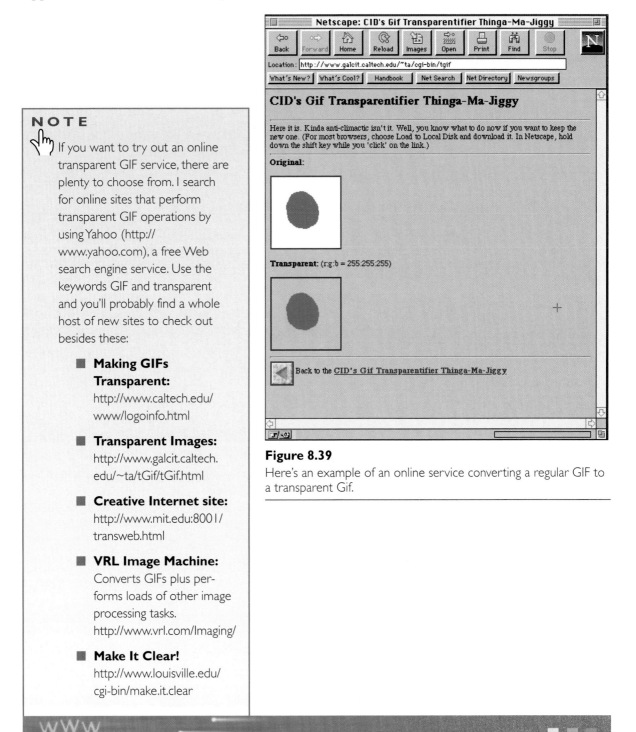

Figure 8.39
Here's an example of an online service converting a regular GIF to a transparent Gif.

NOTE

If you want to try out an online transparent GIF service, there are plenty to choose from. I search for online sites that perform transparent GIF operations by using Yahoo (http://www.yahoo.com), a free Web search engine service. Use the keywords GIF and transparent and you'll probably find a whole host of new sites to check out besides these:

■ **Making GIFs Transparent:**
http://www.caltech.edu/www/logoinfo.html

■ **Transparent Images:**
http://www.galcit.caltech.edu/~ta/tGif/tGif.html

■ **Creative Internet site:**
http://www.mit.edu:8001/transweb.html

■ **VRL Image Machine:**
Converts GIFs plus performs loads of other image processing tasks.
http://www.vrl.com/Imaging/

■ **Make It Clear!**
http://www.louisville.edu/cgi-bin/make.it.clear

HTML for Transparent GIFs

The only way to preview the way a transparent GIF will look against the other elements of your Web page is through a Web browser. You don't actually have to be online, or have the image stored on a server to preview. Simply launch your browser and open an HTML file right from your hard drive. Make sure that the GIF images are in the same folder as this HTML document, and that the text document is saved in a "text only" or ASCII mode of your word processor. It should be saved with the extension .html at the end of the file name. The most stripped down HTML code required to include a TGIF on a Web page follows:

```
<html>
<img src="tgifimage.gif">
</html>
```

More information on HTML and previewing Web files from your hard drive can be found in the Appendix: HTML for Visual Designers.

Summary

Gif89a's are essential to sophisticated Web design, but it's important to know how to prepare the art properly when using them. Here are some tips to remember when working with transparent and interlaced images:

- You should only use transparent GIFs on Web pages with background patterns (see Chapter 6, "Making Background Patterns"). If the background of your Web page is solid, it's easier to make the image against the same solid color and insert it on the page as a regular graphic.

- If the edges of the artwork for the transparent GIF are aliased, there is no possibility of unwanted matte lines, or fringing.

- Interlaced GIFs should not be used on images that have small type, because it actually takes longer for the end viewer to read the words than if the graphic were a standard GIF or JPEG.

- Be sure to test your transparent and interlaced GIFs from your hard drive before you post them to the server, to catch any art preparation errors in advance.

http://

CHAPTER 9

Typography for the Web-Impaired

If you gave designers a tool that offered little or no control over fonts, sizes, spacing, and position, you could almost guarantee the type design they created would suffer. Such is the case with HTML—most pages on the Web cause trained type designers to cringe. Add the fact that browsers display text in a default font, such as Times Roman, but *allow* end users to change their preferences to display text in fonts of their choosing (see fig. 9.1), and the designer is left with even less control than the little amount he or she started with.

Contents:

Music

Current Trends

Local Events

typography

YOU

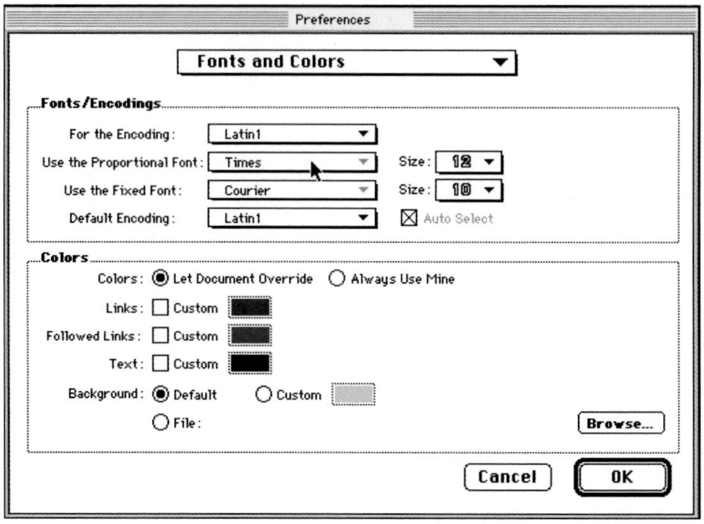

Figure 9.1

Changing the type default preferences in Netscape 1.1N for the Macintosh.

There are basically two kinds of typographical elements on the Web (or the printed page, for that matter)—body type and headline type. Body type, often referred to as *body copy*, composes the bulk of the written text. Body type is typically smaller and contains the majority of the written content of a Web page. Headline type is typically larger, and is used to quickly draw the viewer's eye to it, help define a page break, or organize multiple ideas.

You can make body and headline type a couple of different ways on the Web. One way involves using HTML and/or Netscape-originated HTML type extensions (see fig. 9.2).

The alternative is to create images that have type as the visual content instead of pictures. This kind of image-based type is referred to in this chapter as *graphic-based type* (see fig. 9.3). HTML type is ideal for body copy and graphic-based type is ideal for headlines.

This chapter examines procedures for using standard HTML type, adding Netscape-originated HTML type tags, and methods for making graphic images with headline type using Photoshop and Illustrator. Understanding some of the aesthetic issues related to type design principles is important before we move toward specific production methods.

Figure 9.2

Art Center College of Design's graduate student Thomas Mueller's Liquid Type site composed of HTML type using the <pre> tag.

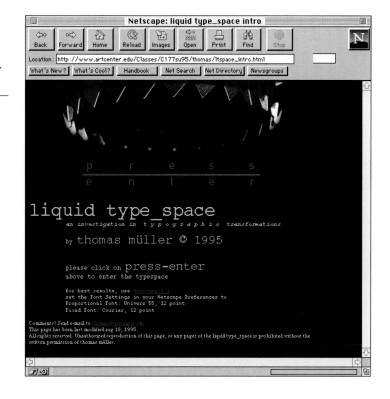

Figure 9.3

Art Center College of Design's undergraduate student Jennifer Chang's Korean Entertainment site composed of Photoshop graphic-based type and HTML.

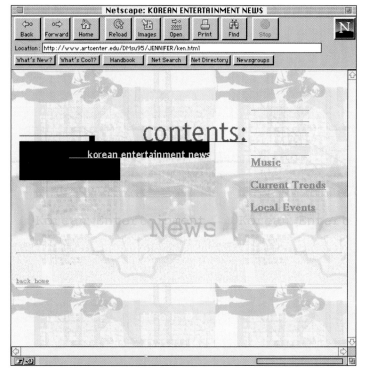

Type Design Principles

I think the Web is an incredibly great way to gather information. Typically, when I find a page with a lot of text on it though, I'll print the page on my printer rather than sit and read through the text on my screen. Who wants to have the light of the monitor blaring in their face while having a recreational read? Give me crisp type on paper any day over that! I feel the same way about all computer-based text delivery systems, such as CD-ROMS and interactive kiosks. If you want me to read a lot of text, I'd rather do so on paper. As designers, we have to recognize that computer-based presentations pose distinct challenges, and not treat our type-ridden Web pages the same way as we would print.

So what design principles can you follow to help out your computer-screen-based reader? I advocate breaking up type into small paragraphs. Also, use different weights, such as bold and italics, to make it possible to skim the page easily and catch the important points. Add hypertext judiciously, (text that links you from one spot to another, which is typically underlined or bold depending on the way the viewer's browser preferences are set) is another way to break up screen text into more digestible portions. The idea is to break up blocks of text as much as possible. Assume your reader is skimming, and make it easy for them to do.

Understand that you're asking a lot of your viewer to sit and read pages and pages of type on a screen. It's your job to invent ways to hold their interest and to bring out the important ideas. This is possible through using both HTML and graphic-based text. Let's examine HTML first.

Font Choices

Chances are, the person looking at your Web page is using the default settings for whatever browser they're viewing the page from. Most browsers default to using a Times Roman font. I've seen sites that include instructions to the viewer to change their default font to some other typeface. I wish them luck! I know very few Web surfers who would take the time to change their settings to see an individual page. If you want your HTML type to be something other than Times Roman, don't count on asking your viewer to change their Web browser settings as a fool-proof method. In fact, I would imagine a very low percentage of viewers would actually act on the suggestion.

If you want your audience to see your body copy in a font other than the default, there is no way to program it with HTML. This is a thorn in many designers sides—mine included! We have our hands tied by the medium at the moment. You can choose to disregard this fact, fight it, ignore it, or gripe about it, but there are few work-arounds I can offer. Using graphic-type for body copy is the only option, which will be discussed later in this chapter. I would only use graphic type for body copy when there isn't much copy on a page, due to the longer download time requirements.

HTML-Based Typography

The advantages of using HTML for most body type needs are obvious. First of all, the memory and download time required for using native text is much lower than that used for graphics. Many sites are text-intensive, and using HTML-based type is the only choice to present large quantities of written information in a timely and efficient manner.

Officially sanctioned HTML offers limited type tag choices. Be sure to return back to the browser comparison chart in Chapter 1 to see which browsers support even the barest HTML tags to control type.

Here are the basics from officially sanctioned HTML, which most browsers (but not all!) recognize:

- **Using headings.** Headings are created using the `<H></H>` tag. The heading tags always have to be in the `<head>` part of an HTML file (see fig. 9.4). Here's some sample Heading code.

```
<html>
<head>
<H3>Welcome to this Site!</H3>
<H4>Welcome to this Site!</H4>
<H5>Welcome to this Site!</H5>
</head>
</html>
```

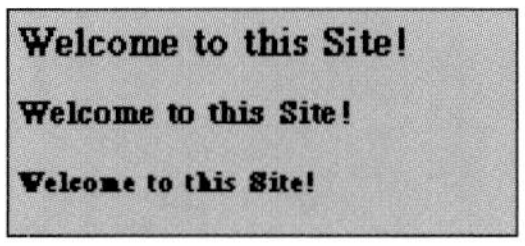

Welcome to this Site!

Welcome to this Site!

Welcome to this Site!

Figure 9.4
Result of the heading tag example.

NOTE

The Times Roman font, to which most browsers default, is called a *serif* font. Typefaces with thicks and thins are serif typefaces. Sans serif type has no thicks and thins. The body copy for this book is a serif font. Many people believe that serif-based typography is easier to read for body copy and that sans-serif is best reserved for headlines; however, you'll see many exceptions to this custom.

There is much controversy in the type community today about type readability and aesthetics. Some hybrid fonts that are popular today use serif and sans-serif in the same face. Other popular typefaces are intentionally abstract and obtuse. You'll find spirited discussion groups debating these subjects online. Check out the following:

- Hugh Dubberly, Creative Director at Netscape: Interview about Type on the Web: http://www.agfa-home.com/features/design.html

- Usenet group devoted to font discussions: Usenet-Comp.fonts

- Frequently Asked Questions about Fonts (Fonts FAQ): http://www.cis.ohio-state.edu/hypertext/faq/usenet/fonts-faq/top.html

Figure 9.5

Using the <b> or the <strong> tag yields the same result—making type bold.

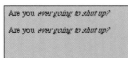

Figure 9.6

Using the <i> or the <em> tag yields the same result—making type italicized.

Figure 9.7

Using the <i> or the <pre> uses a monotype font and accepts spacing as you typed it.

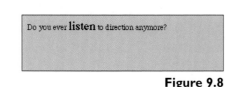

Figure 9.8

Using the <font=#> tag allows you to change the font size in mid-sentence.

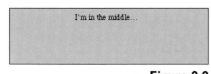

Figure 9.9

Using the <center> tag centers text.

■ **Making type bold.** There are a couple of ways to make type bold (see fig. 9.5) Here they are:

```
<html>
Talk <b>LOUD!</b><p>
Talk <strong>LOUD!</strong>
</html>
```

■ **Making type italicized.** There are a couple of ways to italicize type (see fig. 9.6). Here they are:

```
<html>
<i> Are you <i>ever going to shut up? </i> <p>
<em> Are you <em> ever going to shut up? </em>
</html>
```

■ Using pre-formatted text. Usually shows up in Courier or monotype (see fig. 9.7). Here's the code:

```
<html>
<pre> When are you    g    o    i    n    g    to be
QUIET?</pre>
</html>
```

Here's the trick—use Netscape originated HTML extensions. Netscape and Microsoft's Internet Explorer were the only browsers found to recognize these tags at the time this book was finished.

Font sizes can be changed, using the <font size> </font> tag (see fig. 9.8). Here's how:

```
<html>
Do you ever <font size=5>listen</font> to direction
anymore?
</html>
```

Text can be centered by using the <center> tag (see fig. 9.9). Use the following code:

```
<html>
<center>
I'm in the middle...
</center>
</html>
```

Netscape has a site that has a style sheet for using the <font size> tag as well: http://www.cen.uiuc.edu/~ejk/fontsizes.html. By logging on to this site it will automatically generate an entire range of font sizes using the font your browser is set to. In addition, figures 9.10 and 9.11 are two helpful style sheets that Yoshinobo Takahas, from Disney Online, shares.

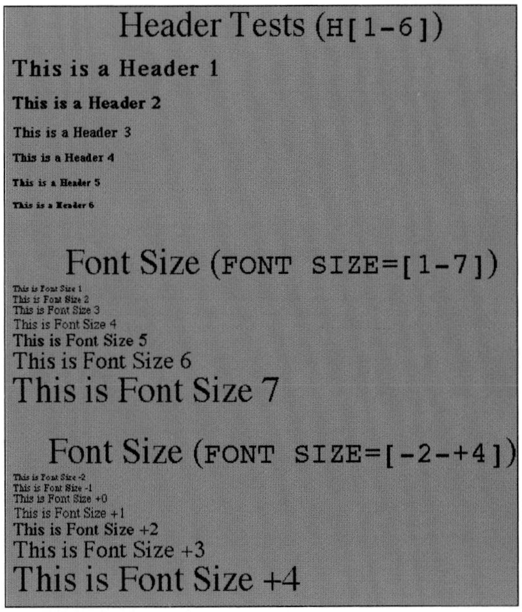

Header Tests (H[1-6])

This is a Header 1

This is a Header 2

This is a Header 3

This is a Header 4

This is a Header 5

This is a Header 6

Font Size (FONT SIZE=[1-7])

This is Font Size 1
This is Font Size 2
This is Font Size 3
This is Font Size 4
This is Font Size 5
This is Font Size 6
This is Font Size 7

Font Size (FONT SIZE=[-2-+4])

This is Font Size -2
This is Font Size -1
This is Font Size +0
This is Font Size +1
This is Font Size +2
This is Font Size +3
This is Font Size +4

Figure 9.10

Using standard HTML text headings, positive value <font size> settings, and negative value <font size> settings.

Header Tests (H[1-6])

This is a Header 1

This is a Header 2

This is a Header 3

This is a Header 4

This is a Header 5

This is a Header 6

Font Size (FONT SIZE=[1-7])

This is Font Size 1

This is Font Size 2

This is Font Size 3

This is Font Size 4

This is Font Size 5

This is Font Size 6

This is Font Size 7

Font Size (FONT SIZE=[-2-+4]

This is Font Size -2

This is Font Size -1

This is Font Size +0

This is Font Size +1

This is Font Size +2

This is Font Size +3

This is Font Size +4

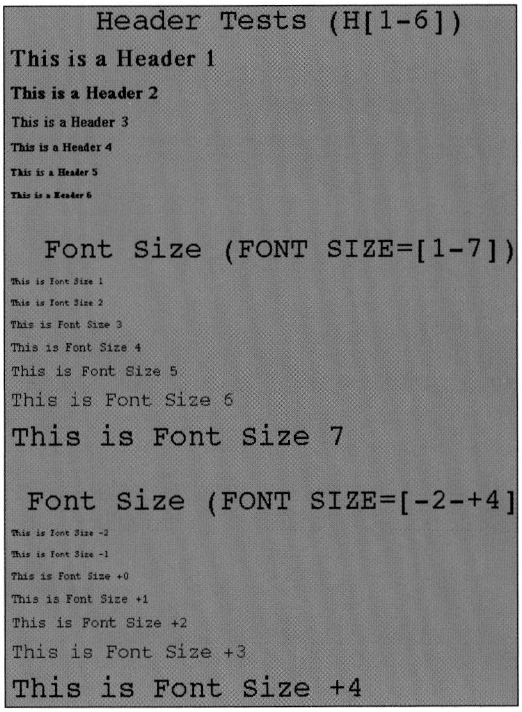

Figure 9.11

Using preformatted <pre> or <code> HTML text headings, positive value <font size> settings, and negative value <font size> settings.

TIP

There are tens of thousands of Postscript and TrueType fonts available to personal computer users today. It's a great benefit to be able to view and *order* fonts online; especially those late nights when you're designing something that's due the next day and you need a specific font you don't yet own. If you're looking for new fonts check out these URLs:

House Industries: http://www.dig-itmad.com/house/house.html

Letraset Online: http://www.letraset.com/letraset/

Handwriting Fonts: http://www.execpc.com/~adw/

Fonthead Design: www.media-bridge.com/fonthead/

Fonts Online: http://www.dol.com/fontsOnline/

Emigre: http://www.value.net/~emigre/index.html

Agfatype: http://www.agfahome.com/

Internet Font Libraries: http://jasper.ora.com:90/comp.fonts/Internet-Font-Archive/index.html

Graphics-Based Typography

We've just examined many HTML possibilities, now it's time to move on to graphics-based text. This section walks you through making a sample type graphic, using Photoshop layers, and learning how to change colors and add effects.

Using graphics for text instead of HTML is where you get the chance to flash your type design aesthetic for the world to see. You'll be able to use any font your heart desires and add special effects to it, like drop shadows, glows, and blurs. A great advantage to using this technique is that the end user will not have to own the font you used, or have it installed on their system. Because it's a graphic, it shows up like any other graphic regardless of what system your end-viewer is on.

Some of the chapters we've already presented demonstrate techniques we recommend you combine with your text-based graphics. Using transparency and solid colors that match the background color of your page are two processes in particular that could be employed in combination to achieve some of the effects described here.

Using Photoshop for Type Design

Photoshop is the ideal environment to create type and graphic Web elements in. Layers in Photoshop 3.0 let you do all kinds of special type effects for headlines that you can use on the Web. Here's a step-by-step example of some type design treatments and how you would accomplish them.

I'm going to assume that the background color to our Web page is white. If you want a different color background, feel free to alter my instructions. Remember; this is just a starting point. Here's how to set up a drop shadow type-based graphic file using layers.

1. Open a new file. For practicing, I've chosen a small file of 100 by 100 pixels, at 72 dpi. Remember to set the background to be Transparent (see fig. 9.12).

2. Double click on the layer and rename it Letter T. Click OK (see fig. 9.13).

3. Using the type tool, click inside the checkerboard document (a checkerboard background means it's transparent and other layers can be laid behind it) and type the letter T. I used a font called OCRA at 80 points, and clicked on the Anti-Aliased checkbox (see fig. 9.14). Feel free to change the font to the font of your own choice. Note that anti-aliasing is checked. If you ever want to create aliased text, uncheck this box. For now, leave it checked.

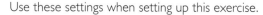

Figure 9.12

Use these settings when setting up this exercise.

Figure 9.13

This launches a New Layer dialog box, where you can change the layer's name.

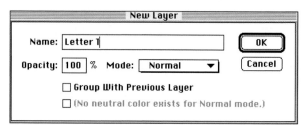

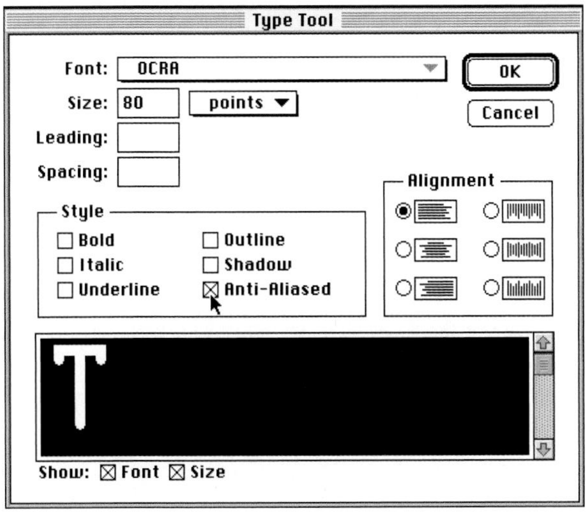

Figure 9.14
By clicking the type tool inside the checkerboard area, this dialog appears. I've used OCRA at 80 pts.

4. Be sure your Show Layers palette is open, located under the menus Windows, Palettes, Show Layers. The type you just added will appear as a Floating Selection. Click on the bottom layer and the floating selection will drop on to the Letter T layer cell (see fig. 9.15).

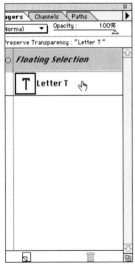

Figure 9.15
The type will appear as a Floating Selection in the layers window. Choose None under the Select menu, or click on the Letter T layer to remove it.

5. Click to highlight the Letter T layer and holding the mouse button down, drag it to the New Layer icon at the bottom of the screen as shown in figure 9.16.

6. You will now have two layers. Double click the new layer and rename it T shadow (see fig. 9.17).

7. Making sure the T shadow layer is highlighted, select the move tool on the tool bar. Drag the layer to offset it slightly from the original.

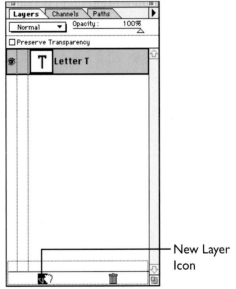

New Layer Icon

Figure 9.16
Click the layer and drag it down to the New Layer Icon. This will make a copy of it in the Layers Palette. To name this layer, repeat step 2.

8. With the T shadow layer still selected, go to the menu Filters, Blur, Gaussian Blur (see fig. 9.18). Adjust the slider until you like the results you get. There is no one set amount—the appropriate blur radius will always vary depending on how big your original art is and how blurry you like your drop shadows. You can adjust opacity in the Show Layers window if you think it's too opaque. Because this is separated as a layer, you can change your mind about how you want your drop shadow to appear at any time.

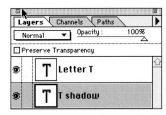

Figure 9.17

Rename the new layer T shadow.

Figure 9.18

With the T shadow layer highlighted, use the move tool to offset the two identical T letter forms. You now have a black letter T with a drop shadow. Congratulations.

Figure 9.19

Highlight the T shadow layer and go to the menu Filter, Gaussian Blur. Adjust as needed.

Figure 9.20

Open one of the Browser Safe color palette files from the CD-ROM and use the eydropper tool to select the color you want. Make sure Preserve Transparency is checked. Change the color by selecting the menu Edit, Fill, Normal, Foreground Color, 100%. The color of the T should change.

9. You should now see a black T with a black drop shadow as in figure 9.19. Changing the color of the T layer is easy. Make sure that layer T is highlighted in the Show Layers palette. Click on the Preserve Transparency box. Pick a new color. Go to the menu Edit and select Fill. Click OK. The original T should now be colored according to what color you chose (see fig. 9.20).

10. You're ready to save the file. Because this type treatment has a soft-edge to the drop shadow, choosing JPEG would be the best file format. (See the discussion of appropriate file formats in Chapter 3.) If you want to save this file as a GIF you will have to convert it from RGB mode to index mode (see Chapter 4).

There are many variations on this one technique, but it lays the foundation for understanding how to work with layers, filters, and changing colors. See figures 9.21–9.23 for examples of slight variations on the same principles presented here.

Figure 9.21

Using the same Photoshop document, I set preserve transparency to the Letter T layer and airbrushed in red and orange. I added a background layer and filled it with turquoise.

Figure 9.22

Using the same Photoshop document, I positioned the T shadow layer so it was directly behind the T, filled it with red and made the T and the background black.

Figure 9.23

Using the same Photoshop document, I set preserve transparency to the Letter T layer and airbrushed in red and orange. I took the T shadow layer, used a Wave distort filter, scaled and skewed it for a drop shadow that looks like it's falling on a curved surface.

Working with Illustrator Type in Photoshop

Unless I have a very simple logo, such as a single letter T like the previous example, I rarely set type in Photoshop. The type setting tools in Photoshop are limited and disappointing. Photoshop excels in its coloring treatment capabilities. You couldn't make soft-edged shadows or work with layers and filters as easily in any other graphics program.

Illustrator, however, has far more sophisticated and professional type controls, and is a much better type design program. It does things like type along a path, type within a defined space, size, kern, space, superscript, plus more (look to the glossary for explanations of these terms). The problem is, Illustrator was created as a Postscript program, and writes files in formats that the Web does not recognize. Here's how to set the type in Illustrator and bring the results into Photoshop, so the type can be utilized on a Web page:

1. Open a new Illustrator file.

2. Set your type. You'll find all the controls your typesetter heart has been waiting for (look to the glossary for explanations, if you aren't familiar with these terms) sizing, kerning, spacing, superscript, and so on (see fig. 9.24).

3. Once you've got everything set the way you want it, save the file as a default Illustrator 5 document and quit.

4. Open Photoshop. Open the Illustrator file and this dialog box appears (see fig. 9.25).

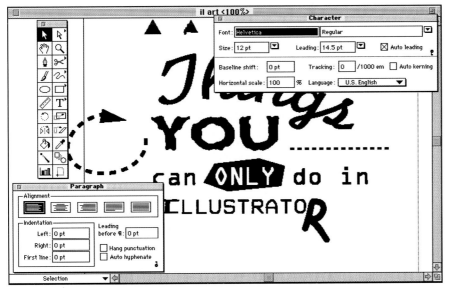

Figure 9.24

Here's an example of an Illustrator file. It shows type along a curved path, dotted lines, blending from one object shape to another, custom type-spacing and mixed fonts—operations that are either impossible or very difficult to do within Photoshop.

Rasterize Adobe Illustrator Format

Image Size: 565K

Width: 7.461   inches ▼

Height: 4.99   inches ▼

Resolution: 72   pixels/inch ▼

Mode: RGB Color ▼

OK

Cancel

☒ Anti-aliased   ☒ Constrain Proportions

Figure 9.25
When you open the Illustrator file in Photoshop, you'll get a
Rasterize Adobe Illustrator Format dialog box. If you say OK
to these settings, the file converts to a bitmap graphic and
will be able to be saved in a Web file format.

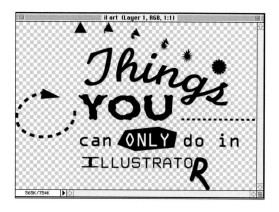

Figure 9.26
Here's how the document opens in Illustrator. Note the checkerboard background that signifies it's on a transparent layer.

Figure 9.27
Once the file is brought into Photoshop as a bitmap graphic, all the
Photoshop features that aren't available in Illustrator can be used,
like adding layers, glows, photographs, and color.

5. Once you've opened the file in
Photoshop it automatically
comes in on its own layer (see
fig. 9.26) and is a perfect candidate for the techniques
described previously.

Figure 9.27 shows the final image
after it has been touched up with
Photoshop. What teamwork!

Fun with ASCII!

Two clever Web designers—Eric Hardman and Alex Lieu of Disney Online—impressed me recently with an unusual twist on typographic design on their Hollywood Records site (see fig. 9.28). ASCII art! Those of us old enough to have lived through the 1970s remember this type of nostalgic computer art fondly. This site sure provides an innovative diversion from typical Web art fare.

To deliver ASCII art over the Web is a brilliant idea. It has all the advantages of speedy HTML-based text delivery, and the advantage of working on almost every browser, since the only HTML necessary to produce involves the <pre> tag, which is widely supported.

Figure 9.28

One of the many great pages from the www.hollywoodrec.com site that features ASCII art.

Here is the HTML source code for figure 9.28:

```html
<HTML>
<HEAD>
<TITLE>GWEN MARS Press</TITLE>
</HEAD>
<BODY TEXT="#A99A05" LINK="#A99A05" VLINK="#FFFFFF" BGCOLOR="#001000">

<CENTER>

<PRE>
<FONT SIZE=+0>
<B>
<A HREF="/HollywoodRecords/Bands/GwenMars/Press/GwenMarsPressM.html">
HI-FI GRAFX</A> /
<A HREF="/HollywoodRecords/Bands/GwenMars/GwenMarsV.html">SCI-FI VR</A>
/ <A HREF="/Note">EMAIL US</A> / <A HREF="/Help">HELP</A>
<A HREF="/HollywoodRecords/HollywoodRecordsL.html">HOLLYWOOD
RECORDS</A>/<A HREF="/HollywoodRecords/Bands/BandRosterL.html">
MUSICIANS</A> / <HREF="/HollywoodRecords/Bands/GwenMars/GwenMarsL.html">
GWEN MARS</A>
</B>
</FONT>
</PRE>

<PRE>
                                 ..uoeeuu.
                        z$$$R#"""``"""#R$bL              .uodW$Wu
                    :$$$"                    ^"%.    .o$R#"""``#$$$
                   :$$F                             +"          8$$
                  8$F                                           $$P
                 $$"                                          d$$"
                $$~                                          d$$"
               $$F                                         d$$"
              t$$                                         d$$"
              $$F                                       x@$P`
             '$$.                                    .@$$"
             9$$.                          .~    .@$$#
             9$$.                    .e"    .@$$#`
            z$$$$$&               .o$"   u@$$#
          .@$$$"$$$L           .z$$"   z$$R"
         :$$$#    ?$$$   .o$$*"  .d$$#
         :$$$"       .o$$$#  z$$#`                        :
        @$$"     u@$$$P" u@*"                            d
       :$$$L .o$$$$$" .d$$$N                            xR
      :$$$$$$$$$R"`  `   '#$$$k               d$"
      '****""              "$$$$eu           .u@$$"
                            "*$$$$$$$$$$$$$$$$#"
                                      ` ` `
</PRE>

<FONT SIZE=+2><B><CODE>PRESS INFO</CODE></B></FONT><P>

</PRE>
</FONT>

</CENTER>
</BODY>
</HTML>
```

There are two shareware programs that convert artwork to ASCII. The Mac-based program is called GIFscii, and the PC-based product is called PIXCHAR. Both are on the Designing Web Graphics CD-ROM.

Writing the HTML to Place Your Text Graphics into the Page

Placing graphics on a Web page is addressed in depth in Chapter 13, "Hot Spots," and "Fun with Alignment" in Chapter 10. The basic way to insert a graphic on a page is to use the <img src> tag. Here's how to put the Drop Shadow artwork, made earlier, on a page.

```
<html>
<img src="dropshad.JPEG">
</html>
```

If you wanted to link the Drop Shadow image to another source, you'd combine the <img src> tag with an <a href> tag. Here's how:

```
<html>
<a href="http://www.domain.com><img src="dropshad.JPEG"></a>
</html>
```

Summary

Type design on the Web has a long way to go before it will make trained typographers happy. HTML doesn't let artists choose fonts or use sophisticated type tools, like those we're accustomed to in Photoshop and Illustrator. Most sophisticated Web sites use a combination of HTML tags and text-based graphics that take advantage of Photoshop's and Illustrator's superior type design tools.

- Use HTML to set body type, but be aware that many browsers won't recognize some of the Netscape-originated tags described here.

- Graphics that include type or are composed entirely of type are a great alternative to limited HTML-based text.

- Use transparency with graphics-based text, or create the text against the same color background on your Web page, and you'll get text that floats freely on backgrounds.

- Illustrator and Postscript drawing programs typically have better type tools than Photoshop. You'll need to convert Illustrator files to Photoshop files before they can be colored, filtered, and saved as GIFs or JPEGs.

- An advantage to using graphics-based text is that the end viewer doesn't need to have the fonts you used installed in their systems.

CHAPTER 10 Fun with Alignment

Shall we start with the bad news first? A Web page has no fixed size. Some browsers have pre-defined sizes that the viewing window fits to; others let you size the screen to fill your monitor. Some of your audience will see your page through tiny portable computer screens. Others will have 21" monitors. Imagine if you had to fit lots of information on a piece of paper, but no one could tell you the size of the paper you had to work with. And imagine trying to fit that information onto the paper artistically, with a little more finesse than left-justifying every image, headline, and text block? Also imagine that the tools to change position and alignment were strange and unintuitive, and didn't work everywhere.

Is it any wonder that few designers know how to do Web page layout well? Making a Web page behave the way you want it to is a challenging task. Let's look at the lack of defined size of your viewer's window and monitor screen first.

Defining the Size of a Web Page

"Small is better" seems to be the credo of Web design. Because there is no fixed size to a Web page, you get to define one yourself. Taking into account that people might be looking at your work in small windows, it makes the most sense to define a small page size to work with. Yes, but how small is small?

I tend to err on the conservative side when suggesting width restrictions for graphics on a Web page. 640 pixels is the average width of an average computer monitor, even on many portables, and I think there should be some breathing room around that. On Macintoshes, Netscape's opening screen defaults to 505 pixels across. I've picked 480 pixels as a good width for an opening graphic or headline. That's the approximate width of the menu bar for Netscape's home page. This rule is not cast in stone. I'm simply describing the sizes of some of the environments your page will be viewed in and arriving at a size based on how I would want my graphics to be viewed.

Lack of a defined Web page size can be dealt with creatively. Carina Feldman, who recently received an M.F.A. in Graphic Design from Art Center College of Design, challenged the unlimited size of a Web page by making a long, vertical text graphic that forces viewers to scroll down many computer screens to finish reading (see fig. 10.1).

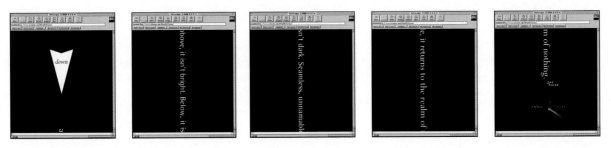

Figure 10.1
Carina Feldman's long, vertical graphic that plays with the lack of defined space.

Because Web pages can scroll vertically, there are no length restrictions to contend with on a Web document. If you want your opening graphic to be visible on most computer monitors however, you might want to think about composing your opening page graphic (splash screen or menu bar) so it could be seen on a portable computer. Most portable computer screens today are 640×480, and some are 640×400.

Based on this information, I think opening screen graphics and headline text, or whatever *you* hope the viewer will see at first glance on your page, should be no taller than 350 pixels.

Some artists choose to make wider screens than my conservative estimate of 480 pixels. There are lots of clever ways to tell your audience how wide to open their browser window, and figures 10.2 and 10.3 show some examples.

As you can see, the size of your page is up to you. Take into account people's monitor capabilities to make informed design decisions about sizing. Carina's pages are great for personal expression, but if you are hired to design a page for a client it most likely would be important to make their page read at first glance under most monitor conditions.

Now that the page width and height is understood to be a variable, let's examine techniques for lining up artwork within it.

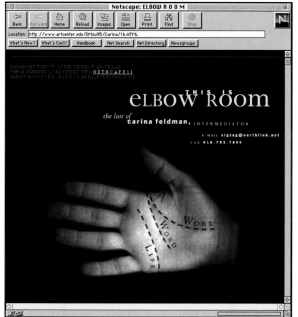

Figure 10.2

Carina Feldman's instructions to viewers of her Web page to size their screen.

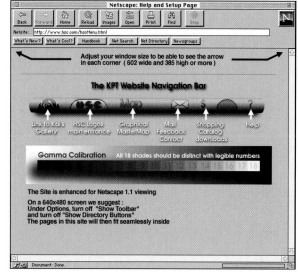

Figure 10.3

Metatools Web site's instructions for screen width.

Using HTML for Alignment

HTML was not designed to be a QuarkXpress or PageMaker. I don't think the original authors ever dreamed of it as a tool for page layout that would satisfy the needs of graphic designers. It was originally invented to support the scientific community and include diagrams and image tables that were associated with massive quantities of technical writings. Formatting handles like left justifying and indenting a list of words suited the needs of that community just fine. We're asking a lot more of it than it was ever designed to do, but hey, that's life. HTML originators thought they were inventing one thing, we've judged that their efforts are seeds to grow into something more refined.

HTML has limited alignment capabilities, but Web designers worth their weight should know how to use all of them. The following section reviews the HTML alignment tags.

Here is a list of HTML tags for aligning text and images.

Text Alignment Tags

These tags relate to text elements. For an example of how they look on a Web page, see figure 10.4:

- **Paragraph breaks:** Insert this tag where you want spaces between paragraphs:

  <p>

> **NOTE**
>
> With alignment tags, you'll see standard, sanctioned HTML, and Netscape's own enhanced brand that some browsers will not support. Check the browser comparison test in Chapter 1 to see which browsers support these tags and which do not.

- **Line breaks:** Put this tag where you want to have the text wrap return around to the next line:

- **Centering Text:** Use this tag before you center text and/or images, and the closed tag when you want text below it to return to left-justified formatting.

  <center>

- **Preformatted Text:** Preformatted text typically uses a different font, like a typewriter-style Courier, instead of the default Times Roman. The <pre> tag lets you set the spacing and indents of your type. (For more examples of the <pre> tag, check out Chapter 9, "Typography for the Web-Impaired," and Appendix A, "HTML for Graphic Designers."

  <pre></pre>

- **No Break:** Use this tag if you want the browser width to dictate where the text breaks. The closed tag signifies when you want the no break formatting to end.

  <nobr></nbr>

- **Making Text blink:** Use with caution; has been known to cause irritable responses from Web audiences worldwide who hate this feature.

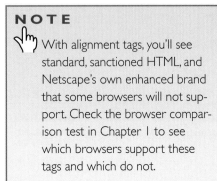

Figure 10.4

An example of all the above text tags in action on a Web page.

Image and Type Alignment Tags

These tags cause text to align in relationship to the images it's next to. For examples, see figure 10.5.

- Align text to the top of your image:
  <img src=filenamehere.gif align=top>

- Align text to the bottom of your image:
  <img src=filenamehere.gif align=bottom>

- Align text to the middle of your image:
  <img src=filenamehere.gif align=middle>

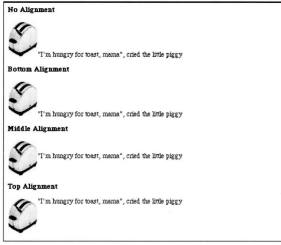

Figure 10.5

An example of text and image alignment tags.

Image Alignment Tags

The following tags align the images to the left or right of the screen. For the results, see figure 10.6.

- Image left justified:
  <img src=filenamehere.gif align=left>

- Image right justified:
  <img src=filenamehere.gif align=right>

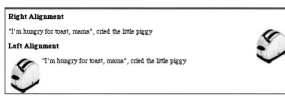

Figure 10.6

An example of right and left image alignment tags.

Horizontal and Vertical Space Tags

The Horizontal and Vertical space tags were originated by Netscape and are now supported by a few other browsers (see the Browser Comparison chart in Chapter 1). These tags allow you to insert empty space around a graphic, creating breathing room.

I've used the <hspace=value> tag in the following code to put forty pixels breathing room to the left and right of the toaster image (see fig. 10.7).

```
<html>
<head> <title> Alignment Test</title>
</head>
<body bgcolor="ffffff">
<img src="ltoast.jpg" align=left
hspace=40>"I'm hungry for toast, mama!",
<br>cried the little piggy.<br clear=all>
</body>
</html>
```

Figure 10.7

Using the <hspace=value> tag creates breathing room between text and graphics on the page.

To demonstrate what adding <vspace=value> does, I experimented with the following code (see fig. 10.8).

```
<html>
<head> <title> Alignment Test</title>
</head>
<body bgcolor="ffffff">
<img src="ltoast.jpg" align=left hspace=40
vspace=80>"I'm hungry for toast, mama!",
<br>cried the little piggy.<br clear=all>
</body>
</html>
```

Figure 10.8

Using the <vspace=value> tag lowered the graphic by 80 pixels. Because there's also a <hspace=value tag of 40 pixels, the image still has left and right "breathing" room around it.

Width and Height Tags

These tags work by allowing you to specify the width and height values (in pixels) of a graphic. This can accomplish two things. It causes the text on the page to load before the graphic, while making space for the graphic to come into the proper location.

If you put smaller or larger values in these tags, they will actually shrink or scale your image larger. The actual dimension of the toaster image is 102×115 pixels. By putting a width of 53 and height of 60, I shrunk the image in half. By putting a value of 240 by 214 I scaled it to be twice as big. The following sections illustrate these alignment tags (see fig. 10.9).

```
<html>
<head> <title> Alignment Test</title>
</head>
<body bgcolor="ffffff">
<img src="ltoast.jpg" width=60 height=53
align=left>"I'm hungry for toast, mama!",
<br>cried the little piggy.<br >
<p>
<p>
<img src="ltoast.jpg" width=240 height=214
align=left>"I'm hungry for toast, mama!",
<br>cried the little piggy.<br >
</body>
</html>
```

This exhausts the possibilities that HTML tags offer for alignment. There are some new tags in proposal stage for HTML 3.0, but so far they

Figure 10.9

One small toaster and one big toaster, courtesy of height and width tags.

are unsupported. If you want to stay on top of HTML 3.0 announcements, contact: http://www.hp.co.uk/people/dsr/html3/CoverPage.html or use Yahoo Search, a great resource for finding useful things, to find anything that's new on this subject: http://search.yahoo.com/bin/search?p=html+3.0.

Next, we move on to alignment techniques without using HTML. These involve making custom artwork that serves to align images, rather than relying on code.

Alternatives to HTML Using Artwork

Using images for alignment involves creating spacer art. This art exists on the Web page for the sole purpose of making spaces between text and images. For the spacer art to be invisible you have two options.

■ Make the spacer art the same color as your background. To do this, use the background color tag or create a solid color pattern, or both. These two methods are described in more depth in Chapters 5 and 7. For an example, see figure 10.10.

■ Make sure your spacer art is one color, and assign that color to be transparent saving the one color artwork as a transparent Gif, as described in Chapter 7.

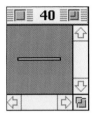

Figure 10.10

An example of a spacer image. It need only be one pixel high if all it's meant to do is create horizontal space. You might do the opposite if it was created to produce vertical space.

Using Spacers for Alignment

The following is what the HTML code would produce without using any spacers or alignment techniques. The toaster photographs are from a CD-ROM collection from Classic PIO Partners (800)370-2746. I've named the artwork respectively: ltoast.jpg, ftoast.jpg, and rtoast.jpg. Figure 10.11 shows the final result.

```
<html>
<head> <title> Alignment Test</title>
</head>
<body bgcolor="ffffff">
<img src="ltoast.jpg"><img
src="ftoast.jpg"><img src="rtoast.jpg">
</body>
</html>
```

The following is the HTML code to use white spacer art between each image to give them a little breathing room. I made a file in Photoshop that was 40 pixels wide and 1 pixel high, and named it 40space.jpg (refer to fig. 10.8). Figure 10.12 shows the result.

```
<html>
<head> <title> Alignment Test</title>
</head>
<body bgcolor="ffffff">
<img src="40space.jpg"><img
src="ltoast.jpg"><img
src="40space.jpg"><img
src="ftoast.jpg"><img
src="40space.jpg"><img src="rtoast.jpg">
</body>
</html>
```

If I used the same spacer in front of each image, I could create a consistent left indent as shown in figure 10.13.

```
<html>
<head> <title> Alignment Test</title>
</head>
<body bgcolor="ffffff">
<img src="40space.jpg"><img
src="ltoast.jpg">
<p><img src="40space.jpg"><img
src="ftoast.jpg">
<p><img src="40space.jpg"><img
src="rtoast.jpg">
</body>
</html>
```

We've covered the possibilities for aligning images to a page, but what about aligning an image to match a background pattern perfectly? There's a bit of trickery to share, because it involves understanding how patterns tile on a page, and creating offset registration into the foreground imagery.

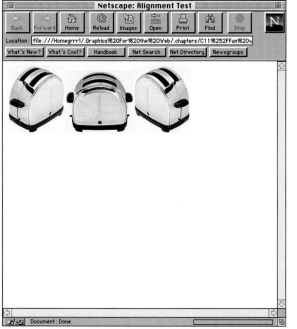

Figure 10.11
The three toasters touching each other.

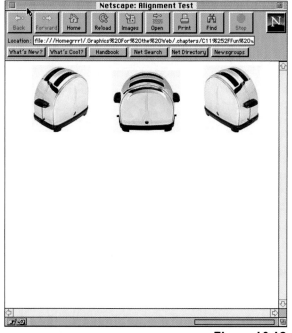

Figure 10.12
The three toasters with space between them.

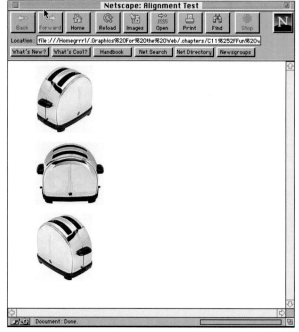

Figure 10.13
The three toasters with a consistent left indent.

Aligning a Graphic to a Patterned Background

Creating pattern backgrounds is discussed thoroughly in Chapter 6. This chapter addresses those cases where you want to align a graphic perfectly to a pattern background, and have it match up. You can make an image line up to a background, assuming that your browser supports transparency. Transparent images can float freely above a pattern background and line up to look like one seamless image. Transparency is discussed in Chapter 8.

This chapter deals with alignment, and aligning an image that fits to a background pattern is a little tricky. This is due to an offset that occurs to graphics when they are displayed within a Web browser. All pattern backgrounds automatically line up flush top and flush left on a Web page. All overlaying images automatically load into a Web page with a space of 8 pixels to the left and 8 pixels on the top. You'll have to make the foreground art with this offset built-in, if you want the art to perfectly match your background pattern. See the following case study for an in-depth example of aligning a graphic to a patterned background.

Playing with Space: Bruce Heavin's Gallery Page Art

Bruce Heavin came up with an original idea when asked to design *The Net Magazine's* Web-based gallery space (http://www.thenet-usa.com/ gallery/gallery.html). He decided to make a room out of his page, complete with wallpaper, cracks in the wall, a floor, ceiling, and mouse hole (not to mention his trademark monkey acting in his usual mischievous manner). He did this by first creating the wallpaper. He made one pattern (see Chapter 6 for tips on making patterns) then created vertical color bands within the pattern that would simulate lighting changes on a room's walls. Figure 10.14 shows the original wallpaper tile.

Using the Select All, and Define Pattern features in Photoshop, Bruce then filled a larger image to see how the pattern would look once it was tiled on the Web. He used the Fill dialog box set to "Fill with Pattern" (see fig. 10.15). This allowed him to preview the wallpaper once it was tiled as shown in figure 10.16.

Bruce brought each piece of art (the ceiling, the wall crack, and the floor) into the large Photoshop file in which he tested his wallpaper, turning it into a layered document in order to previsualize placement of the graphics over the wallpaper (see fig. 10.17).

Using Photoshop, he trimmed the 8 pixels off the top and left side of the

Figure 10.14

The original wallpaper tile designed by Bruce Heavin.

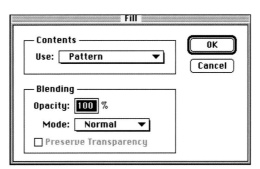

Figure 10.15

The Fill dialog box in Photoshop.

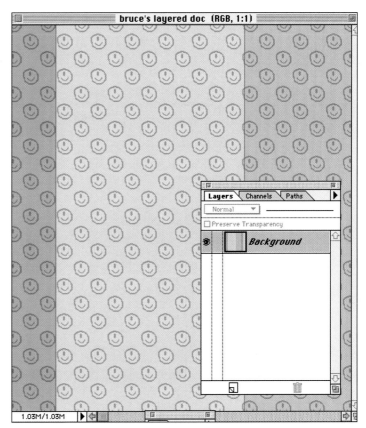

Figure 10.16

The image tiled to fill the background of the Web page.

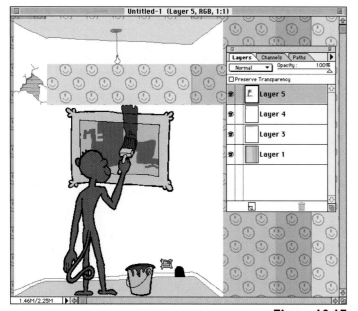

Figure 10.17

Bruce's Photoshop document with all the layers registered in place.

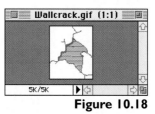

Figure 10.18

The wall crack.

Figure 10.19

The floor.

graphics that needed to match up to the pattern. Once he was finished, he saved each piece of registered artwork out as separate Gif files. Figures 10.18 through 10.20 show each piece of art separated out from background wallpaper.

The following the HTML code (written by The Net's Webmistress, Kathy Tafel) that puts everything together. An interesting note is the fact that Bruce Heavin does not know a word of HTML. Here's a perfect example of an exceptional designer and illustrator using his talents in conjunction with an exceptionally talented HTML programmer. Figure 10.21 shows the complete page.

```
<HTML>a
<HEAD>
<TITLE>Eye Candy</TITLE>
</HEAD>
<BODY
BACKGROUND="../../Images/tiles/
happypaper.gif">
<IMG
SRC="../../Images/rooms/ceiling.
gif" ALT="Ceiling"><BR>
<IMG
SRC="../../Images/rooms/crack.gif
" align=right ALT="Crack in the
wall"><P>
<DL>
<DL>
<DL>
<DT><a
href="downs/downs.html">Richard
Downs</a>
<DT><a href="mark/mark.html">Mark
Todd</a>
<DT><a
href="esther/esther.html">Esther
Watson</a>
<DT><a
href="bruce/bruce.html">Bruce
Heavin</a>
</DL>
</DL>
</DL>
<IMG
SRC="../../Images/rooms/gallery2.
gif" border=0 ALT="Monkey
painting"><Ahref="rat/rat.html
"><IMG
SRC="../../Images/rooms/frame.gif
```

```
" border=0 ALT="Rat
gallery"></a><A
href="nest.html"><IMG
SRC="../../Images/rooms/hole.gif"
border=0 ALT="Rat's
Nest"></a><BR>
[<a
href="../../Welcome.html">Nest</
a>]<BR>
</BODY>
<HTML>
```

Figure 10.20
The ceiling.

Figure 10.21
The finished page.

Summary

You might feel like you're fighting an uphill battle, but it is possible to trick browsers into recognizing image alignment requests. If HTML doesn't work, try making artwork that will. You can do this by:

- Using HTML tags to control alignment. Be sure to check that the Browser you're designing for recognizes the HTML tags you're using. (Check our Browser Comparison chart in Chapter 1 or contact the URLs that are listed there for current browser information.)

- Using invisible placeholder graphic can create alignment. Either make the placeholder graphics the same color as the background to your Web page, or make it a transparent GIF (see Chapter 8).

- Aligning a graphic perfectly to a background pattern involves shaving 8 pixels off the left and top sides before you post the image to the Web.

Check out the Chapter 14, "Table Manners," to see another, newer technique that's useful for aligning text and images.

CHAPTER 11 Horizontal Rules!

A horizontal rule line that serves as a page divider is something you'll rarely see in print design. These divider lines are commonly observed across Web sites the world over, however. Some are embossed, some are thick, some are thin, and some are colored or have different shapes. The Web term for these lines is *horizontal rule*, and they are used for many things:

- Defining a page break
- Completing an idea
- Beginning a list
- Separating one picture from another

Horizontal rules are used often; some might even say too often. That's no wonder, if you ask me. Web pages have no set length like printed pages. The visual techniques and metaphors available to print designers—such as using a block of color behind text or images, changing the text color in an isolated paragraph or sidebar, or using a different screened-back image or picture frame to separate an idea or theme—are not easily replicated on the Web.

If you want to add horizontal rules to your pages, you have some choices. You can use straight, old-fashioned HTML code, Netscape Extension HTML code for fancier horizontal rules, or you can insert your own artwork to make custom horizontal rules, and vertical rules too. When all else fails, there are libraries of horizontal rule clip art too.

Horizontal Rules, the HTML Way

The basic TML 2.0 and 3.0 standard horizontal rule tag looks like this: <hr>. Here it is in the context of code:

```
<html>
<body>
Some Text
<hr>
Some More Text
</body>
</html>
```

This will put an embossed, double-pixel line horizontally through your page at whatever point you insert it into an HTML document (see fig. 11.1). If you stretch your browser window wider, the horizontal rule will get wider, and vice versa if you narrow your window. Horizontal rules have no set width, except to fill the horizontal distance of your browser screen.

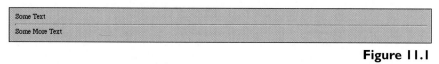

Figure 11.1
A standard HTML horizontal rule.

Sometimes you might want to add some breathing room, because the horizontal rule will butt up underneath whatever text or image that was in the HTML code before it. The following code will add a row of empty space above and beneath the rule, as shown in figure 11.2.

```
<html>
<body>
Some Text
<p>
<hr>
<p>
Some More Text
</body>
</html>
```

Figure 11.2
Inserting the <p> tags adds more space around the rule.

Horizontal Rules, the Netscape Extensions Way

As usual, Netscape has added some nifty extensions to the horizontal rules feature that other browsers may or may not support:

- Changing the rule's width
- Changing the rule's weight (thickness)
- Changing both the rule's width and weight
- Left-aligning the rule
- Eliminating fake emboss shading

Notice that if you define a width, the resulting horizontal rule is automatically centered. Any value you put after the = (equals) sign will tell the rule how wide to be in pixels. Here's the code telling the rule to be 10 pixels wide, as shown in figure 11.3:

```
<hr width=25>
```

Figure 11.3
Rules with a defined width, such as this 25-pixel rule, are automatically centered.

The following code changes the weight, or thickness, of the line. Notice that this stretches the length of a page, as shown in figure 11.4.

```
<hr size=10>
```

Figure 11.4
Changing the rule's "size" creates a thicker line.

The following code changes the thickness and width at the same time. Figure 11.5 shows the results of code telling the rule to be a square, with equal height and width.

```
<hr size=25 width=25>
```

Figure 11.5
By changing the rule's weight and width to equal measurements, you end up with a square.

The following aligns the square left and sizes it at 25 pixels high and 25 pixels wide (see fig. 11.6):

```
<hr align=left size=10 width=10>
```

Look ma, no fake emboss shading! (see fig. 11.7):

```
<hr noshade>
```

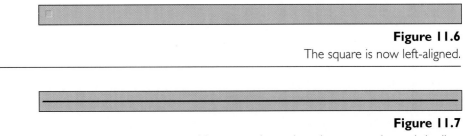

Figure 11.6
The square is now left-aligned.

Figure 11.7
You can code a rule to have no embossed shading.

Horizontal Rules the Do-it-Yourself Way

Anything gets old when you see it too often, and horizontal rules are no exception. If you want to be a little more creative, here are some tips to creating custom artwork to design your own rules.

When you make your own horizontal rule art, your artwork dictates the length, width, and height. It's a graphic like any other graphic. It can be aliased, anti-aliased, a GIF, a JPEG, interlaced, transparent, blurred, 2D, 3D—you name it. If you know how to make it, it can be a horizontal rule.

To include a graphic as a horizontal rule, the HTML code would be:

```
<img src="your_horizontal_rule_art_here.gif">
```

Using Illustrator and Photoshop to Create Custom Horizontal Rule Art

Adobe Illustrator has lots of features that are wonderful for making horizontal rules. I've used some of my favorites here. Filters, for example, are great for making quick and easy art. I used the spiral, free polygon, and star filters found under the Filter, Create heading of the Filters menu. I also like to draw freehand with my pressure sensitive tablet using the brush tool in Illustrator. You can set the line to have thick and thin weights, thereby lessening the predictably uniform, perfectly symmetrical look that Illustrator files so often have. A neat way to repeat a piece of art along a horizontal axis in Illustrator is to copy it and place the copy next to the original at a set distance, then use the Duplicate command to repeat the established offset indefinitely.

Figure 11.8 shows a sampling of some of my favorite Illustrator techniques, and are not meant to limit you from using your favorite Illustrator tools and techniques. However, you can choose to create artwork in Illustrator that can be used in Photoshop, as described in the following section.

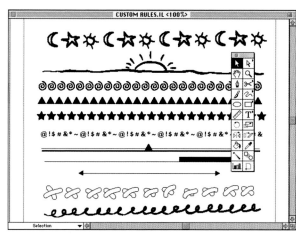

Figure 11.8

This is how my custom horizontal rule art file looked in Illustrator.

Case Study

Here's a step-by-step example of making custom horizontal rule art using Illustrator and Photoshop.

As we discussed in Chapter 7, Illustrator files have to be converted to bitmaps before they can be converted to Web graphics. I've saved the Illustrator art as a bitmap and have brought it into Photoshop. At this point, the art is rasterized. I chose to not check the anti-alias box, so these graphics would be smaller when saved. (See Chapter 3 for more tips on making low-memory graphics.) Notice that the files came into Photoshop as black and white, against a checkerboard background (see fig. 11.9). This means that they're on a transparent layer, which is going to help me out tremendously when I go to color them.

When an object is placed on a transparent layer in Photoshop, you can modify the object easily. Check Preserve Transparency box found in the upper left hand area of the Layers palette (see fig. 11.10), then paint on the image area. Notice the object is masked to accept color only where there's image. This allows you to paint the black areas of the horizontal rule line, without worrying about painting outside the shapes created in Illustrator. The final image is shown in figure 11.11.

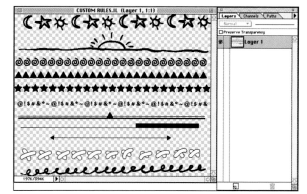

Figure 11.9

An example of how the Illustrator art looked in Photoshop once it was rasterized. Notice that it appears against a checkerboard background.

Figure 11.10

An example of the Layers palette in Photoshop with Preserve Transparency checked.

Figure 11.11

The final image.

I also thought it would be funny to use this same artwork to poke fun at the "embossed" nature of typical Web horizontal rules. I used the RGB value 192 192 192 to approximate the color of a typical gray background of a Web browser. I took a screen capture of a Web page (Command Shift+3 on a Mac and F13 on a PC), pulled it into Photoshop, and used the eyedropper tool in Photoshop to get the RGB values of the highlight and shadow colors of the standard embossed horizontal rules. (Shadow: 252 242 243 Midtone: 241 241 241 Highlight: 234 234 234). I copied the layer I brought in from Illustrator three times, and using the Preserve Transparency feature, filled each layer respectively with a shadow, midtone, and highlight color. By selecting the move tool and using arrow keys on my keyboard, I was able to nudge the layers up and down to create the emboss effect. The results can be seen in figure 11.12.

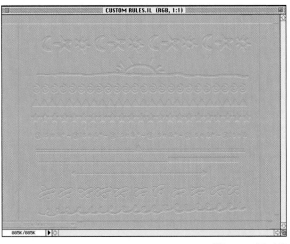

Figure 11.12

The finished custom horizontal rule embossed artwork.

Of course, after reading Chapter 1, "Browser Hell," you know that one standard gray background color does not exist on the Web. I'm getting as close to that color as I can, and once I choose to save my file with a transparent background (see Chapter 6) the slight variations in gray are going to go unnoticed to my unassuming Web audience. Now the rule is

ready for Web use. Figure 11.13 shows a finished page using my custom fake embossed rule. If you like it, feel free to borrow it from the Horizontal Rule folder on the CD-ROM that comes with this book. Or, better yet, make your own with the tips I just shared.

Once I'm done, I can copy and paste each horizontal rule into its own file, and save it. I think saving the rules as transparent GIFs (see Chapter 8) makes the most sense, because I want the irregularly shaped lines to look like they're floating freely on my Web pages. Figure 11.14 shows two of the custom horizontal rules I made.

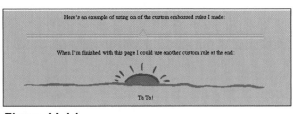

Figure 11.13

Separating custom horizontal rule art into its own file.

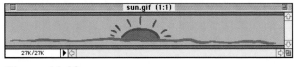

Figure 11.14

More of the art demonstrated in this chapter put to use on a Web page.

Vertical Rules

Vertical rules are not an easy task to take on with Web pages. Making the custom artwork is identical to making any other custom artwork and all the Photoshop and Illustrator tips shared in this book should be of help. The trick is how to get vertical lines aligned to a Web page, as there is no easy way to assign vertical columns using HTML. We have lessons on how to position vertical ruled lines in Chapter 14, "Table Manners."

Clip Art Rules, Too

There are many kind, generous souls on the Web (see figure 11.15) who lend their wares for free. Or other gifted souls who might charge for their art so they can do what they're good at—satisfy you and me—and still feed themselves and their families. Clip art is a wondrous thing in a pinch, and with tools like Photoshop, Illustrator, and Painter, there's no end to cool ways you can personalize it further.

Here are some URL's and samples of horizontal rule art you can find on the Web. There are some in the Horizontal Rule folder on the CD-ROM too.

- Gifs R Us, Jay Boersma's prolific image collection:

  http://www.ecn.bgu.edu/users/gas52r0/Jay/home.html

- Sandra's Clip Art Server, a great resource for clip art over the Net:

  http://www.cs.yale.edu/homes/sjl/clipart.html

- Buttons, Cubes, and Bars; a great collection of custom art from Chris Stephens:

  http://www.cbil.vcu.edu.8080/gifs/bullet.html

- Yahoo search for Clip Art, always a great bet to find the best and latest clip art listings:

  http://www.yahoo.com/Computers_and_Internet/Multimedia/ Pictures/Clip_Art/

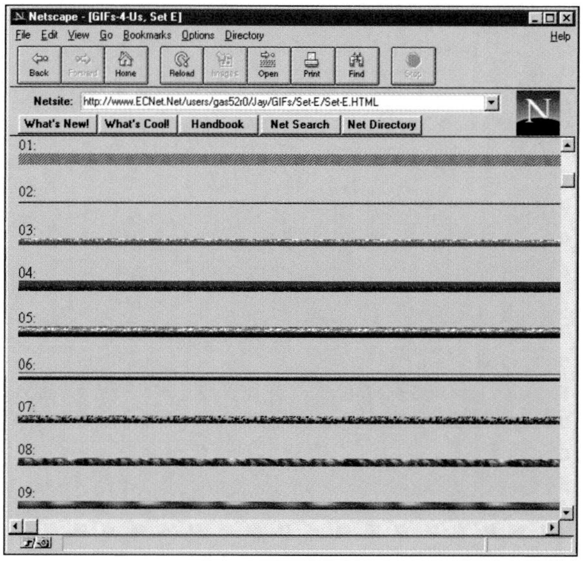

Figure 11.15

A sample from Jay Boersma's great shareware clip art collection.

Summary

Now that you're ready to make your own horizontal rules, this chapter should provide a valuable resource for finding the correct HTML code or production techniques to create your own custom art. Here are a few things to remember when working with horizontal rules:

■ Horizontal rules are available using standard HTML tags, or by using Netscape Extension tags that let you create different widths and positions.

■ You can make any artwork of your choosing a horizontal rule, by using the `<img src>` tag and inserting custom-made horizontal shaped artwork.

■ It's possible to do vertical rules, if you build them into your background pattern tile, or pre-build them into bitmapped artwork that would be included in an HTML document using the `<img src>` tag, and then using alignment spacers such as those described in Chapter 10. Check out using Tables for alignment of vertical rules in Chapter 14.

CHAPTER 12 Bullets-o-Rama

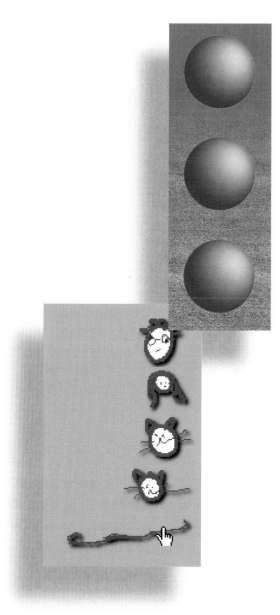

You'll see plenty of pages with diverse information content on the Web, but lists of one type or another are universally needed in the majority of sites. List items can appear indented with numbers, or preceded by icons known as *bullets*. Bullets on the Web can look standardized, using solid circles in front of text (much like those generated by a word processor), or they can include custom artwork that looks more typical of a CD-ROM or magazine page layout. Creating custom bullets is similar to creating custom horizontal rules—basically any artwork that you're capable of creating is a candidate for bullet art.

You've got your HTML variety bullets and your image-based bullets to choose from. Let's look at HTML first. When designing bulleted lists for the Web, you can choose from either HTML bullets or image-based bullets. HTML bullets are created by using code tags that identify the type of list you are creating; such bullets appear as basic circles or squares. Image-based bullets are those you generate from clip art or your own artwork, and can be used to enhance a list or provide added functionality, such as links. This chapter shows you how to create both HTML and image-based bullets, including several variations on both themes.

Creating HTML Bulleted Lists

Using HTML-based bullets is certainly less work than creating your own custom artwork. Sometimes, they're more appropriate, as well. Simple and clean design often looks best without a lot of custom artwork on a page. There will be many instances where an HTML-based bullet or indent will do the job more effectively than custom bullet artwork.

To make a list with solid circle bullets use the <UL> tag, which stands for *unorganized list*. To create such a bulleted list within text items, use the <UL> tag along with the <LI> (list item) tag, as shown in the following code:

```
<p>
<UL>
<LI> The first thinga-dingy
<LI> The second thinga-dingy
<LI> The third thinga-dingy
</UL>
```

Using this code produces the result shown in figure 12.1.

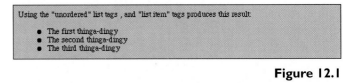

Figure 12.1
Using the <UL> and <LI> tags produces a standard bulleted list.

Lists can be nested by inserting a new tag where you want the list to indent or move to another level. The following code uses an additional <UL> tag to create a bulleted list nested within another bulleted list:

```
<P>
<UL>
<LI> The first thinga-dingy
<LI> The second thinga-dingy
<LI> The third thinga-dingy
<UL>
<LI> More types of thinga-dingies
<LI> Yet More types of thinga-dingies
<LI> Even more types of thinga-dingies
</UL>
```

Using this code produces the result shown in figure 12.2.

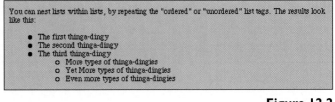

Figure 12.2
You can use additional tags to create nested lists.

You can have the items in your list be links to other pages or sites by using the <a href></a> tag within an organized list or an unorganized list. The following code shows how to use link tags to include links within a bulleted list:

```
<p>
<UL>
<LI> <a href="http://www.domain.com">The first thinga-dingy</a>
<LI> <a href="http://www.domain.com">The second thinga-dingy</a>
<LI> <a href="http://www.domain.com">The third thinga-dingy</a>
</UL>
```

Using this code produces the result shown in figure 12.3.

Figure 12.3
Using the <a href></a> tag to create links within a bulleted list.

Creating Ordered and Definition Lists

At times, you might not want your lists to be preceded with bullets. When creating a list of steps to be followed in order, for example, using numbers rather than bullets will help get your point across. Such numbered lists are called *ordered lists*. Likewise, lists such as glossaries can appear with indents rather than bullets or numbers. These lists are known as *definition lists*.

To make a list that automatically generates numbers in front of its items, use the <OL> (ordered list) tag. The following code lines show how to use the <OL> code to produce the numbered list shown in figure 12.4.

```
<p>
<OL>
<LI> The first thinga-dingy
<LI> The second thinga-dingy
<LI> The third thinga-dingy
</OL>
<p>
```

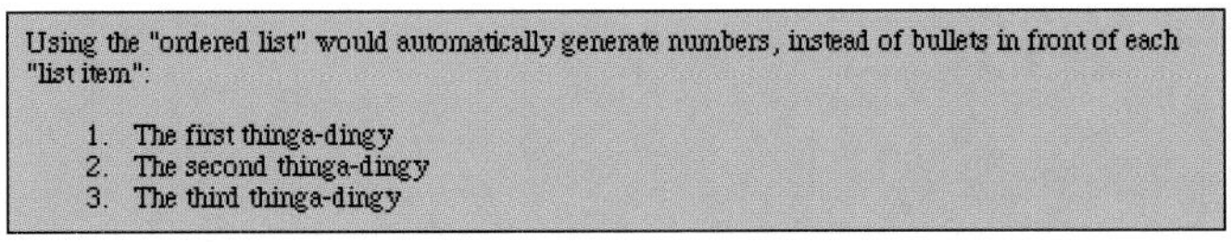

Figure 12.4
Using the <OL> code results in a numbered list.

If you want to indent items in a list without seeing a bullet shape, you might want to use a <DL> (definition list) tag, instead of creating an organized list or unorganized list. You use the <DT> tag for the flush left items and the <DD> tag for the indented items, as shown in the following code:

```
<p>
<DL>
<DT>
First Category
<DD>The first thinga-dingy
<DT>
Second Category
<DD>The second thinga-dingy
<DT>
Third Category
<DD>The second thinga-dingy
</DL>
```

This definition list is shown in figure 12.5.

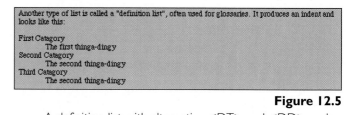

Figure 12.5
A definition list with alternating <DT> and <DD> codes.

Here's a variation on the same code, with the results shown in figure 12.6.

```
<DL>
<DT>
Thingy Dingies<P>
<DD>The first thinga-dingy
<DD>The second thinga-dingy
<DD>The second thinga-dingy
</DL>
```

Figure 12.6
A definition list with a single <DT> line preceding three <DD> lines.

Netscape Extension-Based HTML Bullets

Netscape, once again, adds value to HTML by offering tags that give the designer a little more artistic control over bulleted lists. All the tags described so far in this chapter are also supported within Netscape. Keep in mind that these extensions are not supported by other browsers. They will produce the standard circle bullet, if viewed by browsers other than Netscape.

If you want to change the shape of the automatically generated bullets you can use the <type=circle>, <type=disk>, or <type=square> tags, as shown in the following code (note that the disk and circle shape look identical):

```
<UL>
<LI type=circle>Circle-shaped Bullet
<LI type=square>Square-shaped Bullet
<LI type=disk>Disc-shaped Bullet
```

This code results in the list shown in figure 12.7.

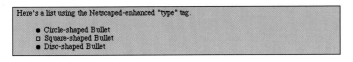

Figure 12.7

This list uses Netscape-enhanced <type> tags.

Netscape also allows you to set up organized lists using alphabetical and roman numeric criteria by adding the variations shown in the following table:

Tag	List Type	Example
<type=1>	Numbers	1, 2, 3
<type=A>	Uppercase letters	A, B, C
<type=a>	Lowercase letters	a, b, c
<type=I>	Uppercase Roman numerals	I, II, III
<type=i>	Lowercase Roman numerals	i, ii, iii

N O T E

As with bulleted lists, ordered lists and definition lists can be nested or serve as links. See the section "Creating HTML Bulleted Lists" earlier in this chapter for information on creating nested lists and links within lists.

The following code shows variations of the <type> tag, which produces the results shown in figure 12.8.

```
<OL>
<LI type=1> Thingy One
<LI type=1> Thingy Two
<LI type=1> Thingy Three
<p>
<LI type=A> Thingy One
<LI type=A> Thingy Two
<LI type=A> Thingy Three
<p>
<LI type=a> Thingy One
<LI type=a> Thingy Two
<LI type=a> Thingy Three
<p>
<LI type=I> Thingy One
<LI type=I> Thingy Two
<LI type=I> Thingy Three
<p>
<LI type=i> Thingy One
<LI type=i> Thingy Two
<LI type=i> Thingy Three
```

Figure 12.8

Varying the <type> tag can produce lists with numbers, letters, or Roman numerals.

Creating Custom-Made Bullets

If you want to use bullets that show more creativity than the basic square or circle, or if you need added linking functionality, you can create your own custom-made bullets.

Custom-made bullets can be ornamental, where their sole purpose is to decorate the beginning of a list item. Or, they can be functional, where they serve as icons that link you to another page or site.

If you plan to make your own artwork or use clip art for buttons, you'll need to use different HTML tags to make the art behave as you want. For visual enhancement only, use the <img src> tag to include image-based bullets at the front of a list, as shown in the following code example. You won't use the <OL> or the <UL> tags, because the image itself is what is creating both the bullet and the indent. Note that you do have to put a <br> tag at the end of each list item, to tell the browser to jump to a new line for the next entry in the list. This wasn't necessary when working with the HTML tags, as it's a built-in part of the list functionality. I've also used an alignment tag (see Chapter 10) to flow the type properly next to the artwork. The following code produces the list shown in figure 12.9.

```
<img src="garrow.gif" align=
middle> Important Item One<br>
<img src="garrow.gif" align=
middle> Important Item Two<br>
<img src="garrow.gif" align=
middle> Important Item Three<br>
<img src="garrow.gif"align=
middle> Important Item Four<br>
```

If you want to use the bullets as icons, to link to another site or page, you'd use the <a href></a> tag, as shown in the following code example. Because linked images typically have a blue border around them, you'll want to use the border=0 tag inside the <img src> tag. (Read more about this in Chapter 13, "Hot Spots.") Note the hand-shaped cursor on the snake in figure 12.10. Your viewer's cursor will change like this when gliding over a linked image to let the viewer know the image is a link.

```
<p>
<a href><img src="lynda.gif"
   align=middle border=0></a>
   Lynda<br>
<a href><img src="jamie.gif"
   align=middle border=0></a>
   Jamie<br>
<a href><img src="stinky.gif"
   align=middle
   border=0></a>Stinky<br>
<a href><img src="elmers.gif"
   align=middle
   border=0></a> Elmers<br>
<a href><img src="jasonjr.gif"
   align=middle border=0></a>
   Jason Jr.<br>
<a href><img src="climber.gif"
   align=middle
   border=0></a>Climber<br>
<a href><img src="sam.gif"
   align=middle
   border=0></a>Sam (whose tail
   is growing back)<br>
```

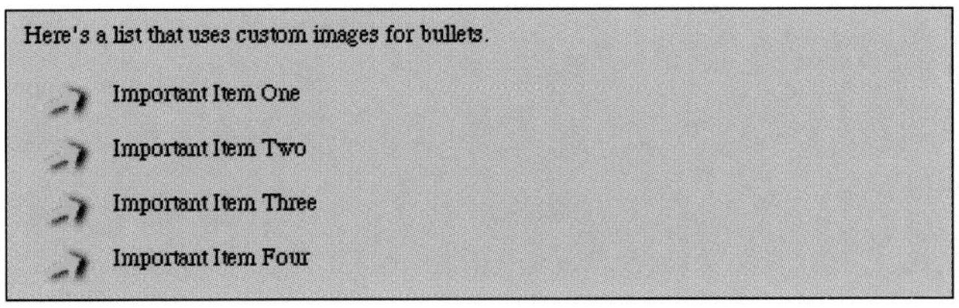

Creating Custom Bullet Art

Any paint program provides a good experimentation ground for making custom bullet artwork. There are no specific guidelines except to keep in mind the scale of the type the bullets will preceed. It's very difficult to design anything with much detail that is small enough to match the scale of 12 point type, such as those typically generated by HTML. If you want to make larger icons for custom bullets, be sure to enlarge the type in the list as well. More info on controlling type size is availaible in

Figure 12.9

Custom-made bullets can be attention-getting additions to lists.

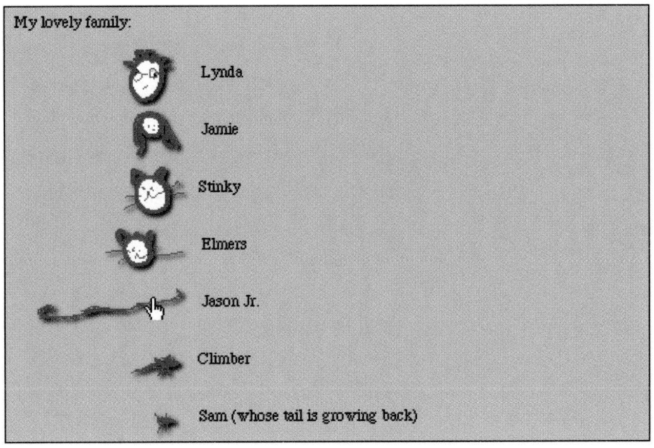

Figure 12.10

Lists can include ornamental bullets that also serve as links.

Chapter 9, "Typography for the Web-Impaired."

Here are some tips I can share from my bullet-making explorations, but please don't let them limit your imagination.

Using Kai's Power Tools

KPT filters, which are available for Mac and PC versions of Photoshop, have a nifty plug-in called KPT Glass Lens. If you are looking to make a shiny, 3D bubble button, this simple filter does it automatically for you. Just perform the following steps:

1. Open a new Photoshop file and fill the background with whatever color your background is going to be.

2. Use the circular marquee tool to select a small circle. (You can choose to anti-alias, depending on whether you'll use transparency or not. See Chapter 8.)

3. Fill the shape with your background color, or whatever color you'd like your button to be.

4. Go to the Filters menu, and choose Distort, KPT Lens Glass Bright. A dimensional bubble button will magically appear.

5. Use the rectangular marquee when finished, and make a tight selection around the bounding shape of the bubble. Choose Crop, located under the Edit menu. This makes the file the appropriate size and it's ready to save. If you want to create an indent in front of or after the custom art, make the shape of the selection account for it *before* you crop (see fig. 12.11).

6. Follow the rules of Chapters 6 and 7 for saving the artwork; for example, depending on whether it is meant to have a transparent background, goes over a pattern background, or incorporates the solid background color dictates whether to save in Gif87a, Gif89a, or JPEG file formats.

Figures 12.12 and 12.13 show the custom bullet in context. Figure 12.13 shows the bullet with color against a colored background.

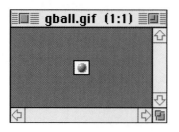

Important Item One
Important Item Two
Important Item Three
Important Item Four

Figure 12.12

Custom bullet examples in context, generated from using KPT filter Glass Lens and HTML.

Figure 12.11

Cropping the individual button down to size.

Important Item One
Important Item Two
Important Item Three
Important Item Four

Figure 12.13

Variation of the same example, in using a background color and colored Glass Lens generated ball art.

Using Typefaces for Custom Bullets

Because bullets have to be small to match scale to small type, looking to typefaces themselves can provide a great starting point for custom icon art. I've chosen the font Zapf Dingbats in figures 12.14 and 12.15. Many typefaces have neat dingbats like this that are perfect for bullets.

Faking Interactive Buttons

What is an interactive button, you might ask. An *interactive button* is one that changes to let the viewer know it's in use. These types of buttons are commonly found on interactive CD-ROMs, such as those that change color when clicked, trigger a sound effect, or change form. True button interactivity on the Web doesn't exist yet, but you can simulate the effect. The drawback to simulating interactive buttons online is the speed limitation, because it involves setting up two pages and waiting for the link to load. An interactive button on a CD-ROM is much more responsive and believable, because it changes the moment you click it. But let's not let that stop us from doing the closest imitation we can muster on the Web.

One type of interactive button is to get an arrow to twirl down when clicked, similar to those you see in Macintosh directory folders. The process requires that you make two pieces of art: one arrow pointing to the right, and another pointing down.

Figure 12.14

Using the typeface Zapf Dingbats, and typing against a transparent layer in Photoshop.

Figure 12.15

By using Preserve Transparency and filling with colors, you create a simple example of transforming type into custom bullet art.

Following is the HTML for an example of how you could make this button appear to twirl down and reveal a list, as shown in figures 12.16 and 12.17. For this example, I've added tags to make the background black and the text green. Using two pieces of simple green triangle art, I saved them as GIFs. Notice that I aligned the text to the top of the graphics as well, using the align=top HTML tag.

The first page:

```
<html>
<head><title>right arrow</title></head>
<body bgcolor="000000" text="66ff33" link="66ff33"vlink="66ff33">
<img src="rarrow.gif" align=top> <a href="darrow.html"> Expand List</a>
</body>
</html>
```

The second page:

```
<html>
<head><title>right arrow</title></head>
<body bgcolor="000000" text="66ff33" link="66ff33"vlink="66ff33">
<img src="darrow.gif" align=top> <a href="rarrow.html"> Collapse
List</a><p>
<UL>
<LI> Important Item One
<LI> Important Item Two
<LI> Important Item Three
<LI> Important Item Four
</body>
</html>
```

Figure 12.16
The interactive button before twirling down.

Figure 12.17
Clicking on the interactive button twirls the button and displays the bulleted list.

Button Clip Art

You'll find clip art for buttons all over the World Wide Web. There are bookmarks on the CD-ROM in the bookmarks folder, plus all of my examples and some other clip-art libraries we've gotten permission to distribute. Clip art buttons follow the same rules for custom bullet art; use the <img src> tag if you want the button for decoration only, and the <a href="" border=0></a> tag if you want them to link. Clip art typically already exists in Web file formats GIF or JPEG, and if not, use Photoshop to convert them.

Bullets can be abstract, such as dots and cubes, or an icon that actually means something. Michael Herrick, of www.matterform.com, has invented something called QBullets, after "cue-bullet" or bullets that cue you to their hint or function. These buttons are part of a proposed interface standard that his site discusses in detail.

Basically, the idea is that QBullets let your audience know what the subject is of your list by using visual metaphors. The e-mail button is a miniature envelope, the download button looks like a floppy disk, a new item has the word "new item," and so on. Herrick's opinion is that bullets should inform your reader about what is at the other end of the link—large download, outside Web site, ftp, telnet, form, and so on. Figure 12.18 shows the Legend page from his site. Qbullets can be used free of charge in exchange for a credit and a link to his page (http://www.matterform.com).

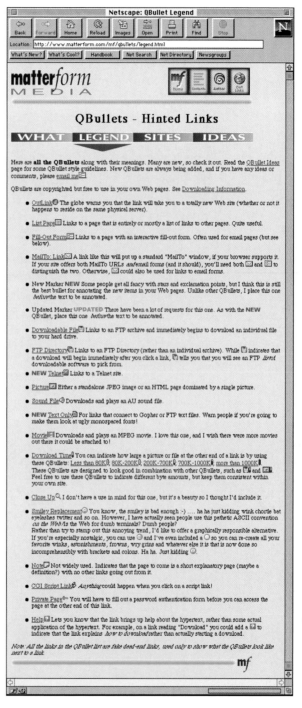

Figure 12.18

The Legend page from Michael Herrick's QBullets site. QBullets are used as visual metaphors that inform readers as to what is at the other end of a link.

Summary

There is little doubt that bullets are a required fact of Web design life. They are used on sites the world over, and are a useful tool for presenting information in lists. You are the judge of when HTML bullets are more appropriate than custom made artwork-based icons. This chapter has covered how to do HTML and custom-artwork-based bullets in detail. Here's a summarization of important tips:

- Bulleted lists can be automatically generated using standard HTML tags, or by using Netscape Extension tags that let you create different shapes.

- You can make any artwork of your choosing into a custom bullet, by using the <img src> tag and inserting custom-made bullet artwork inside. The amount of space surrounding the custom bullet automatically creates alignment and indentations.

- You can fake interactivity, an example being an arrow on the first page, and a twirled down arrow in the same position on the page it links you to, by making two sets of art and two sets of linked pages.

CHAPTER 13 Hot Spots

The meaning of hot for the Web is no longer restricted to what is new or popular. Nowadays we speak of images as being hot. When an image is hot, it means it will send the viewer somewhere else after it's clicked. A hot button can link a viewer to another image, page, site, or external file, depending on how the link is programmed.

A single image can be programmed to be hot if it has been placed on the page using HTML tags that instruct it to link to an outside URL. There are two types of hot images: those single images that are linked to one outside URL, and single images that have been divided into regions using image maps to direct viewers to multiple URLs.

Figure 13.1

Hot images can be identified by an enclosing border.

Figure 13.2

Example of an image without obvious linking properties. Without a blue border, many viewers would not think to click on a graphic that looks like this.

Figure 13.3

By adding a bevelled edge or drop shadow, the graphic looks like something should happen if you click it.

If an image is static (has no linking HTML tags), it's called an *inline graphic*. *Inline* means it's embedded as part of your page, and has no other purpose except to be visible. When a graphic is hot it is sometimes referred to as a map, link, hyperlink, or interactive button. All these words describe the same thing—that clicking on such an image will transport you elsewhere.

This chapter reviews the two types of hot images: linked graphics and image mapped graphics. You'll learn how to do both, and when to use one type of hot graphic over another.

Identifying Hot Images

Images that are hot have certain visual markings that are different from inline graphics. Typically, a border appears around an image that links you somewhere else (see fig. 13.1), and this border defaults to a blue color in most browsers. If your audience has had any experience on the Web, they will be trained that any time they encounter a border around an image it means it can be clicked on as an active link.

There are some instances where a hot image will not have a telltale border around it. If you'd prefer that your hot graphic be without one, this chapter will describe how to program the border to be "invisible." The only way a viewer will know to click on these types of borderless hot images is if your graphic invites them to bring their cursor closer (see figs. 13.2 and 13.3, for further discussion of this). In most browsers, once the viewer's cursor passes over a hot spot it changes from a pointer to the hand cursor shown in figure 13.1. This indicates, just like the border symbol, that an image is a clickable button, instead of a static inline graphic.

Creating Hot Images

The easiest way to create a link that connects one graphic to another Web source is to use the <a href></a> tag with an <img src> tag nested inside. This combination of tags automatically defaults to putting a border around the graphic. Here's an example of this standard HTML code:

```
<html>
<a href="http://www.earthlink.net/
~lyndaw><img src="mylogo.gif"></a>
</html>
```

This code results in the page shown in figure 13.4.

Figure 13.4
The HTML above produces a blue border around this graphic.

Playing with Image Borders, the Netscape-HTML Extensions Way

Netscape offers HTML extensions that let you control the appearance of hot images and their borders. Remember, not all browsers support these features. Refer back to our browser comparison section in Chapter 1 if you want to check which browsers offer support, and which don't.

Sometimes that pesky blue border around an image is totally wrong for the page it was designed for. If you've gone to a great deal of trouble to make an irregular shaped image float freely on a background, using techniques described in Chapters 7 and 8, you aren't going to want to ruin the illusion you worked so hard to achieve by having a glaring rectangular shape around your graphic.

Good news. If you want the border to go away, you can program it to. The following Netscape-specific code eliminates the border shown in figure 13.4 (see fig. 13.5).

```
<html>
<a href="http://www.earthlink.net/
~lyndaw><img src="mylogo.gif" border=0></a>
</html>
```

Figure 13.5
You can program an image so that its border will disappear.

Just as you can make the border disappear, you can also make it appear stronger. The following Netscape-specific code gives a thicker border to the image shown in figure 13.5 (see fig. 13.6).

```
<html>
<a href="http://www.earthlink.net/
~lyndaw><img src="mylogo.gif" border=5></a>
</html>
```

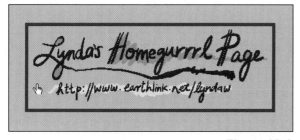

Figure 13.6

A graphic with a thick rectangle signifying the link.

Sometimes your page has a specific color theme and the standard blue rectangle doesn't fit in. You can also change the color of your borders, if you program the links on your page to include hexadecimal values inside the <body link> tag (see Chapter 5). These code lines change the border color of the current image (see fig. 13.7).

```
<html>
<body link="ff00ff">
<a href="http://www.earthlink.net/
~lyndaw><img src="mylogo.gif" border=5 >
word</a>
</body>
</html>
```

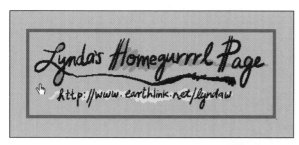

Figure 13.7

A graphic with a colored rectangle signifying the link.

Working with Image Maps

At many Web sites you will see a list of underlined text links on a page (often referred to as a *hotlist*). This is simply a list of multiple URLs, assigned to multiple text objects. Instead of using multiple text links, however, the list of URLs could be attached to a single image object. Such an object is called an *image map,* which is a fancy way of presenting a list of links. This takes a little longer to download than a hotlist, because of the added time required by the graphic to load. Image maps are certainly a convenient, visual way to present multiple choices to your audience.

Image maps are more complicated to code than creating single linked images using the <a href><img src></a> tag. They are complicated on a number of fronts. Each hot region's dimension in pixels has to be determined and documented in an image map definition file. Once that's done, these definition files have to be composed slightly differently depending on which kind of server your Web site uses.

The server is where your artwork and HTML gets stored. There are two types of servers, NCSA and CERN, and each requires the image map instruction code to be slightly different. This means that you have to ensure that the way you've coded the image map is compatible with the type of server your site is stored on. The first step to deciding how to build your image map is to call your online service provider, with whom you have your Internet account and Web site, to find out what kind of server they use.

Image maps can be behave unpredictably on a server. Our Art Center site (where I teach full-time, check it out: http//www.artcenter.com) has crashed a number of times because of image map overload. What happens is, when multiple users from the outside hit your site at the same time, the image map needs to send each of them to multiple locations at the same time. This multiple routing sometimes causes a bottleneck by processing so many requests at once. So, the rule of thumb is to use image maps sparingly. They are harder to program and harder for your server to process than standard, single image links.

Carefully analyze whether you really need an image map, or if there's some other way to accomplish the same goal. For example, if your image is composed of rectangles, or can be seamed together using rectangular shapes (or transparent irregular shapes, see Chapter 8), it's easier to load multiple single graphics with independent links than one graphic with multiple links. In my opinion, the only time image maps should be used is when the hot spot regions of your graphic are irregularly shaped, and demand it. A simple example would be the case of a map of the USA, where you wanted to click on each state to send the viewer to their geographical destination.

You will see examples of image maps used on opening menu screens all over the Web. Sometimes an image map is used, even when the menu bar is composed of rectangular shapes. Some sites do this because the one image will load faster than multiple images. This is a valid reason to use an image map, but even so, the difficulty of creating and maintaining one might outweigh the performance increase. Other sites do it just because they can. Perhaps it's trendy and shows off a certain amount of Web-design machismo? I don't know, but it's another decision you get to make when building your site. I, being the lazy sort, would probably opt for avoiding the image mapmaking task whenever possible.

The Four Stages of an Image Map

Let's walk through the imagemap-making process quickly, then break out with more detail. The first step to making an image map is to create or choose a graphic as the source for the map. It's easiest to define regions if your graphic has obvious areas, such as a map or illustration, but you can use anything, including photographs and typography.

Once you've chosen an image, you will need to create a *map definition file*: a text file you create that contains information about where the hotspots are located on your image. You can define the regions using polygons or circles with the location of each region defined by pixels. This information is then composed as a text file specifically prepared for either a CERN or NCSA server.

Next, a map-processing CGI script is required to instruct the server to recognize the map definition file. Different scripts work for different platforms and servers, and it's best to contact your provider to ask what type of CGI works with their server. Chances are they already use a CGI script that they'll let you have access to and can instruct you on how to use it properly.

The last step is to set up the HTML tags to support the image map using the ISMAP tag. Now, let's break this down to find out just how to create image maps.

Creating an Image Map

This section walks you through the process of creating an image map. For this example we'll be using the file map.gif located in the Image map folder on the CD-ROM.

Starting with the Graphic

First, make sure your source graphic is saved as a GIF (standard, transparent, or interlaced will all work) or a JPEG. In the file name, don't forget to use the proper extensions, .gif and .jpg in lowercase, with no spaces in the name; for example: map.gif.

Defining the Regions of an Image Map

Defining the coordinates of an image map used to be a hellacious chore. You'd need to plot each point and arrive at the x and y coordinates of each region. Once you collected all the data, you'd need to write a text file for the server (slightly different ones for NCSA and CERN servers). This type of grunt work would have been best handled by a "helper app," and we're lucky that several have cropped up that do the repetitive chore well. We'll work with two helper apps: MacWeb for Mac image map authoring, and MapEdit for PC image map authoring. Both of these helper apps are available on our CD-ROM.

Using WebMap

MacWeb is shareware image map software written by Rowland Smith. The evaluation version of WebMap is available at the following URL: http://www.city.net/cnx/software/webmap.html.

Launch WebMap. Open your file (or the map.gif file supplied on the CD-ROM) and the graphic will appear in a window (see fig. 13.8).

Use the tool bar containing the circle, rectangle, and free polygon to draw the shape of each state (see fig. 13.8). Once you've defined the area, click on the region and double click on the [Undefined] list to the right. Enter the URL you wish to link to with an absolute path name (must include http://www.), as shown in figure 13.9.

When you're finished making and naming the regions, define a default URL by going to the Edit menu and selecting Default URL. This should be the name of the URL that the image map resides on. If your shape is irregular, like this map example, the default URL is where the file leads the viewer if they accidentally click off one of your defined regions.

Once you've done these things, go to the File menu and select Export as Text, choosing if you want an NCSA or a CERN script. The image map definition file must end with a .map extension. I've named mine "map.gif.map". It's a good idea to include the name of the graphic "map.gif" with the .map extension at the end for keeping track of all your files. Typically, your map definition file and map graphic reside in the same folder on your server. Be sure to check this out with your Web administrator.

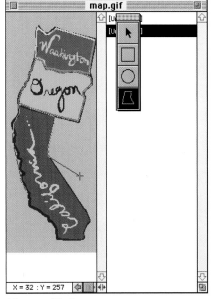

Figure 13.8
The map.gif graphic opened in MacWeb. Use the drawing tools to define each state's area.

Using MapEdit

MapEdit is shareware image map software written by Thomas Boutell. You might recognize his name as the author of the PNG file format (see Chapter 3). It resides on our CD-ROM in the Software/PC folder, or can be downloaded from: http://www.boutell.com/mapedit/.

Begin MapEdit by pulling the menu bar down to File, Open/Create to open your file in MapEdit. You'll be asked to locate the map file (map definition file) in advance, and to load the graphic that you want to plot at the same time (see fig. 13.10). If you haven't already started a map file, you can name it here now. I chose to give it the name of the Gif, with the extra map extension afterwards: map.gif.map (see fig. 13.11). You also decide at this point whether you want to write a NCSA script or a CERN script by checking the appropriate Create Type/NCSA/CERN radio button.

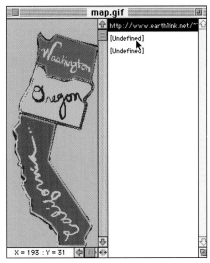

Figure 13.9
Linking an URL to the selected region.

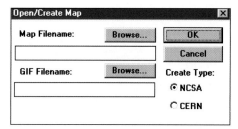

Figure 13.10

The Open/Create Map dialog box prompts you to locate or name the map file, and to specify the name of the graphic to load and the script type.

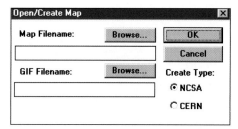

Figure 13.11

The Open/Create Map dialog box showing the new map name and the location of the graphic.

After you have specified the map file name, the Gif file name, and the script type, choose OK to display the image in MapEdit. Choose Tools, Polygon (see fig. 13.12) and drag around the shape of each state (see fig. 13.13).

When you want to close a polygon path, click the right mouse button. This displays the Object URL dialog box, shown in figure 13.14, in which you must identify which URL the area you've just defined is linked to. Be sure to use an absolute path name (http://www...) as opposed to a relative path name (/myfolder/myWebsite).

When you're finished, you can set the default URL by going to Edit, Default URL. Enter the absolute URL of the site your map is sitting on. This sets the default address, to keep your viewers on this page in case they click off a defined region of your image map. When you're finished, choose File, Save As to display the Save As dialog box and the name of your map definition file is automatically inserted.

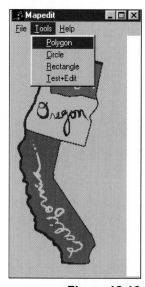

Figure 13.12

Select the polygon style, under Tool.

Figure 13.13

Use the polygon tool to define the state's shape.

In this case, that name is map.gif.map, as shown in figure 13.15.

As before, the finished files all need to be stored in the same folder on your server. Check with your Web systems administrator for exact instructions.

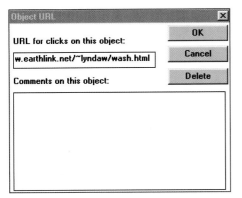

Figure 13.14
Identify the URL to which the area you have defined is linked.

Figure 13.15
The Save As dialog from MapEdit.

Writing the HTML to Support Image Maps

The HTML required for image maps has a few added components besides the example supplied earlier for single linked images. Your HTML code has to tell the server the following two things:

1. What name was used for the image map definition file, and what CGI script you're using to process it.

2. That the <img src> file is an image map, using the ISMAP command.

Here's the HTML code that I wrote for the NCSA server at Earthlink, where my personal Web site resides:

```
<html>
<center>
<a href="http://www.earthlink.net/
cgi-bin/image map/~lyndaw/map.gif.map">
<img src="map.gif" border=0 ISMAP></a>
</center>
</html>
```

By using the <a href></a> tag, I've instructed the server to locate the CGI script that Earthlink supplies to all its subscribers who want to use image maps. Unless you're an Earthlink subscriber like me, your online provider will require that you use a different CGI script that is compatible with its server. The image map CGI script is something you'll have to scout out on your own. There's a good chance your online service provider has one they use for all its subscribers, or can suggest one that will work with its server. The HTML code I wrote also tells my server to use the map definition file I created, called map.gif.map.

By using the <img src> tag, I've instructed the Web page to use the map.gif artwork for the map, to have no border around the graphic, and that the graphic is an image map because I included the ISMAP tag.

I named this HTML document map.html and loaded it to the server, with my artwork map.gif and the image map definition file map.gif.map. Unlike most HTML, there is no way an image map can be tested from your local hard drive. You must upload the proper files to the server or the image map will not work.

Troubleshooting

If your image map does not work the first time, check the following things:

- Did you load all the necessary files to the server—the map graphic, the map definition file, and the HTML file that supports it?

- Is the HTML requesting the CGI script properly?

- Did you use the ISMAP tag in your <img src> tag?

- Is the URL name an absolute path (the entire address—http://www.etc)?

If you still have problems, your online service provider might be willing to offer tech support for you, but always check the previous on your own first.

Summary

As a Web designer, making hot graphics look good and work smoothly is something you'll want to know how to do. It's much easier to make individual graphics link to outside sources than it is to use an image map. Still, if an image map is what's required, there's great support software to ease the hassle of tedious prep work. Here are some helpful tips:

- Single images with single links are programmed by using the <a href><img src><a/> command.

- Single image links and image maps will default to using a border around them unless you use Netscape-extension border tags in your HTML code.

- It's easier to put multiple single image links next to each other than to create an image map, where one graphic supports multiple links.

- Image maps require a graphic, a map definition file, a CGI script, the ISMAP tag, and absolute path names to work.

CHAPTER 14 Table Manners

Some tables are meant to eat supper on and keep your elbows off of, but the Web has another definition in mind. We're talking information tables here, folks—the kind that have columns of text or numbers in individual cells, much like a spreadsheet or chart.

Tables were invented to support text and numbers, but you can put graphics inside table cells, too. All the graphic tags we've described so far work within the table tags. Because of this, I've made a distinction between data tables and graphic tables. You'll see a lot of attention in other books and online sources paid to data tables. The same tags that support data can also support graphics, and herein lies a great power waiting to be unleashed. The graphic designer who knows how to use tables for page layout control will be a much happier camper than the one who doesn't. Learning to program tables will offer lots of formatting options that HTML hasn't been able to support so far.

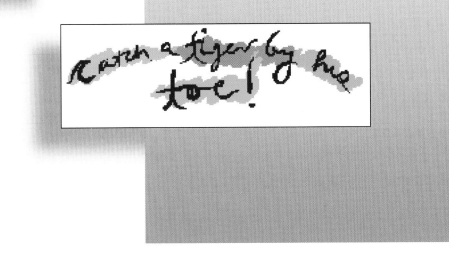

NOTE

At the time this book was written, Netscape and Microsoft's Internet Explorer 2.0 were the only browsers that supported HTML tables. There are plans for tables to be part of HTML 3.0 sanctioned code, but early browser adopters are few and far between. (Look at the browser comparison chart in Chapter 1.) So here's a big warning, right off the top: Tables will look wonderful in Netscape and look like an unforgivable mistake everywhere else.

Hopefully, by the time this book is on shelves near you more browsers will support tables. Until you've checked this out, proceed with caution. I'm here to show you how HTML tables work regardless. Even though I think they are way cool, you should think about offering substitute screens to your general audience if you plan to implement them. I'll address some alternative options for tables later in this chapter.

eenie	meenie	mynee	mo
catch	a tiger	by his	toe

Figure 14.1

Data tables on the Web use embossed lines to divide the cells and sections.

eenie	meenie	mynee	mo
catch	a tiger	by his	toe

Figure 14.2

Using a pattern background or solid color background allows the embossed lines of tables to show through, creating an interesting lighting effect.

There's great online support for learning to program tables. I've only seen online support for data tables, not graphic tables. Still, data table principles are crucial to understand if you're going to use graphic tables. Some of my favorite online sources for table instruction follow. We have bookmarks to these sites (and more) on the CD-ROM.

- **http://ncdesign.kyushuid.ac.jp/howto/text/Normal/table.html:** This is a site to watch for all kinds of great online tutorials. The authors are Japanese, so the English is a little stilted, but the instruction on Tables and many other HTML tags is indispensible.

- **http://home.mcom.com/assist/net_sites/tables.html:** Table instruction from the Netscape site itself.

You will learn about how to program graphics tables later in this chapter, but first you should understand the basic kind of Web tables: data-based tables.

Data Tables

Data-based tables are probably what HTML programmers had in mind when they invented the code. These are the typical kind that you'll see on most sites. They contain text and numbers, links and occasional graphics. They have tell-tale borders around the cells, which look slightly dimensional, by employing embossed lines of varying width to divide individual chart sections (see fig. 14.1). One neat thing about tables is if you use a pattern background or solid color background, the embossing shows through and looks as if it's a lighting effect (see fig. 14.2).

Table borders are kind of like horizontal rules on steroids—the HTML code magically manufactures vertical and horizontal lines of different widths and thicknesses with a few choice strokes of code and tags. They seem complicated by appearance, but I was surprised at how easy they really were to create and use. If only they were more widely supported! Looking at preliminary HTML 3.0 specs, it only seems a matter of time before they are. Nonetheless, let's jump in and begin creating data-based tables.

Working with Table Tags

When creating data or graphics tables for the Web, you work with HTML tags. The table tags allow you to put information inside individual cells. Understanding the tag structure for data tables enables you to work with graphic tables later in this chapter.

You always begin a table with <table> and end it with the </table> tag. The <tr> </tr> tag stands for starting and ending a new row. The <th></th> tag delineates the header, and makes the text in that row bold. The <td></td> tag stands for the content of each data cell. Here's an example of such code, with the results shown in figure 14.3:

```
<table>
<tr> <th>eenie
     </th><th>meenie</th><th>mynee
     </th><th>mo</th></tr>
<tr><td>catch</td><td>a tiger</td><td>by
     his</td><td>toe</td></tr></table>
```

The <table border> tag gives the table that embossed look and feel, as shown in figure 14.4:

```
<table border>
<tr> <th>eenie
     </th><th>meenie</th><th>mynee</th>
     <th>mo</th></tr>
<tr><td>catch</td><td>a tiger</td><td>by
     his</td><td>toe</td></tr></table>
```

The <colspan> tag allows one row to fill more than one column, as shown in figure 14.5:

```
<table border>
<tr><th colspan=4> A poem, by someone</th>
<tr> <th>eenie
     </th><th>meenie</th><th>mynee</th>
     <th>mo</th></tr>
<tr><td>catch</td><td>a tiger</td><td>by
     his</td><td>toe</td></tr></table>
```

The <rowspan> tag (as shown in fig. 14.6) takes up columns and rows. It is not any specified size or shape; the dimensions are dictated by the content you insert.

```
<table border>
<tr><th rowspan=4> A poem, by someone</th>
<tr><th>eenie
</th><th>meenie</th><th>mynee</th>
  <th>mo</th></tr>
<tr><td>catch</td><td>a tiger</td><td>by
     his</td><td>toe</td></tr></table>
```

The <table width=# of pixels> and <table height=# of pixels> tags let you dictate the shape of the table by pixels (see fig. 14.7):

```
<table border width=300 height=100>
<tr> <th>eenie
     </th><th>meenie</th><th>mynee</th>
     <th>mo</th></tr>
<tr><td>catch</td><td>a tiger</td><td>by
     his</td><td>toe</td></tr></table>
```

eenie	meenie	mynee	mo
catch	a tiger	by his	toe

Figure 14.3

The beginning of a data table, with rows, a header, and cell contents.

eenie	meenie	mynee	mo
catch	a tiger	by his	toe

Figure 14.4

Using the <table border> tag adds the borders that give the table its embossed look.

A poem, by someone			
eenie	meenie	mynee	mo
catch	a tiger	by his	toe

Figure 14.5

Using the <colspan> tag enables a row to fill more than one column, as shown in the top row here.

A poem, by someone	eenie	meenie	mynee	mo
	catch	a tiger	by his	toe

Figure 14.6

Use the <rowspan> to have some information take up more than one row across.

eenie	meenie	mynee	mo
catch	a tiger	by his	toe

Figure 14.7

A 300x100 pixel table, formatted with the <table width> and <table height> tags.

The tag <table cellspacing=# of pixels> puts a thicker line weight around the cells, as shown in figure 14.8:

```
<table border cellspacing=10>
<tr> <th>eenie
    </th><th>meenie</th><th>mynee</th>
    <th>mo</th></tr>
<tr><td>catch</td><td>a tiger</td><td>by
    his</td><td>toe</td></tr></table>
```

Figure 14.8

Use the <table cellspacing=# of pixels> tag for a thicker border around the cells.

The <table cellpadding=# of pixels> tag puts a uniform space inside the cells, governed by the number of pixels entered after the = (equal) sign, as shown in figure 14.9:

```
<table border cellpadding=10>
<tr> <th>eenie
    </th><th>meenie</th><th>mynee</th>
    <th>mo</th></tr>
<tr><td>catch</td><td>a tiger</td><td>by
    his</td><td>toe</td></tr></table>
```

Figure 14.9

By inserting a border height of 100, extra breathing room has been introduced in the table cells.

You can adjust the alignment of data inside cells by using the <valign> tag, which allows you to specify top, middle, bottom, and baseline alignments. Here's how it might work. Figure 14.10 shows an example using my eenie, meenie, mynee, mo chart and all four alignment positions. The code follows:

```
<table border height=100>
<tr> <th>eenie
    </th><th>meenie</th><th>mynee</th>
    <th>mo</th></tr>
<tr><td valign=top>catch</td><td
valign=middle>a tiger</td><td valign=bot-
    tom>by his</td><td
    valign=baseline>toe</td></tr></table>
```

Figure 14.10

Top, middle, bottom, and baseline alignments for cell data can be set with the <valign> tag.

You can also specify, right, left, and middle alignment values within the <tr>, <th>, and <td> tags using the word align. Figure 14.11 shows an example of everything aligned left, and figure 14.12 shows an example of right-alignment. The following code snippets show left-alignment, then right-alignment.

```
<table border width=300>
<tr> <th align left>eenie </th><th align
    left>meenie</th><th align
    left>mynee</th>
    <th align left>mo</th></tr>
<tr><td align=left>catch</td><td
    align=left>a tiger</td><td
    align=left>by his</td><td
    align=left>toe</td></tr></table>
```

```
<table border width=300>
<tr> <th align=right>eenie </th><th align-
    right>meenie</th><th
    align=right>mynee</th> <th
    align=right>mo</th></tr>
<tr><td align=right>catch</td><td
    align=right>a tiger</td><td
    align=right>by his</td><td
    align=right>toe</td></tr></table>
```

Figure 14.11

You can use the align comment within the <tr>, <th>, and <td> tags to specify horizontal alignment of cell data. Here, all the input is left-aligned.

Figure 14.12

The result of using the <tr>, <th>, and <td> tags to specify right-alignment.

You can also put graphics inside tables, by using the <img src="name.gif"> tag, instead of text or values (see fig. 14.13). Here's an example:

```
<table border>
<tr> <td><img
    src="catcha.gif"></td></tr></table>
```

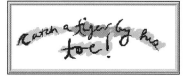

Figure 14.13
Use the <img src="name.gif"> tag to insert graphics inside a table.

Figure 14.14 shows an example of mixing text and graphics inside cells of a table; the code follows:

```
<table border>
<tr> <th>eenie </th><th><img
    src="meenie.gif"></th><th>mynee</th>
    <th>mo</th></tr>
<tr><td>catch</td><td >a tiger</td><td>by
    his</td><td ><img
    src="toe.gif"></td></tr></table>
```

Figure 14.14 shows that you can insert graphics into your tables by using by using the <img src> tag. The following section explains how you can work with graphics more seamlessly, by eliminating the tell-tale border around table cells.

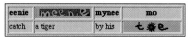

Figure 14.14
You can integrate graphics into a data table by using the <img src="name.gif"> tag.

Graphic Tables for Page Layout Design

This is where Web design finally gets interesting. Table support is the first real hook we've had to being able to control layout of page design. If you use tables to create a design grid, all the things that HTML has kept you from doing are suddenly possible. You want a vertical row of linked type in the middle of your page, or a vertical rule graphic? No problem! You want your graphics aligned left or right to a specific grid defined by pixels? No problem! You want to define the size of your page, and not let the browser do that for you? No problem! Basically, if you're used to working with PageMaker or Quark, you're used to working with design grids. Tables take much more effort, but if you do some pre-planning, you can use them much the same way.

This section serves as a guide to designing a graphics-based table for the Web. It shows a step-by-step example of creating a three column résumé. There is no other way to make vertical columns on the Web, aside from tables. This is just one example, but it demonstrates how the same principles and HTML code that went into the data tables described previously can be applied to a graphical Web page.

Case Study

I hadn't updated my résumé in a long time, so I thought I'd use tables to make a new one for myself. I chose to work with a white background and warm pastel, earthtone colors. I worked with blurring and diffusing my art, to give the résumé artwork a soft focus, intriguing look. I created three images: figures 14.15 through 14.17.

Figure 14.15
My name in blurry Photoshop-treated type.

Figure 14.16

A vertical dotted ruled line with arrows at both ends.

Figure 14.17

A blurry, washed out picture of me.

TIP

Typically, when you use tables for aligning graphics, you don't want to use an embossed border. You're trying to hide the fact that you're using tables at all, with the goal of a seamless page layout that makes your audience none the wiser about how it was accomplished. If you use the <table border=0> tag, it will make all the border rules disappear. Yay!

I chose a blurry type treatment for my name. Because of the continuous tone nature of this graphic, I saved it as a JPEG. It is 4.6 KB.

I made the vertical arrow in Illustrator, using the Dotted Line feature in the Stroke dialog box, and added arrowheads using the Filter, Stylize, Add Arrowheads options. I copied and pasted it into Photoshop, where I colored it from my pastel, earthtone color palette. I saved it as a GIF because it is mostly flat color. It weighs in at 1.3 KB.

I lightened this video scan of myself by using output levels in the Photoshop Levels dialog box. This lightens the image without building contrast. Then I took a feathered lasso and Gaussian-blurred some of the areas, leaving my face and glasses in sharper focus. I colorized it using the Adjust Hue, Saturation, and Brightness commands, clicking the Colorize check box. Then I found a hue and lightness setting that I liked and clicked the OK button. Because this was continuous tone, I chose JPEG again. It is a whopping 8.9 KB!

Total size of this page: under 15 KB!

I started my HTML document by laying out these images first to see how the table was starting to work. The result is shown in figure 14.18; the code follows:

```
<html>
<head><title>resume two</title></head>
<body bgcolor="FFFFFF" text="999966" link="cc9966"
vlink="996600">
<table border=0>
<tr><td valign=top><img src="lyndawein.jpg"><td
valign=top><img src="arrow.gif"></td>
<td valign=top><img src="grey4lynda.jpg"></table>
</html>
```

Once I got the skeleton code in place, I went to work adding my text and links. I like the way <pre> formatted text looks, so I played with that tag and changed font sizes. I set my background color hex to pure white, and picked soft earthtone colors for my links and visited links too. Here's the final code; the final page is shown in figure 14.19.

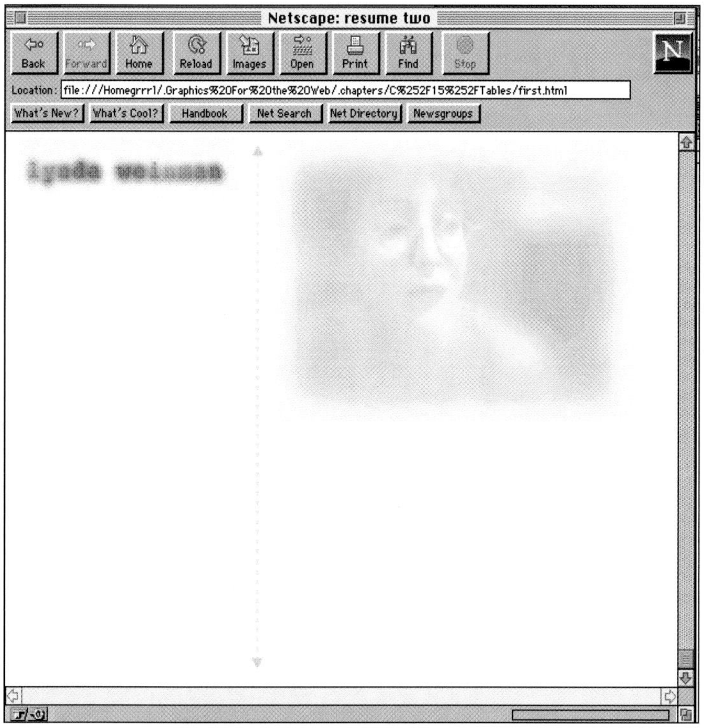

Figure 14.18
The beginning stages of the résumé page table layout.

Figure 14.19
Here's the finished result. Not bad, considering that before tables, this type of alignment was physically impossible on the Web.

```
<html>
<head><title>resume two</title></head>
<body bgcolor="FFFFFF" text="999966" link="cc9966" vlink="996600">
<table border=0>
<p>
<tr><td valign=top><img src="lyndawein.jpg"><pre><font size=2>
<a href="http://www.earthlink.net/lyndaw>www.earthlink.net/~lyndaw"</a> - web address
<a href="mailto:moshun@aol.com"> _____MoShun@aol.com</a> - email address
</font><font size=6>
<strong> <a
href="http://www.earthlink.net/~lyndaw/resume4.html">resum&#233;</a></strong></font>
<pre>
<font size=4>
private
clients:</font>
<font size=3>  cbs
   disney
   apple
   nbc
   adobe
   paramount pictures</font><pre>
<font size=4>
publi-
cations:</font>
<font size=3>  macuser
   macweek
   newmedia
   the net
   digital video
   step-by-step graphics
   animation magazine
   macromedia users journal</font>
<pre><font size=4>
pub-
lisher:</font>
<font size=3>  designing web graphics (1996)
   new riders/macmillan</td></font>
<td valign=top><img src="arrow.gif"></td>
<td valign=top><img src="grey4lynda.jpg"><pre><font size=4>
instructor:</font>
<font size=3><a href="http://www.artcenter.edu">  art center college of design</a><br><a
href="http://www.cel.sfsu.edu/msp/MSP.html">  san francisco state multimedia studies pro-
gram</a> <br>   american film institute</font></pre><pre><font size=4>
courses:</font>
<font size=3><a href="http://www.artcenter.edu/ACCD/departments/computer/courses/C164-
1su95.html">  motion graphics</a><br><a
href="http://www.artcenter.edu/ACCD/departments/computer/courses/C170Psu95.html">  photo
motion graphics</a> <br> <a href="http://www.artcenter.edu/ACCD/departments/computer/cours-
es/C167su95.html">  interactive media design</a>
   web graphics</a></font><pre> <font size=4>
edu-
cation:</font>
<font size=3>  the evergreen state college,
   b.a., 1976<br></font>
</table>
```

We've got images and HTML on the CD-ROM for you to play with, as well as templates (see Chapter 18) that let you work more with graphic tables.

The Bad News—Browsers That Don't Support Tables

I warned you! This page will look horrible with any browser other than Netscape and Internet Explorer. (I hope this has changed by the time you buy this book!) Figure 14.20 shows the output in America Online's Window browser. This browser is a fixed size, so I had to scroll through five screens to see this mess! Figure 14.21 shows the output in MacMosaic 2.0, which supports tables, but not background color.

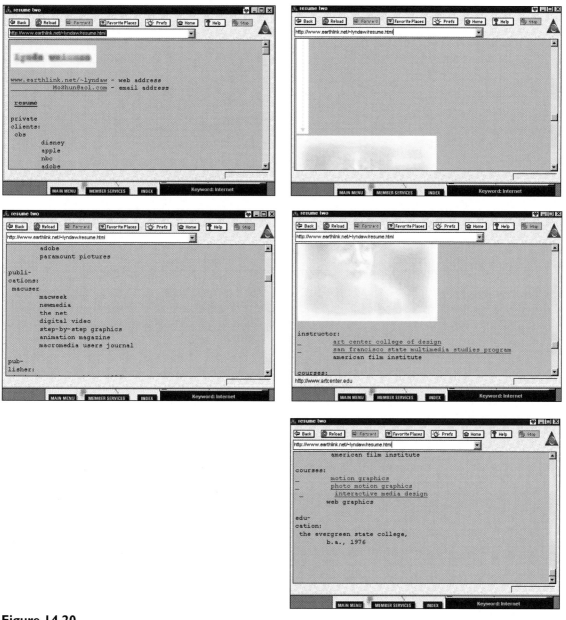

Figure 14.20

The final résumé on America Online's Window browser. Because the browser is a fixed size, what appeared in one screen in Netscape takes five screens in the AOL browser.

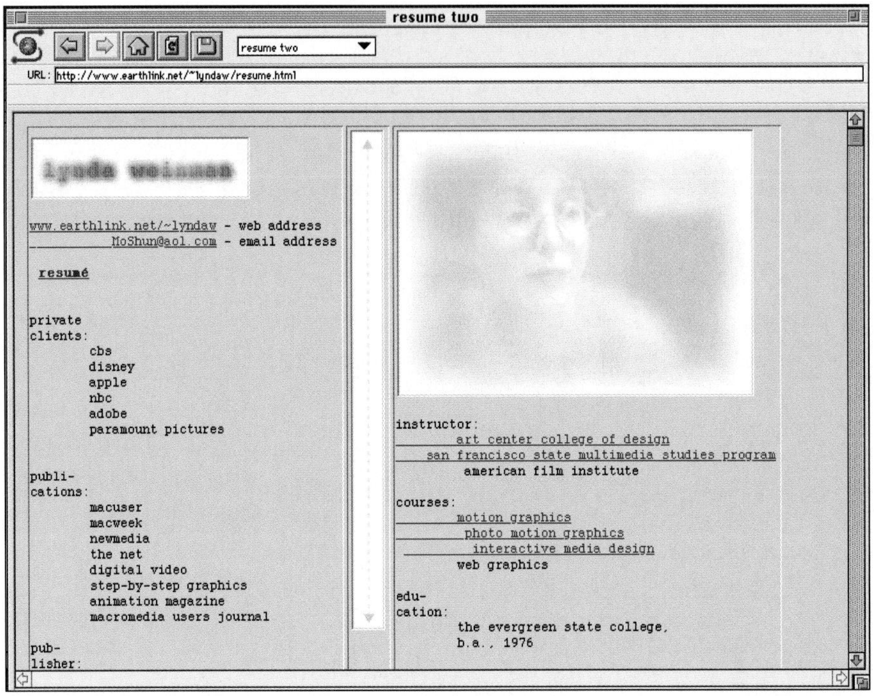

Figure 14.21

My résumé as shown on the MacMosaic 2.0 browser. This browser supports tables, but not background color.

What can you do for browsers that don't support tables? You can make an alternative page, using accepted HTML commands. I chose to use the <pre> tag for my entire résumé. The <pre> tag accepts the alignment of my text exactly as I type it. I was able to do two columns here by using this trick. I wouldn't be able to insert any pictures into this, the way I did using tables. There could be a picture above, below, or inside the <pre> tags, but alignment control is very finicky.

Return to Chapter 1 for suggestions on how to prepare multiple pages for different browsers.

Figure 14.22 shows the result of the following code:

```
<html>
<head><title>text based resume</title></head>
<pre>
Lynda Weinman
email: moshun@aol.com
web address: http://www.earthlink.net/~lyndaw
R E S U M E
private         instructor:
clients          art center
  cbs          san francisco state
  disney          american film institute
  apple
```

```
   abc         courses:
   adobe         motion graphics
   paramount pictures      photo motion graphics
         interactive media design
publi-        web graphics
cations:
   macuser      pub-
   macweek      lisher:
   newmedia       designing web graphics
   the net        new riders/macmillan
   digital video      edu-
   step-by-step graphics   cation:
   animation magazine    the evergreen state
   mm users journal      b.a., 1976
</pre></html>
```

Another method, if you have a small graphic table, is to go ahead and make a bitmap graphic in Photoshop or elsewhere and load it as an <img src> instead of using tables (see fig. 14.23).

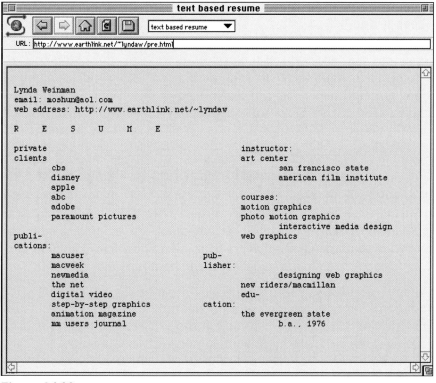

Figure 14.22

The résumé from the earlier example, redone using the <pre> tag.

Figure 14.23

An example of a bitmap graphic of a table as opposed to an HTML-generated table.

Summary

Tables allow you to control alignment of graphics with more precision than any other method available on the Web. Tables are a lot of work; they are tricky to figure out and require practice and pre-planning. The results are worth it; but then once you factor in the fact that many browsers don't support tables you're left wondering again. Browser support is limited for many of the features this book describes, and that's why so many sites put up disclaimers, like Netscape Enhanced.

If you're going to use tables, remembering these few tips will be helpful:

- Tables look great, but are not available to all viewers.

- Make an alternative page for those viewers who can't see tables.

- If you create tables using the <table border=0> tag, the borders will be invisible.

- Tables offer enhanced page layout control that other HTML tags don't offer.

CHAPTER 15 **Dynamic Documents**

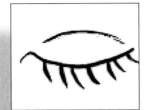

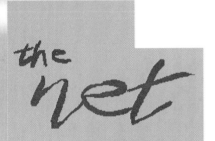

We've already seen that the Web does a pretty poor job of imitating the printed page. Its strengths lie in those things it does that print can't, like offering cross-platform global interaction, hypertext links, and database search capabilities. We're witnessing the emergence of a new communication medium. With maturity, missing ingredients such as sophisticated graphics and text layout tools that print designers have long relied upon are certain to follow.

Adding motion to pages is key to moving Web technology a step further. There is no denying the power of movement on a screen, and here's something a printed page can't do that a computer page can. We're probably not talking about anything as sophisticated as video or film Web delivery for years to come, but the Web has to start somewhere, and that's what this chapter is about.

NOTE

News Flash! At the finish of this book, Microsoft's Internet Explorer 2.0 browser was released. It can be downloaded from: http://www.microsoft.com/ie/msie.htm. It introduced the addition of several new HTML extensions that relate to this chapter. Anyone can author Web pages using the new Internet Explorer tags, but like any proprietary tags, only those with the Internet Explorer browser can view the results.

For information on tags that let you add AVI movies, sounds, and scrolling text marquees, check out: http://www.microsoft.com/windows/ie/ie20html.htm. If you have Microsoft's Internet Explorer browser, this page will show you examples of the new tags in action: http://www.microsoft.com/windows/ie/iedemo.htm.

Once again, Netscape has taken the leadership role in bringing another important feature—adding motion to pages—to the Web. I haven't seen any proposals to incorporate Netscape's set of dynamic tags into official HTML 3.0 specs, so chances are other browsers won't follow with their support. Know that when you add Netscape's fare of Server Push, Client Pull, and animated GIFs that your efforts will only be seen by the Netscape browser crowd. Unlike tables, where outside browsers will view your creations as abysmal failures, the Netscape animation tags will be overlooked and simply not be visible. That's not such a bad trade-off, if you ask me. As long as there's no penalty for using them, why not?

Unfortunately, some of the dynamic Netscape feature offers are not easy to implement. They might require teaming up with a programmer or buying a script from an outside source. This will probably stand in your way far more than whether outside browsers recognize the code or not.

This chapter offers insight into these dynamic Netscape features and instructions to use them. In this chapter, you will learn about the three types of dynamic documents that make your Web pages move in Netscape: animated GIFs, client pull, and server push.

Animated GIFs

With the release of Netscape 2.0, a hidden feature emerged that made it easily possible for anyone to create animated graphics for Web pages. There's already been a lot of discussion about GIFs within this book, but until Netscape 2.0, no Web browser had elected to support part of the GIF89a specs that offered the capability to include multiple images within one single GIF document.

These animated GIFs, which function much like an automated slide show, are formally called multi-block GIFs, and have been part of the GIF89a specs since it was originally written in 1987. The animation feature went unrecognized for all those years because no Web browser or authoring environment honored this aspect of the file format's specs. All has changed for the better with Netscape 2.0's support for these GIFs, and the result is one of the most exciting new features on graphics Web pages in recent memory.

GIF animations hold great promise for many reasons. First of all, the software required for creating this type of animation format is easily obtained via the Web. For Macintosh users, download GIFBuilder at http://iawww.epfl.ch/Staff/Yves.Piguet/clip2gif-home/GifBuilder.html. For Windows users, download GIF Construction Set from http://www.mind workshop.com/alchemy/alchemy.html. Both programs require that you create multiple images first and number them sequentially before importing them. GIFBuilder translates multiple PICTs, GIFs, and Quicktime movies. GIFConstruction Set requires that your multiple source images be saved first as GIFs before importing them. Creating animations that cycle endlessly is supported through simple "loop" instructions found within both GIFBuilder and GIF Construction Set. The programs additionally support transparency, interlacing, and color palette control.

Making animation source files can be done anywhere. If you have Premiere, Macromedia Director, After Effects, 3D Studio, or Infini-D, you can create your motion there and export the files as individual, sequentially numbered PICTs. You might need to convert them to GIF files before using GIFConstruction Set for Windows, but the Mac-based GIFBuilder can even convert Quicktime movies. Don't think you are excluded if you don't already own or work with an animation program—you can create animation anywhere. All it takes is making images that are different from each other and naming them in a sequential, numeric order. Try using a Photoshop filter in various increments over the same still image and name each file in a numeric sequence. There are limitless possiblilities for animation ideas, and sophisticated software is not necessary.

An advantage of using the GIF89a animation file format is how simple it is to insert into an HTML document. Basically, an animated GIF can be embedded into a Web page the same way as a regular GIF image, meaning that

---

With the release of Netscape 2.0 there are various new options for creating dynamic documents using Java (http://java.sun.com/), Shockwave (http://www.macromedia.com/Tools/Shockwave/index.html), and numerous plug-in offerings from other companies. Here are some URLs to watch for more information on these new opportunities:

- Astound Web Player (AWP): http://www.golddisk.com/awp.html. Plays both Astound and Studio M Multimedia files directly from a Web page.

- Sizzler: http://www.totallyhip.com. Allows users to view inline sizzler (Multimedia) files.

- Smartsketch Animator: http://www.futurewave.com/animatorpress.htm. Uses Smartsketch's compact file format for animation of vector-based source art.

- Emblaze: http://Geo.inter.net/Geo/technology/emblaze/downloads.html. Offers real-time, online, full-motion animation with no preloading, buffering, or delay of any kind.

- Plug-in Plaza: http://www.browserwatch.com/plug-in.html. Most up-to-date new plug-in guide found on the Web.

NOTE

We owe it all to Royale Frazier for being the first to discover that Netscape 2.0 supported multi-block GIFs. He was experimenting with GIFConstruction Set's support of this feature, and on a whim decided to try Netscape 2.0 to see if it worked. It did, even though Netscape made no mention of the new feature anywhere within the formal Netscape 2.0 specs! For great information on GIF animations, including the full GIF 87a and 89a specs, tutorials, links to software, list of known bugs, and a gallery of GIF animations (including my site's trademark 50's man, who now waves and bobs his head—http://www.lynda.com/multigif.html) visit Royale Frazier's amazing personal Web site devoted to this subject at http://member.aol.com/royalef/gifanim.htm. Another good source for information on animated GIFs is called the GIFBuilder's FAQ, at http://iawww.epfl.ch/Staff/Yves.Piguet/clip2gif-home/ GifBuilder Doc/GifBuilder-FAQs.html.

it is not necessary to learn any new HTML codes. No additional programming is involved, as in the case of Server Push, or Java. If the Web browser doesn't support the format, the first image is displayed and that's the only penalty.

As Netscape loads the animated GIF, it displays each frame in sequence. There's no waiting for downloading, and once all the images have been displayed, they can replay indefinitely from memory (cache), meaning that the Web server is never taxed by the process. Multiple GIF animations can reside on a single Web page, which was not possible using older Server Push techniques. (See the following section for more information on Server Push.)

There are a few annoying things about GIF animations. If you use one as the source for a link or image map, it will be impossible to read the URL in the bottom bar of Netscape. I've had visitors to my site report that my animated GIF crashed their systems when using earlier versions of Netcape. An animated GIF also increases the file size of a normal GIF, though downloading performance is only affected in browsers other than Netscape. There's speculation that many other browsers will follow Netscape's lead to support animated GIFs. Let's hope so!

Client Pull

Client Pull is a technique that enables pages on your site to change without your audience clicking anywhere to make them come and go. It's called Client Pull, because the HTML code tells the client (your audience) to change pages without them asking. Their browser is recognizing code that's changing their pages like an automatic slideshow.

Client Pull is relatively easy to program as well. The <meta> tag must always be inserted at the beginning of an HTML document, inside the <head></head> tag:

```
<html>
<head>
<Meta HTTP-Equiv="Refresh" CONTENT=1; URL=http://
your URL address here></head>
```

The CONTENT=1 part of the tag tells the screen how long (in seconds) to wait before it goes to the next URL. Be aware that each time a new page is invoked, the new page has to load. This results in a flash of "browser gray" background, and whatever time it takes to load all the images, text, links and tags of the forth-coming page. It's not seamless animation or even a smooth running slide-show, but it can be an interesting device to get your message broadcast.

Creating a Client-Pull Animation

Here's an example of an eye-blink animation I did with two simple sprites (animation fig-ures). I wrote HTML code that made two pages, each with one of these images on it that cycle back and forth indefinitely until the user clicks "Please Stop!" (You can check out the results at http://www.earthlink.net/~lyndaw/open.html.)

My first page looks like figure 15.1; the code for this page follows:

```
<HTML>
<head><Meta HTTP-EQUIV=Refresh Content="5;
URL=http://www.earthlink.net/~lyndaw/closed
.html">
<title> Blink ON></title>
</head>
<P>
<p>
<img src="oeye.gif">
<P>
<p>
<body>
<a href
"http://www.earthlink.net/~lyndaw/index.
html"> Please Stop! </a>
</body>
</html>
```

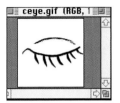

Figure 15.1
The first part of the Client Pull code causes the eye to blink.

My second page looks like figure 15.2. The code for the second page is as follows:

```
<HTML>
<head><Meta HTTP-EQUIV=Refresh Content="5;
URL=http://www.earthlink.net/~lyndaw/open.
html">
<title> Blink OFF></title>
</head>
<center>
<P>
<p>
<img src="ceye.gif">
<p>
<p>
<body>
<a href"http://www.earthlink.net/~lyndaw/
index.html"> Please Stop! </a>
</body>
</html>
```

Figure 15.2
The second part of the Client Pull code causes the eye to open.

NOTE

When you are considering whether to use Client Pull, keep in mind that your viewers might get annoyed that they've lost control of their browsers. Another drawback is that each page your Client Pull requested is stacked up in your viewers' caches. This means, if they want to scroll back to the page that they started from, they might have a long, cumbersome path of clicking backwards arrows in their way.

Because Client Pull has to load each file as a separate page, the animation illusion is mostly lost. I tried changing the Content = tag to lower numbers to make the pull effect happen faster, but when I tested it, the pages didn't have time to load the images. I put more time in the tag after I got the dreaded broken picture icon Netscape puts up when images refuse to load. Even with a simple two sprite animation, Client Pull is a bit of a disappointment. It works best with pages of text that have no graphics, because they are the most responsive and can load the fastest.

Server Push

Server Push (see fig. 15.3) is one of the coolest dynamic feature Netscape has to offer. If you use Netscape for browsing, you might have seen screens where limited animation appears without anything else on the page changing. If not, check out the Server Push folder on the CD-ROM; we have lots of bookmarks to pages with this feature for you to check out. Server Push allows animation artwork to change on pages, without the entire page having to reload or flash. The speed of the frames is dependent on the access speed of your modem, as well as the size of the animation graphics the Web site is displaying.

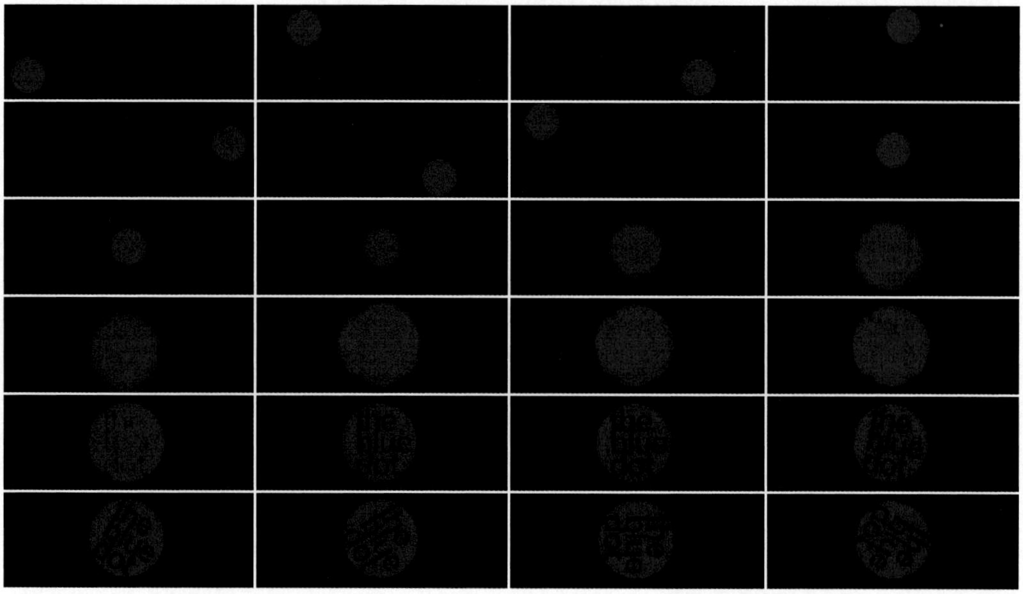

Figure 15.3

These animation "sprites" were used on the www.razorfish.com Web site (_razorfish). This site has great examples of dynamic documents, and is in the bookmark.html file on the Designing Web Graphics CD-ROM.

Typically, if you're designing *sprites*—independent images that change progressively—for a Server Push, you want to keep each individual piece of artwork under 10 KB. (Look to Chapter 3 to learn how to make images this small, or smaller.) You can get away with a little less quality when things are moving. No one is lingering on one piece of artwork long, so aliased edges and limited colors are generally more forgiving. Because of the time-loading issue, it's best to use GIFs over JPEGs, because JPEGs take longer to download.

Unfortunately, the Server Push function within Netscape is sadly the hardest for "mere mortals" to create. That's because Server Push involves writing CGI scripts, which involves knowing how to write code in C, C++, or Perl code.

Working with CGI Scripts

Server Push relies on the server that your site is stored on to access a CGI script. Just like image maps (see Chapter 13), you need to know what type of server you have, CERN or NCSA. Ask your Web systems administrator before you proceed with CGIs. The Web administrator of your site will let you know which type of script your site requires. You will definitely need to consult with a programmer if you hope to use Server Push on your site. Programming in C++ is not something you teach yourself overnight. Speaking to your online service provider will also be necessary, because they'll have to instruct you where to store the script and what kind their server can handle.

Netscape has published a CGI script written in C that does push. It's public domain, so you can use it, if you can figure it out! This is what it looks like:

```
/*
 * doit.c: Quick hack to play a sequence of GIF files.
 *
 * Rob McCool
 *
 * This code is released into the public domain. Do whatever
 * you want with it.
 *
 */
#include <sys/types.h>
#include <sys/mman.h>
#include <unistd.h>
#include <fcntl.h>
#include <sys/stat.h>
#include <stdio.h>
#define LASTCHAR 'j'
#define HEADER \
"Content-type: multipart/x-mixed-replace;boundary=ThisRandomString\n" \
#define RANDOMSTRING "\n——ThisRandomString\n"
#define ENDSTRING "\n——ThisRandomString——\n"
#define CTSTRING "Content-type: image/gif\n\n"
```

```
int main(int argc, char *argv[])
{
 struct stat fi;
 char fn[32];
 caddr_t fp;
 unsigned char x;
 int fd;
 if(write(STDOUT_FILENO, HEADER, strlen(HEADER)) == -1)
 exit(0);
 if(write(STDOUT_FILENO, RANDOMSTRING, strlen(RANDOMSTRING)) == -1)
 exit(0);
 x = 'a';
 while(1) {
 sleep(1);
 if(write(STDOUT_FILENO, CTSTRING, strlen(CTSTRING)) == -1)
 exit(0);
 sprintf(fn, "images/A%c.gif", (char) x);
 if( (fd = open(fn, O_RDONLY)) == -1)
 continue;
 fstat(fd, &fi);
 fp = mmap(NULL, fi.st_size, PROT_READ, MAP_PRIVATE, fd, 0);
 if(fp == (caddr_t) -1)
 exit(0);
 if(write(STDOUT_FILENO, (void *) fp, fi.st_size) == -1)
 exit(0);
 munmap(fp, fi.st_size);
 close(fd);
 if(write(STDOUT_FILENO, RANDOMSTRING, strlen(RANDOMSTRING)) == -1)
 exit(0);
 if(x == LASTCHAR) goto thats_it;
 else ++x;
 }
 /* This goto is Marc's fault. Marc digs goto. */
thats_it:
 exit (0);
}
```

If this causes your brain to freeze over, as it does mine, you might now agree that C scripting is not for "mere mortals." There is good news on this front, though. A few generous programmers on the Web have put out some user-friendly interfaces to Server Push.

If you're on a Unix-based server, check out Lior Saar's shareware Server Push tools at http://www.blue.org/pushy.htm. He's made it possible to write a very simple list of files, such as the following:

```
image01.gif
image02.gif
image03.gif
etc.
```

Put those files in an ASCII text document that could be named, for example, list.txt. Using his tools, you can add Server Push to your Web site and have the GIF images play on your page. Visit Lior Saar's site to download the software and get complete instructions on how to use it at http://www.blue.org/pushy.

AniMaker for WebStar Server Push

If you are fortunate enough to be on a WebStar server (part of Apple's official server software), you could use AniMaker, written by Chuck Shotter. This software is included with the WebStar Server authoring package, and is also on the CD-ROM in the Server Push folder. It only works on Macs and WebStar servers, so many of us can't take advantage of what it does.

It's very easy to use, and I was able to do some tests for The Net Magazine, which has a WebStar server. It's part of the Web Design-O-Rama section of their site (http://www.earthlink.net-usa.com/mag/design). The following list describes how I set up this server push.

1. I made three images of The Net's logo in a layered Photoshop document, then saved each separately as a transparent GIF. I made three separate drawings that were almost identical. This will cause the word to sizzle on-screen. Each file was 1.2 KB. Figure 15.4 shows what my artwork looked like.

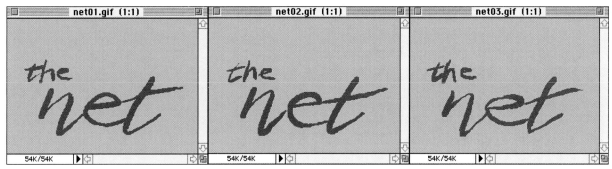

Figure 15.4
A series of three images for the Server Push test.

2. I opened AniMaker and selected New under the File menu (see fig. 15.5).

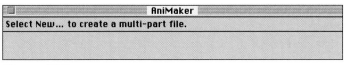

Figure 15.5
AniMaker's opening screen prompts you to create a new file.

3. Choosing File, New displays the dialog box shown in figure 15.6, in which you have to first save the file name. The software prompts you to add the raw file format extension to your name. This is a custom file format that is native to WebStar software. I named the file thenet.raw.

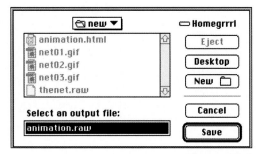

Figure 15.6

AniMaker prompts you to save the file with the raw extension.

4. Next, I was prompted to locate the art I wanted to include in my server push (see fig. 15.7). In this example, I wanted the three images—net01.gif, net02.gif, and net03.gif—to cycle, so I clicked each file name in sequential order 10 times. (AniMaker does not support looping, or endless cycling of an animation sequence).

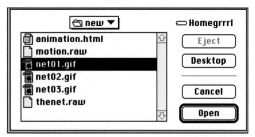

Figure 15.7

After the file is named, AniMaker prompts you to select the art for the Server Push.

5. When I was done, I clicked on Cancel to end the process of making the CGI. Wow, that was sure easy! Thank you Chuck Shotter! The results are can be viewed at http://www.earthlink.net-usa.com/mag/design/animation.html.

Summary

Adding motion to pages is a great enhancement to make a Web site more interesting and lively. We're witnessing the first baby steps of the Web as it emerges as a true multimedia environment. Not all of the dynamic capabilities are easy to use, but that will change as the technology matures. Here are some tips to remember, if you are authoring dynamic documents for Netscape:

- Netscape's dynamic extensions can only be seen from a Netscape browser.

- For the most part, this set of tags does not harm other browsers; the effects simply don't show up.

- Keep your artwork for Server Push as small as possible as it will affect the speed of playback over slow modems.

CHAPTER 16   **Toons and Tunes**

The Web as we know it today is on the verge of major transformation. This is particularly true regarding the way movie and sound files will be handled. Up to this point, viewing a movie or hearing sound files directly from within a browser has been impossible due to bandwidth and speed restrictions. Sound and video files have been referred to as "external media" because they can't be embedded into native Web pages. In order to view or hear these types of files today, it is necessary to possess the correct external viewer or player (often referred to as a MIME (Multipurpose Internet Mail Extension).

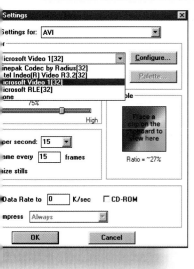

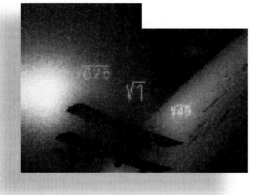

This means that to view sounds or movies, the person looking at your site had to click on your movie or sound file and wait a significant amount of time for the file to download before it was visible or audible. Following the 1 KB per second rule of download transfer speed, on a 14.4 modem it will take approximately one minute to download a 60 KB movie file. Well, those of you who've made movies on computers before know that a 60 KB movie file is almost impossible to create. Most movies, even at the smallest size and highest compression setting, are at least 1 MB. Therefore, in order to view a movie posted to your site, your audience could be waiting as long as ten or fifteen minutes before they could view the smallest conceivable file.

New advancements in Web technology are making it possible to stream audio and video. This means that the audio and video file will be able to come across the phone wires on demand, in small digestible chunks, rather than as an entire file. The speed of your connection will dictate how fast the information streams in. This is going to be a much better system once it becomes a standard. If you need to author sites today that supply audio and video files, however, streaming is not widely implemented or supported; it is still in the promise stage only.

Therefore, this chapter concentrates mostly on how to work with audio and video as external files. This means that you will have to know how to prepare your media files for downloading off your site. We'll look at the HTML tags required to do this, how to make your movies and sounds small, and decide which types of helper applications you and your audience will need. If you look in the software folder on our CD-ROM, you'll find many of the helper applications that are mentioned here, plus other related helpful goodies.

Movie File Formats

The Web accepts a few different movie file formats, each with their respective strengths and weaknesses. Choosing the right one is the first decision you'll need to make before you begin creating movies. This section introduces you to the three major file formats for movies on the Web: QuickTime, AVI, and MPEG.

QuickTime

QuickTime (http://quicktime.apple.com/) has become a popular movie file format on the Web because Apple offers free players for Macs, Windows, SGIs, and Suns. This makes it a great choice for cross-platform movie authoring. QuickTime is native to Macintosh, and the only disadvantage to using it is that it needs to be installed on other platforms. This is a disadvantage to any of the three formats discussed in this chapter, however, because there is no universal movie format that's native to all platforms. We've included QuickTime 2.1 on our CD-ROM, or you can download it directly from http://www.quicktime.apple.com.

QuickTime Requirements

If you're planning to make QuickTime movies, you need to do the following:

- Get QuickTime software.

- Create a movie using QuickTime movie-making software.

- You must flatten the QuickTime movie in order for the movies to be viewed over the Web. Flattening strips the resource fork (which is code embedded in the file that identifies your movie as being just a Macintosh file), so the file can be read by platforms. We've included flattenMooV on the CD-ROM, a very simple movie converter that accepts Mac QuickTime movies and flattens them.

  If you are using Premiere, there's a command under Export called Flatten that you would select. If you don't have Premiere, you can use the utility flattenMooV. Within flattenMooV, open the QuickTime movie, then click in the upper left corner to close the file. Both Premiere and flattenMooV prompt you to resave the file with the extension .flat filled in for you. Be sure to take the .flat extension off before you post it to your Web site. It must have the extension .mov or .qt to be recognized by Web browsers.

- Choose a compression setting. Cinepak or Indeo will make the smallest sized movies for the Web. See the "Codecs" section later in this chapter for information on compression settings and standards.

- Name the file with the extension .mov at the end. If you want the files to be recognized by PCs, the file name must conform to a 12-character limit (including the period and three letter extension name). Example: sample1.mov will be recognized on PCs. Sampleone.mov would be too long.

- Be sure to put links to QuickTime viewers on your site. You will find many viewers on our CD-ROM, or you can download these files by finding the URL in the section "Video Helper Apps and Utilities" found at the end of this chapter.

NOTE

Late breaking news: Netscape has announced plans for inline support of QuickTime movies. This means you will be able to include movies like any other <img src=mymovie.qt> inline image in the near future. How the movie will be played (what interface controls for play, stop, rewind, and so on) is yet to be seen at the time this chapter was written. Netscape is calling QuickTime a Live Object; meaning a QT movie could be played directly from within a future Netscape browser. This is one of the many Live Object file formats Netscape plans to support. (For more info: http://home.netscape.com/comprod/products/navigator/version_2.0/plugins/index.html.)

AVI

The Video for Windows file format is often referred to as VfW or AVI. Players are widely supported on PCs and Windows-based machines. The advantage to using AVI is that these files are easier for PC users to view, because Windows 95 ships with an AVI player. The disadvantage is that Mac, SGI, and Sun audiences will have to convert the files or have the necessary player to view them.

AVI Requirements

If you're planning to make AVI movies, you need to do the following:

- Create a movie using AVI movie-making software.

- Choose a compression setting. Cinepak or Indeo will make the smallest sized movies for the Web.

- Name the file with the extension .avi at the end.

- Be sure to put links to AVI converters on your site. You will find some on our CD-ROM, or look at the list at the end of this section to learn where to download from.

MPEG

MPEG movies are very popular on the Web, but can be problematic. Many MPEG movies have sound and video separated as two distinct files. The only people who can view MPEG movies with sound have sound cards installed inside their PCs. Additionally, you need to have dedicated MPEG decoding hardware in order to create movies with sound and video combined. Because of this, most MPEG movies on the Web typically have separate movie files and audio files. This is a hassle, when the other two possibilities—AVI and QuickTime—do not have this limitation.

MPEG stands for the Motion Picture Experts Group, and was developed specifically as a compression standard for distributing moving images. Unlike JPEG files, which only compress individual frames, MPEG compresses all the redundant information between frames. So the only thing that is recorded between frames is the motion occurring in the movie; everything else is stored every half second or so.

Creating MPEG movies requires dedicated hardware, and is very time consuming because the files take so long to compress. Once they're compressed, they look great. It's actually one of the best-looking movie compression formats available. There are outside services that will batch process MPEG movies for you, if you have a lot of movie files to present on your site and want to use this file format because of the quality advantages.

The difficulties of combining audio and video in one file, as well as the limitations of many of your Web audience's systems to view such files, most likely will outweigh the quality advantages.

MPEG Requirements

If you're planning to make MPEG movies you need to do the following:

- Create a movie using MPEG movie-making software.

- Have extra hardware compression boards if you plan to combine sound and video into one MPEG file.

- Name the file with the extension .mpg at the end.

- Be sure to put links to MPEG players on your site. You will find them on the Designing Web Graphic's CD-ROM, or you can look at the list at the end of this section for URLs to download them from.

Creating Movies

There are so many movie-making software packages, that entire books have been written about which ones to choose and why. With movie-making software packages you can typically edit digital video, taken from videotape footage, to create pure animation based on custom still graphics or process both to create a hybrid of live-action and graphics.

Just like you might choose to own a scanner if you work with still graphics, you will need to get a video digitizing system if you intend to work with live-action video footage on your site. There are lots of software and hardware choices, ranging from which movie capture card to which video-recording deck is better or worse. You'll find many books on the subject of digital video, as well as great online sources, which we've listed in this chapter. Of course, as always, we've included electronic bookmarks for you on the CD-ROM.

What you won't easily find is how to make movies that are appropriate for Web-based distribution and authoring. That's what this section focuses on.

> **NOTE**
>
> A new movie file format may be coming to the Web, called Xing Streamworks. It boasts incredible compression rates of 200:1 and video streaming, creating full-motion video files small enough to transfer in real time over phone lines. Keep your eye on this site for further updates: http://www.xingtech.com/.

NOTE

If you're interested in getting recommendations on specific video and audio hardware or software, check out these online resources:

Electronic Music Software Guide: http://oingomth.uwc.edu/~whizkid/emspg.html

Making Movies on Personal Computers White Paper: http://www.el-dorado.ca.us/~homeport/white_paper_toc.html

Productions Unlimited: Professional Sound and Video Hardware and Software Reviews: http://www.teleport.com/~produnl2/

ZiffNet Services— Cross-platform Online Hardware and Software Reviews: http://www.zdnet.com/~ziffnet/cis/

Digital Video Magazine Online: http://www.dv.com

GFX News/PC Sound, Multimedia Reviews: http://barchetta.stu.rpi.edu/gn/GFXNews.html

General Movie-Making Tips

When referring to movies, there are two things to keep in mind: frame size and frame speed. The frame size is the dimension of the movie in pixels, and frame speed is how many frames per second the movie is recorded at. When authoring movies, it's necessary to know what the end delivery medium will be. If you were going to market your videos to the film and video market, you would make full-screen, full motion (30 frames–60 fields per second) videos of the highest quality with little or no compression. It should be no surprise that this is NOT the case on the Web.

■ **Make your movies small.** A standard size for Web-based movies is 160×120 pixels. This looks better than you might expect. Web audiences do not expect television quality. They are used to looking at thumbnails and are more forgiving of small movie sizes than audiences in other situations would be. Content with live-action tends to be more forgiving at this size than movies that include graphics and type.

If you have the option, and want to include titles or graphics in your Web movies, compose those elements at a bigger scale than you would if you had the full screen to play with. Fonts should be at least 30 points high to be readable once the movie is shrunk to Web postage stamps. If you work large first, let's say 640×480 or 320×240 (see fig. 16.1), and reduce the movies to 160×120 (see fig. 16.2) you will get slightly better quality than if you create small movies to begin with (see fig. 16.3).

■ **Web-based movies should be anywhere from 5–15 frames per second.** Again, this choice will depend on the content and length of your movies. If you have a 30 minute documentary, forget about Web-delivery! Most movies on the Web are under one minute long! Try to keep to the 1 megabyte rule. A 1 megabyte movie file will take your viewer approximately 10 minutes to download. That's already asking a lot, in my humble opinion!

Many people divide the original frame rate of a movie file in half. If the source was recorded at 30 fps (frames per second), they'll make their Web movies 15 fps. If the source was 24 fps, they'll make their movies 12 fps. I've found you can get away with lower frame rates than this, depending on the content. Typically, live action recorded at normal speed or high speed (slow motion) is much more forgiving than movies that are fast-paced to begin with. You might have to save your Web-sized movie at higher frame rates if there's very fast action, or fast titles in the original source material.

The best thing is to run tests at different sizes and frame rates to see what works best for your sources footage.

■ **Use the highest compression setting your movie can withstand.** See the following section for a listing of compression standards (codecs) appropriate for the Web.

■ **Never re-compress an already compressed movie!** It will introduce unsightly artifacts that don't need to be there! Begin with an uncompressed original if you want to change your mind about a compression setting.

Codecs

To make matters a little more complicated, movie formats also use different types of compression settings and standards. These are called Codecs, which stands for COmpressor/DECompressor.

Table 16.1 lists movie file formats with appropriate Codecs for Web authoring. Just like there are lots of other image file formats besides those this book discusses—GIFs and JPEGs—there are many other movie Codecs. They are missing from this list because I'm specifically only including those that would compress movies to reasonable sizes for modem downloading.

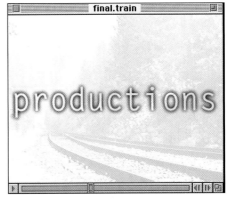

Figure 16.1

The original 320×240 movie with no compression.

Figure 16.2

The same file rendered direct to 160×120, Cinepak.

Figure 16.3

The imported original 320×240 and reduced it to 160×120 Cinepak additional quality improvement (software used: Adobe After Effects).

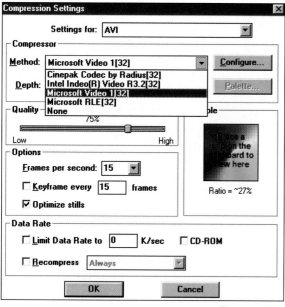

Figure 16.4

Selecting a codec in Premiere on the Mac.

Figure 16.5

Selecting a codec in Premiere for Windows.

Table 16.1	Appropriate Codecs for Web Movies
Movie Format	Web-appropriate Codec
QuickTime	Cinepak
	Indeo
AVI	Indeo
	Cinepak
MPEG	MPEG

The codec is requested when you're saving your movie. The choices are accessed from the movie-making software you use. For example, when you go to save your movie in QuickTime, you are prompted to choose a compression setting (see figures 16.4 and 16.5). At this point, you choose from either Web-appropriate codec: Cinepak or Indeo. The compression setting you choose is invisible to the end users. They only know whether your movie is a QuickTime, AVI, or MPEG.

The following sections look at advantages and disadvantages to the codecs appropriate for Web-based movies.

Cinepak—Available for QuickTime and AVI

Cinepak offers lossy compression, which means that this compression codec causes the original movie file to loose quality. That might sound more alarming than it actually is. All Web-based compression schemes are lossy. If they didn't sacrifice some quality, they couldn't produce small enough files suitable for modem transfer.

Cinepak was designed for CD-ROM authoring, and does an exceptional job at playing back off a disk—be it floppy, hard disk, or CD-ROM. Cinepak has a tendency to make images look slightly blurred, and for this reason works better on animation and graphics that have lots of solid colors rather than live-action, which has lots of subtleties and changing colors. It takes a long time to render a QuickTime movie to Cinepak because of the amount of crunching Cinepak does to the file. What makes the file play back well is precisely what makes it render slowly: Cinepak takes a very large file and makes it very small—a lot of work!

Indeo—Available for QuickTime and AVI

Indeo also offers lossy compression. It has two modes, a normal and super compressor mode. If you use the super compressor mode, Indeo will take as long as Cinepak to render, but the image quality will be much better. Indeo does an exceptional job compressing live-action–based footage. It tends to make those types of movies look sharper than Cinepak. The size in megabytes and playback speed on Indeo and Cinepak movies will be the same. Indeo is not available for Unix-based machines. They can play Indeo compressed movies, but cannot author them.

MPEG

MPEG became an early standard on the Web because it was the only movie format on which Unix platform-based computers could write. The problem with MPEG movies on the Web is that they typically are either video or sound files; combined video and sound movies are a rarity. This is because you need special hardware to render an MPEG movie with sound. If you are using software to compress you must choose to either write a sound or a movie file. Now that QuickTime is available for Unix-platforms, chances are that MPEG will become less ubiquitous.

HTML for Placing Movies on Web Pages

Because your audience has to download movies to see them, the movie files need to be placed inside the <a href></a> tag. Let's say we have a movie file called movie.mov. To make a simple text link, you would do the following (see fig. 16.6):

```
<a href="movie.mov">Click here to download this movie!</a>
```

Click here to download this movie!

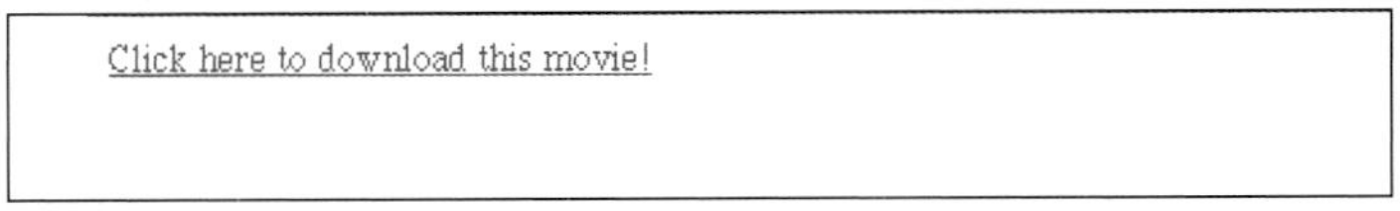

Figure 16.6
This HTML code creates a text-based link to the movie.

Even better would be to include a thumbnail image from the movie, as shown in figure 16.7. (See the following Case Study to learn how to make a thumbnail in Premiere.) Let's say we made a thumbnail image that was named movieframe.gif. Here would be the code:

```
<a href="movie.mov"><img
src="movieframe.gif">Click here to download
this movie!</a>
```

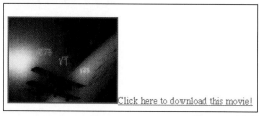

Figure 16.7

You can use the <img src=> tag to include a thumbnail image from the movie.

Figure 16.8

Your audience will appreciate it if you provide the format and size of the movie.

Figure 16.9

Adding a link to a site that has QuickTime movie players.

In order to be kind to your audience, it's best if you tell them up front what kind of movie file format you've used and how big the file is. Figure 16.8 shows a good example; the code follows.

```
<a href="movie.mov"><img
src="movieframe.gif"></a>
<p>
160 x 120 QuickTime movie<br>
1.2 MB
```

If you wanted to include a link to a site that had QuickTime movie players, here's how that code would look (see fig. 16.9):

```
16<a href="movie.mov"><img
src="movieframe.gif"></a>
<p>
160 x 120 QuickTime movie<br>
1.2 MB
<p>

If you need a QuickTime player to view this
movie, click <a
href=""http://wwwhost.ots.utexas.edu/mac/
main.html">here.</a>
```

Case Study—Posting Movies to the Web

Because I teach several motion graphics classes at Art Center, and want all my students to post their finished movies to the Art Center Web site, I made a step-by-step handout for them to follow in order to prepare their movies properly. This case study presents the information from that handout as a list of steps you can follow to prepare your own movie for the Web.

1. The first objective is to remake your movie so it's small enough to post to your Web site. Open Premiere and choose 160×120 preset (see fig. 16.10).

2. Import your finished movie and drag it to the A channel of the Construction window.

3. From the Make menu, select the Make Movie option to display the Save Movie As dialog box. Name the file sample1.mov (see fig. 16.11).

4. Click on the Compression button to display the Compression Settings dialog box, and match the settings as shown in figure 16.12.

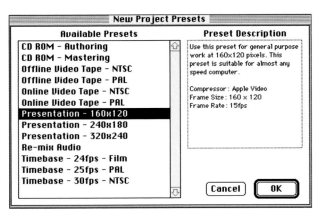

Figure 16.10
Choosing the presentation size in Premiere.

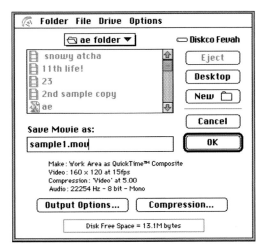

Figure 16.11
Naming the movie in the Save Movie As dialog box.

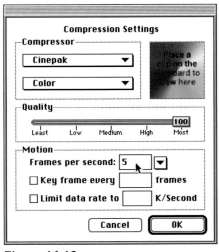

Figure 16.12
Use these compression settings.

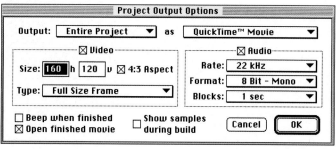

Figure 16.13
Use these output settings.

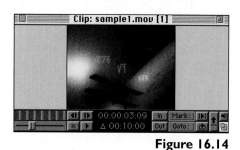

Figure 16.14
Example of Art Center student Fred Nymoen's movie rendered in the thumbnail size for the Web.

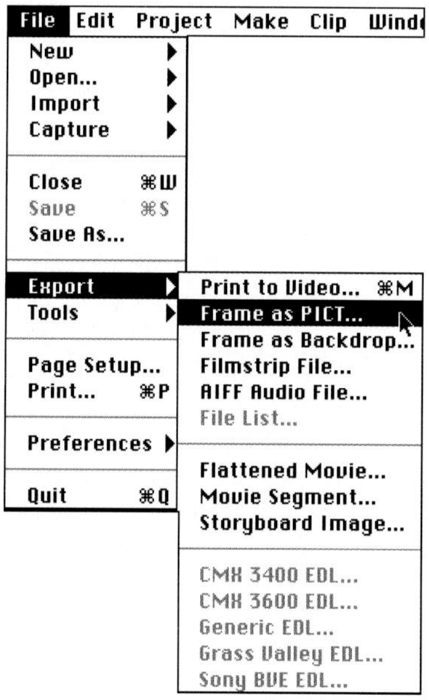

Figure 16.15
Export, Save as PICT Menu selection from Premiere box.

5. Click on OK to return to the Save Movie As dialog box, then click on the Output Options button to display the Project Output Options dialog box. Match the settings shown in figure 16.13.

6. Click OK to make the movie. When it's finished, the movie will appear on the screen.

7. In the File menu open Export and then Flattened Movie. You'll be prompted to rename the file with a MOV extension Premiere has filled in for you. Delete that added extension. Make sure your file name reads sample.1.mov (all lowercase, all strung together). Click Save. The movie will remain on your screen (see fig. 16.14).

8. The next goal is to make a thumbnail image of your movie for the Web site. Use the slider to go to a frame of the movie you want to represent your film. This is the still image your Web audience will see, and it is what they will click on to trigger the downloading of your file.

   Once you've picked the right frame, choose Export from the File menu, and then Frame as Pict. This results in a dialog box that automatically names your file sample1.mov.PICT (see fig. 16.15). Click on Save.

9. Open Photoshop. Open the file sample1.mov.PICT. Go to the top menu bar and choose Mode and then Index Color

to display the Indexed Color dialog box. Make the settings match those shown in figure 16.16.

10. Next, under File choose Save a Copy as. Use CompuServe GIF format, and name your file sample1.gif (see fig. 16.17).

11. This allows you to use the thumbnail image for the following HTML:

```
<a href="sample1.mov"><img
src="sample1.gif"></a>
```

For an example of a finished student page and other templates, see Chapter 18, "HTML Templates for Designers."

Video Helper Apps and Utilities

Here's a list of useful helper applications and utilities for movie creation and viewing. Most of these programs are on the Designing Web Graphics CD-ROM. If you don't have a CD-ROM player, here's where you can download them from:

For Macs:

- **Sparkle:** Converts and Plays QuickTime and MPEG movies: ftp://sumex-aim.stanford.edu/info-mac/grf/util. Sparkle requires sound manager 3.1 to run on Power PC.

- **FlattenMoov:** Coverts QuickTime movies so they can be viewed from platforms other than Macs: ftp://ftp.utexas.edu/pub/mac/graphics/flattenmoov.hqx

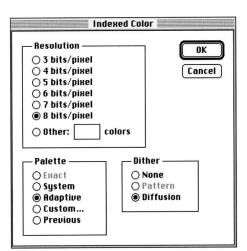

Figure 16.16

Use these settings for the indexed color.

Figure 16.17

Save the file in CompuServe GIF format.

- **QuickTime:** To get the most current version of QuickTime: ftp://ftptoo.support.apple.com/pub/apple_sw_updates/US/Macintosh/System%20Software/Other%20System%20Software/QuickTime_2.1.hqx

- **MPEG Realtime Audio Player 1.b0: Plays MPEG movies:** ftp://mirror.apple.com/.ufs01/info-mac/gst/snd/mpeg-audio-player-10-ppc.hqx

- **MakeItMooV:** AVI>QuickTime Conversion Utility:
  ftp://mirror.apple.com/.ufs01/info-mac/gst/mov/video-for-windows-11p.hqx

- **MoviePlayer:** Plays QuickTime movies from Macs:
  ftp://ftp.support.apple.com/pub/apple_sw_updates/US/Macintosh/Utilities/MoviePlayer
  _2.1.hqx

For PCs:

- **QuickTime for Windows:** Install QuickTime for Windows:
  ftp://ftp.iuma.com/video_utils/Windows/qtw11.zip

- **Xing MPEG Player:** Plays MPEG Movies:
  http://www.xingtech.com/products/xingmpeg/xmpdata.html

- **MPEG Play:** Playes MPEG Movies:
  ftp://ftp.iuma.com/video_utils/Windows/mpegw32h.zip

- **SmartVid:** Converts both ways for AVI>Quicktime: ftp://ftp.intel.com/pub/IAL/
  multimedia/smartv.exe

- **Indeo:** To get the most current version of Indeo: http://www.intel.com/pc-supp/
  multimed/indeo/index.html

- **AVI Pro:** AVI player for Windows:
  ftp://gatekeeper.dec.com/pub/micro/msdos/win3/desktop/avipro2.exe

Tunes

(Special Thanks to Mark Wheaton of http://www.underground.net/Weba/
catasonic.html and Erik Holsinger of Musical Imagery for help with this section.)

Audio on the Web has most of the same limitations as video—the files are too large to hear as inline components of a page. Your audience will be required to download audio files in order to listen to them, and it's your job to choose a file format and compression rate. You will base these decisions on what platform you're authoring sounds from, and how to make the files as small as possible while still sounding as good as possible.

Because there are so many audio standards on the Web, it's a good idea to have links to audio players on your site. For a list of MIMEs and helper apps, check the end of this chapter.

Here's a look at the various audio standards and ways to reduce the size of audio files.

Rates and Bits

There are two components of an audio file that make it sound good (and take up space): the sampling rate and the bit depth, which is referred to as the sample resolution.

Sample rates are measured in kilohertz. The sample rate affects the range of a digitized sound, which defines its highs and lows. Higher sample rates result in larger file sizes, as shown in table 16.2. The sampling rate is set when the sound is digitized (captured) into the computer. Sound editing software is where the initial sample rate settings are established, and it should be set according to the type of sound being sampled. Some types of sounds can deal with lower sampling rates better. Narration, for example, doesn't depend on high and low ranges to sound good. Here are some typical sampling rates:

8 KHz

11 KHz

22.050 KHz

44.1 KHz

48 KHz

Sampling resolution dictates how much range the sound has in highs and lows. Higher kilohertz settings results in a bigger file size, as shown in table 16.2. The sampling resolution is also set when the sound is digitized (captured) into the computer. Sound editing software allows users to dictate which sample resolution the sound is captured at. Because noise is introduced at lower sample rates, it's necessary to evaluate individual sound elements to see how far down the sampling resolution can be set without introducing unacceptable noise. You can create digital sound at the following resolutions:

8 bit mono

8 bit stereo

16 bit mono

16 bit stereo

Generally when you first digitally record or "sample" a sound, you want to record it at 16-bit resolution at the 44.1 KHz sampling rate. Later, after processing the sound to your satisfaction with digital audio editing applications, you would resample the final file down to 8-bit, 22.05 KHz.

Audio File Formats

Many types of audio files are used and found on the Web. Choosing which one to use is often determined by what kind of computer system and software you're authoring sounds from. Here's a breakdown of the various formats:

µ-law

µ-law used to be the only file format you'd find on the Web, as it is generated by Unix platforms. Now that Macs and PCs are the predominant platform, µ-law files are not seen as much. The sound quality is generally considered much lower than the other sound formats described here. It is used much less often now, as a result. If you are going to author µ-law files, they should be saved with an .au extension.

AIFF

AIFF was developed by Apple and is used on Macintoshes and SGIs. It stands for Audio Interchange File Format. It can store digital audio at all the sample rates and resolutions possible. You'll also hear about MACE (Macintosh Audio Compression/Expansion), which is the built-in compression standard for AIFF files. Just like in video, what compression you used is invisible to the end listener. It does dictate the size and quality of your end result, however. If you are going to author AIFF files, they should be saved with an aif extension.

WAVE

Wave was developed by Microsoft and IBM, and is the native sound file format to Windows platforms. Like AIFF, it can store digital audio at all the sample rates and resolutions possible. Basically, WAVE and AIFF files are considered equals in terms of quality and compression, and are easier to use depending on which platform you are authoring from. If you are going to author WAVE files, they should be saved with a .wav extension.

MPEG

MPEG audio is well respected as a high-quality, excellent audio compression file format. The only problem is that encoding MPEG requires extra hardware that is out of reach of many audio content creators. Because MPEG files aren't native to any specific platform, your audience will need to download a helper application to hear them. If you are going to author MPEG sound files, they should be saved with the .mpg extension.

RealAudio

RealAudio is the first example of streaming audio on the Web. Streamed audio files come over the phone lines in small chunks, so the entire file doesn't have to be downloaded before it can be heard. The file can be up to one hour long, because the data is coming in as you're hearing it—not downloading fully first to your hard drive. The sound quality is often compared to that of an AM radio station. Because of quality limits, it's best used for narration and not for music or other sounds. You must have the RealAudio player installed on your system to hear sounds play as soon as you click on a link that supplies real audio source material. You can author RealAudio content by using the RealAudio encoder, which can be obtained by accessing their site (http://www.realaudio.com). You won't be able to offer RealAudio files from your Web site unless your provider has paid RealAudio a server licensing fee. Contact the RealAudio site for more information.

Tips for Making Web-Based Sound Files

Several free or shareware applications can convert from or to μ-law, AIFF, WAV, and MPEG files, so chances are your audience will be able to access your sounds regardless of which file format you choose to support. Typically, Mac authors will choose AIFF, PC authors will choose WAV or MPEG, and Unix authors will pick μ-law, because those are the file formats supported natively by their systems.

To properly prepare the files, however, you might want to use a sound editing program that offers features like peak level limiting, normalizing, down sampling, and dithering from 16-bit to 8-bit. Premiere is a great entry level video and sound editor—though professional videographers and sound engineers will typically own higher-end dedicated editing programs. Figure 16.18 shows some of the audio filters found in Premiere.

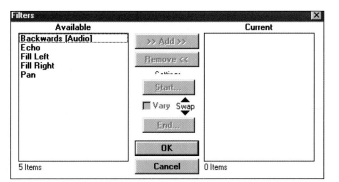

Figure 16.18

Premiere's Filters dialog box, showing some of the available audio filters.

Here are some tips for making Web-based sound files:

■ Digitize at the standard audio CD sample rate and resolution (44 KHz and 16 bit). Down sample the file to the preferred sample size of 22 KHz or 11 KHz. Typically, the lower the sample rate, the less high end or duller the sound will be. For dialogue or sounds where high end doesn't matter, lowering the sample rate creates smaller files that will be of acceptable quality.

■ Halfing the sample rate will half the file size (see table 16.2). Additionally, changing the file from stereo to mono cuts the file size in half. Use the Mix feature of most audio software packages to create a mono version of a stereo file.

■ If the 16-bit file is still too large, you can use dithering algorithms on audio (just like on images) to take the files down to 8-bit. Dithering will add noise, in the form of hiss (and in the worse case electronic buzzing and chattering). Dithering will be most noticeable in files with silences between sounds.

Because of the electronic noise, dithering should be avoided on dialogue. Dithering works great for rich, full music files such as hard rock and industrial. Another alternative is to re-digitize the 16-bit audio file at 8-bit by playing back and recording a pre-recorded 16-bit, 44.1 KHz sound into your digitizer. Often this creates cleaner 8-bit samples with more "punch."

■ When naming audio files, as with all files being prepped for Internet distribution, they must be named with no spaces. Unlike inline images, these files are going to be downloaded by your audience. Therefore names should be under eight characters long, with room for a three-letter file extension, or Windows platform users won't get to hear them!

■ Make sure you've done all your sound editing (such as mixing from stereo to mono, filtering, peak level limiting, normalizing, or down sampling) before you convert to 8-bit. If you edit an 8-bit sound and then resave it, you will add electronic noise to your file. Always start with higher bit depth, and do your editing in that file before you save or dither it to 8-bit.

Table 16.2 was compiled by the Webmaster of Catasonic records (http://www.underground.net), Mark Wheaton, who took the same 30-second sound and compressed it various ways with various results. The sound clip "Spider" was written by WebaWorld publishing (1995 Bubblewrap BMI), and is available on an upcoming Catasonic Records release. This chart gives you a good idea of what happens to file sizes when sounds are saved with different bit-depths, channel depths (mono or stereo), and sampling rates. These sound files are on the CD-ROM, so you can judge the quality gains and losses for yourself.

Table 16.2	File Formats, Sample Rates, Sound Channels, and Bit Depth Comparison Chart				
File Name	File Format	Sample Rate	Mono/Stereo	Bit Depth	Size
Spider/Orig	AIFF	44.1	Stereo	16-bit	687.6
Spider/44/16/M	AIFF	44.1	Mono	16-bit	1371
Spider/22/16/S	AIFF	22050	Stereo	16-bit	343.6
Spider/22/16/M	AIFF	22050	Mono	16-bit	686.2
Spider/11/16/S	AIFF	11025	Stereo	16-bit	1371.5
Spider/11/16/M	AIFF	11025	Mono	16-bit	2741
Spider/44/8/S	AIFF	44.1	Stereo	8-bit	686.2
Spider/44/8/M	AIFF	44.1	Mono	8-bit	1371
Spider/22/8/S	AIFF	22050	Stereo	8-bit	2741
Spider/22/8/M	AIFF	22050	Mono	8-bit	5482.9
Spider/11/8/S	AIFF	11025	Stereo	8-bit	1371.5
Spider/11/8/M	AIFF	11025	Mono	8-bit	2741.9
Spider/44/16/M	AU	44.1	Mono	16-bit	1371
Spider/22/16/S	AU	22050	Stereo	16-bit	343.1
Spider/22/16/M	AU	22050	Mono	16-bit	685.7
Spider/11/16/S	AU	11025	Stereo	16-bit	1371
Spider/11/16/M	AU	11025	Mono	16-bit	5482
Spider/11/8/S	AU	11025	Stereo	8-bit	1371.5
Spider/11/8/M	AU	11025	Mono	8-bit	2741.9
Spider/Orig	WAV	44.1	Stereo	16-bit	5482
Spider/44/16/M	WAV	44.1	Mono	16-bit	2741.5
Spider/22/16/S	WAV	22050	Stereo	16-bit	2741.5
Spider/22/16/M	WAV	22050	Mono	16-bit	1371
Spider/11/16/M	WAV	11025	Mono	16-bit	685
Spider/22/8/M	WAV	22050	Mono	8-bit	685.7
Spider/11/8/M	WAV	11025	Mono	8-bit	343.1

HTML for Sound Files

A sound file gets the <a href></a> tag, just like its video counterpart. Unlike video, where there might be an associated thumbnail image, though, sounds are usually indicated by a sound icon, or hyper-text. Here are a few variations, and the code you would use to produce them.

Here's the code to link your audience to a sound and let them know what file size and format it is:

```
<a href="snd1.aif"><font size=5>Click here to download this
sound!</a></font>
<p>
Excerpt from CD:<br>
WebaWorld<p>
Cut: Spider<p>
AIFF Sound<br>
:30<br>
567k
```

or, if you want to add an icon, too:

```
<a href="snd1.aif"><font size=5><img src="ear.gif">Click here to download
this sound!</a></font>
<p>
Excerpt from CD:<br>
WebaWorld<p>
Cut: Spider<p>
AIFF Sound<br>
:30<br>
567k
```

How to Configure MIMEs in Netscape

As discussed earlier in this chapter, external media such as sound and video require viewers, players, MIMEs, and helper applications in order to see or hear these files. Netscape lets you pre-configure your browser to automatically open these viewers, players, MIMEs, and helper applications depending on what type of media you download. Here's how you set up Netscape:

1. Go to the Options menu and select Preferences.

2. Select the Helper Applications preference page.

3. Select the File type that you want to support.

4. Select Launch and load the proper player, viewer, MIME, or helper application.

Audio Helper Apps and Utilities

Here's a list of useful helper applications and utilities for audio creation and playback. Most of these programs are on the Designing Web Graphics CD-ROM. If you don't have a CD-ROM player, here's where you can download them from:

For Macs:

- **Sound Machine 2.5:** Plays AU, AIFF, and WAVE:
  ftp://ftp.iuma.com/audio_utils/au_players/Macintosh/sound-machine-21.hqx

- **SoundApp:** ftp://mirror.apple.com/.ufs01/info-mac/gst/snd/sound-app-151.hqx

- **MPEG Audio:** Converts MPEG to AIFF: ftp://ftp.iuma.com/audio_utils/
  mpeg_players/Macintosh/MPEGAudNoFPU1.0a6.hqx

- **MPEG CD:** Plays MPEG audio:
  http://www.kauai.com/~bbal/MPEG_CD_2.0.3.sea.hqx

- **Brian's Sound Tool:** Converts WAVE, AU and AIFF:
  gopher://gopher.archive.merit.edu:7055/40/mac/sound/soundutil/
  brianssoundtool1.3.sit.hqx

- **SoundHack:** Converts WAVE, AU, and AIFF:
  ftp://shoko.calarts.edu/pub/SoundHack/SH0866.hqx

For PCs:

- **Xing SoundPlayer:** Plays MPEG audio (you need a sound card for it to work):
  ftp://ftp.iuma.com/audio_utils/mpeg_players/Windows/mpgaudio.exe

- **Windows Play Any:** plays AU/WAV/AIFF:
  ftp://ftp.ncsa.uiuc.edu/Web/Mosaic/Windows/viewers/wplny12a.zip

- **WHAM 1.31:** Sound Converter:
  ftp://gatekeeper.dec.com/pub/micro/msdos/win3/sounds/wham133.zip

Summary

As you can see by the size of this chapter, adding sound and video to a Web site is a complex undertaking. You have a lot of decisions to make, many of which will be dictated by what tools you have available to you and what platform you're authoring from. Here are a few universal tips to follow:

■ Because external media files will be downloaded to your audience's hard drives, be sure to keep your file names under eight characters long so Windows users can enjoy them, too.

■ Test your files at different compression settings. You rarely can find one setting that works for all types of video or all types of audio.

■ Always work from a high-quality original. Don't add compression to an already compressed file, or you'll add unwanted electronic noise and/or image artifacts.

■ Be sure to warn your audience in advance of downloading about the file size, type, and player requirements.

CHAPTER 17 Pre-Visualizing Web Pages

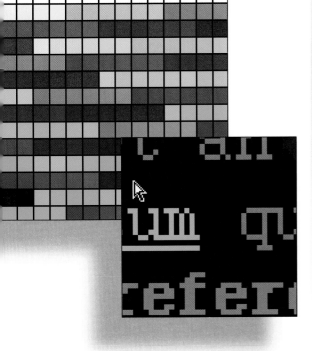

Most designers would never consider publishing their work before running tests and trying at least a few different versions of their concept first. This chapter discusses pre-visualizing your Web graphics, using Photoshop as the pre-visualization tool. Because we've been using Photoshop throughout this book, and because Photoshop works well for Web graphics tasks, we'll feature Photoshop in this chapter as our pre-visualization tool.

There are entire books about Photoshop, and many of us own more than one. The amazing thing about Photoshop is how deep and rich it is, and how many different end applications there are for its features. I've never known any other program to be relied upon by artists of so many disciplines: photographers, illustrators, painters, printmakers, filmmakers, videographers, and textile designers all can cite Photoshop as their single most important software tool.

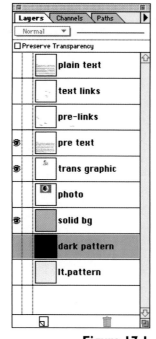

Figure 17.1

The eye icon shows which layers are turned on.

Web visualization is another function at which Photoshop excels. I have set up a Photoshop layered document for this purpose that you can open from the CD-ROM, or you can easily create your own if mine doesn't suit your purposes.

This chapter walks you through setting up a layered Photoshop document and demonstrates techniques that are useful for Web page pre-visualization.

Using Layers

Where I might have a firm concept for a site in terms of its look and feel, balancing images to text sizes and colors against background colors or patterns is something you must *see*, not imagine. I use Photoshop as a testing ground for choosing colors and sizes, by breaking elements of my pages into layers.

Photoshop layers work like transparent overlays. This allows me to see how elements work together and to test them in different combinations with different settings. Layers can be turned on and off. This allows you to try out different ideas; like how your photo looks against a solid background as well as a patterned background. You turn layers off and on by clicking the eye icon, which is located to the left of each layer (see fig. 17.1).

As long as you separate each Web page component on to its own layer, you can independently control its color, size, and position. Here are the layers in the test Photoshop document I've created for this chapter (see the following section), with explanations of what I would choose to do with them:

- **Plain Text.** I want to make sure the color I pick for my type reads well against whatever background I use. By separating the text onto its own layer, I'm able to change the color in relationship to whatever background I decide to put it against.

- **Text Links.** Linked type, active links, and visited links can be in different colors from the rest of your body text. By putting these on a separate layer, I can experiment to see which colors work best.

- **Pre-Text.** Preformatted text (using the <pre> tag) usually defaults to being in a Courier typeface, rather than the standard Times Roman default font. If I want to see how it looks as an alternative to plain text, a separate layer allows me to try it out.

- **Pre-Links.** The links in my pre-formatted type layer can now be colored separately from the text.

- **Trans Graphic.** This layer allows me to preview how a transparent GIF is going to look over a specific background color or pattern.

- **Photo.** I can adjust the color treatment or size of the photo if it's on an independent layer

- **Solid BG.** This is the layer I would put solid color in to test solid background colors.

- **Dark Pattern.** I will choose whether a dark or light pattern works best with my type and photos or illustrations.

- **Light Pattern.** I will choose whether a dark or light pattern works best with my type and photos or illustrations.

Figures 17.2 and 17.3 show examples of the same document with different layers activated, resulting in entirely different effects.

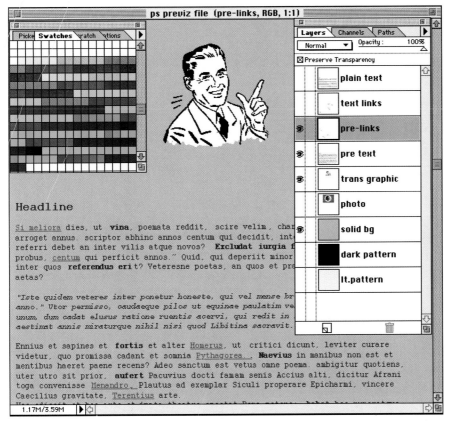

Figure 17.2
As shown in the Layers dialog box, this document appears with the Solid Background layer activated.

Figure 17.3

The same document, but with the Solid Background layer turned off and the Dark Pattern layer activated.

Working with the Supplied PS File

I've put a copy of the layered Photoshop master file I work off of when doing my personal Web Design on the *Designing Web Graphics* CD-ROM. It's located in the Chapter 17 folder and is titled Previz.ps. Open this document if you'd like to follow along with this chapter. Try clicking eye icons on and off, and you'll quickly get an understanding of how to visualize different variations of the same page.

Type

If you want to change the type color, go to a type layer and click on Preserve Transparency (see fig. 17.4). This allows you to change the color of the type without affecting the rest of the layer. Choose the color you want to fill with and use the Edit, Fill command to change the color of the entire block of text (see fig. 17.5).

Using layers is a wonderful way to adjust and tweak colors. Remember the rule of contrast—use dark colors against light backgrounds and light colors against dark backgrounds—and your pages will be a lot easier to read. If you load the browser palette from the CD-ROM, you can choose from the non-dithering color palette described in Chapter 4, "Color Palette Hell!" or use our chart found in Chapter 5, "Fun with Hex," and on the CD-ROM, for the respective hexadecimal translations.

I've made separate layers for linked type, allowing you to select different colors for links, visited links, and active links. With Preserve Transparency checked on this layer, you can take a paintbrush tool and color individual links on the same layer to preview how changing those colors will look (see fig. 17.6).

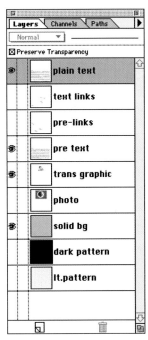

Figure 17.4
Highlight a type layer and click on Preserve Transparency to change the type color.

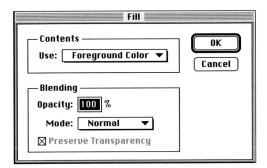

Figure 17.5
Choosing Edit, Fill displays this Fill dialog box, in which you can change the color of the entire block of text.

TIP

A short cut to fill with foreground color is to hold down the Option and Delete keys on a Mac and the Alt and Delete keys on a PC. This completes the fill without going up to the menu bar or clicking on the Fill dialog box.

Figure 17.6
Magnified view of painting an individual text block with a brush.

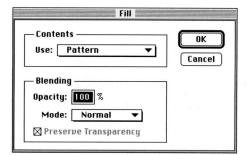

Figure 17.7

Fill dialog box settings for filling a layer with a pattern.

Backgrounds and Patterns

There are a couple of layers in which you can paste your custom patterns and solid background fills to test different color combinations. You can use the pattern I've supplied or paste a pattern of your own in here. If you want to fill this layer with your own custom created pattern, or any clip-art pattern source, follow these steps:

1. Open your custom pattern tile document and select All.

2. Under the Edit menu, choose Define Pattern.

3. Go back to the layered pre-visualization document and activate it. Click on the light or dark pattern layer, depending on which is appropriate.

4. Choose Edit, Fill to display the Fill dialog box (see fig. 17.7). Make sure the Contents is set to Use: Pattern.

5. If you want to fill the solid background layer, pick a single color and choose Edit, Fill, Contents, Use: Foreground Color.

Creating a Layered Document for a Pattern Tile

You can take patterns a step further by isolating your tile source document into layers. I've provided a second Photoshop prototype source file on the CD-ROM, called Pttrns.ps. It allows you to take this sample arrow pattern and use Preserve Transparency and Fill features to try out different color combinations for your pattern fills. Figures 17.8, 17.9, and 17.10 show examples of variations possible by using layers for pattern tile documents.

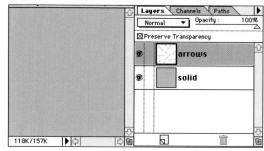

Figure 17.8

The first pattern color variation, made easy by using layers.

Figure 17.9

The second pattern color variation.

Figure 17.10

The third pattern color variation.

Making Your Own Layers

I've provided a document with layers, but learning how to make them yourself is rather simple. Make sure the Layers Palette is open (see fig. 17.11). Click on the new layer tool (see fig. 17.12) to add new layers. You can copy and paste from other files, or use the move tool to drag images into a layer. Make sure the target layer you need is selected first when you choose to paste.

You can fill your custom layers with whatever appropriate elements they require. If you are going to make a type layer represent your HTML text, be sure to not check anti-aliasing when you're in the type dialog box (see fig. 17.13).

Figure 17.12
Use the new layer tool to add new layers.

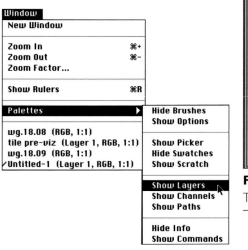

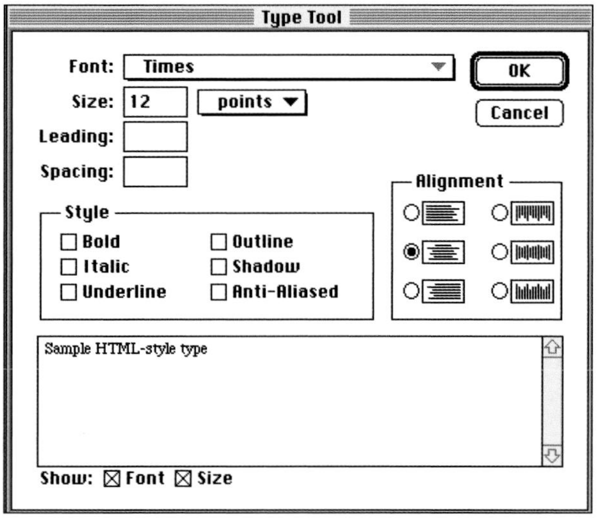

Figure 17.11
Select Windows, Palettes, Show Layers to open palette layers before making your own layers.

Figure 17.13
The Type Tool dialog box.

Turning Layers into Usable Web Graphics

Once you're satisfied with a finished prototype, the next task will be to convert the layered Photoshop document into usable Web graphics. Let's look at a sample prototype and break down what you'd need to do:

1. Let's say the document in figure 17.14 was the prototype I settled on for my Web page. I would need to separate out each component, save it in the proper file format, or choose the appropriate hexadecimal numbers to place inside my HTML code.

   To save the illustration, I first select it with a rectangular marquee (see fig. 17.15).

2. By cropping the image, I'm able to create the size for the individual GIF file (see fig. 17.16).

3. To save the file as a GIF it must be indexed first. Selecting Mode, Indexed Color will display the dialog box shown in figure 17.17; click on OK.

Figure 17.15

To save the illustration, first marquee-select it.

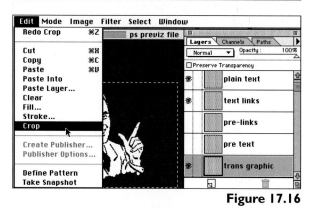

Figure 17.16

Select Edit, Crop to crop the image.

Figure 17.17

The cropped illustration. Select Mode, Indexed Color to begin indexing the file.

4. Choose the index color palette (see fig. 17.19). In this case, going with the exact palette is the choice I want to make. I plan to use this GIF with these colors, so these are the exact colors I want. Exact usually appears as a default when an index palette can be created with the

Figure 17.14

The prototype document for the Web.

exact colors of the original document. If there are more than 256 colors in an original, an exact palette cannot be generated, because it would exceed 8-bits worth of information.

5. It's very important to choose File, Save a Copy, because you don't want to overwrite the original layered document. Even though I've "flattened the layers," which eliminates all the layers I've worked so hard to maintain, by saving as a copy I can easily Revert to my layered Photoshop document. Save it with CompuServe GIF file format and name the file in lowercase with the extension GIF at the end.

6. Choose File, Revert to return to the Photoshop layered master (see fig. 17.20).

Figure 17.18
Because you are working in a layered document, Photoshop requires that the image be flattened (all the layers be removed) before allowing you to change the bit-depth to index color. When you click yes, it will advance you to the Indexed Color dialog.

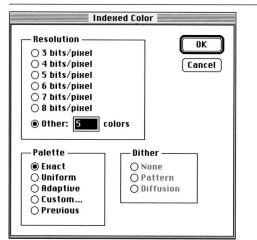

Figure 17.19
Select Index Color as the first step to convert this from a 24-bit layered document to an 8-bit GIF.

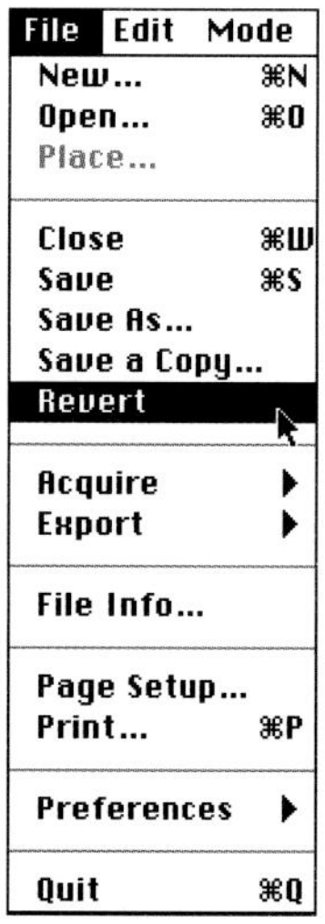

Figure 17.20
The Revert command is found under the Edit menu.

7. Use the eyedropper tool with the Show Info palette open (see fig. 17.21). This will give you the RGB reading of the colored text and backgrounds, so you can translate them to Hex.

Figure 17.22 shows three different versions of this document file.

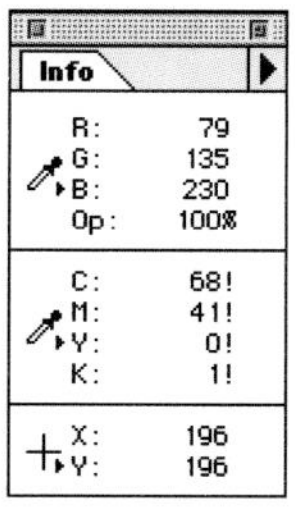

Figure 17.21
Using the eyedropper tool in the Info palette.

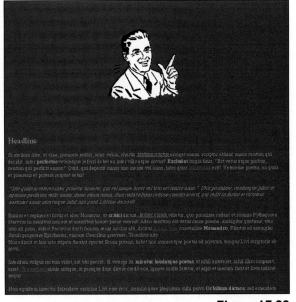

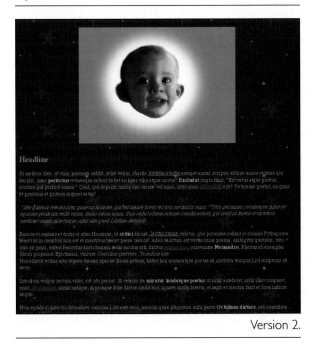

Figure 17.22

By using the Pre-Visualization file, I was able to quickly try three different versions of this document. Version 1.

Version 3.

Version 2.

Summary

Once you get used to using Photoshop layered documents for the purpose of Web pre-visualization, you will probably never give it up. There is no other imaging tool on the Mac or PC that offers this type of flexibility and power in one program. Here's a review of the key points this chapter covered:

- If you separate your graphics onto their own layers in a prototype Photoshop file you can make all kinds of adjustments in relationship to each component. This helps with sizing, position, and color decisions.

- Work with Preserve Transparency if you want to change the color of a layer.

- If you're trying to simulate HTML text, choose the appropriate typeface with anti-alias unchecked.

- Use the Save a Copy command when cropping final elements out of a prototype document so you can revert to the original layered document and continue to make changes or revisions.

CHAPTER 18 HTML Templates for Designers

I first had the idea of making HTML templates during a computer graphics faculty meeting at Art Center less than a year ago. We were discussing our Web site long before we had even purchased a server, wondering how to educate 1200 students in HTML and Web graphics so they could participate on our site. It struck me then: why not create a standard HTML document that students could follow, much like a template? It would be a simple matter of having a master document and having students save their work with the correct size and name, and boom, they could have a Web page.

Not knowing a word of HTML myself at that point, I made a commitment to the rest of the faculty that each of my students would have a Web page by the end of the following term. I teach close to 100 students each semester in subjects that range from print graphics to multimedia to video graphics. These classes are far too demanding to ask students to additionally learn about HTML and making a Web page, so I was pretty excited by the prospect of making it possible for them.

trip with him on a syquest disk that had failed. He and his prospective client instead logged on to the Web and saw his motion graphics projects from half a world away. Another student said someone from a film production company in Washington D.C. called her because he saw her work on the Web site and liked it. I'm sure stories like this will multiply exponentially as our site becomes a hub for prospective students, designers, and design enthusiasts looking for inspiration.

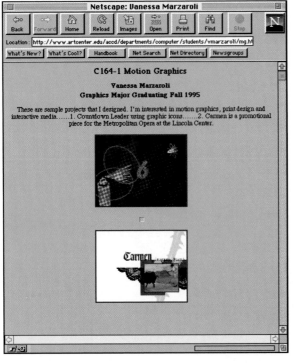

Figure 18.1

The results of a template from the Motion Graphics class at Art Center.

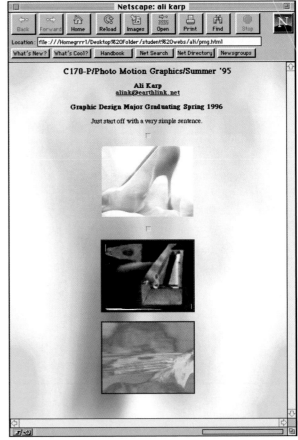

Figure 18.2

The results of a template from the Photo Motion Graphics class at Art Center.

The experiment worked (see figs. 18.1 through 18.3). At the end of last term it took me an entire day to upload 100 MB of images, movies, and HTML text to our server, but you can go to http://www.artcenter.edu and see the student work from any of the classes I taught. Over break, one student emailed me from Norway to say he had brought his work on the

Templates can offer students of all origins (including those of you reading this book) the opportunity to get results by doing, rather than by studying first and then doing. I think most of us want feedback and gratification right away when learning something new. Chances are that the following exercises will demystify HTML and the design process so you have more courage and foundation to try things on your own.

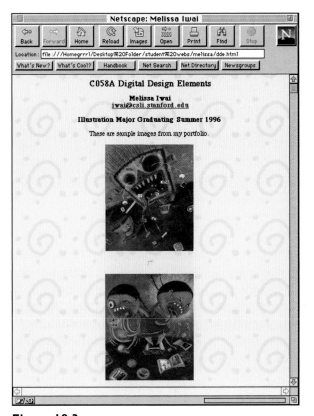

Figure 18.3
The results of a template from the Digital Design Elements class at Art Center.

The disadvantage to working with templates is that they are rigid and look predictable and boring after a while. The truly great work is done outside of a template, but if this is a stepping stone to helping you develop your first Web presence, then use it for that and take it further once you're comfortable. For my purpose—I wanted to gently introduce my students to the advantages of being on the Web without going through the work—the templates were a big success. They certainly pale in comparison to what would be expected from a Web graphics design class where students were writing their own HTML and creating their own concepts.

Working with the Templates

We have included all of the templates demonstrated in this chapter on the CD-ROM that ships with this book. If you don't have a CD-ROM player, you can still follow along, by re-typing the code you'll find here.

It's important that you have a browser on your hard drive to test these templates. I recommend that you download Netscape from http://www.netscape.com. When I wrote this book, beta versions of Netscape were available free to students and staff of academic institutions and charitable non-profit organizations, and for 90-day evaluation by individuals and commercial users. A *beta version* of a product is one that is not in its final release form. When the final release is available, users can purchase supported, licensed copies of Netscape Navigator directly from Netscape Communications or from a Netscape authorized reseller. I predict you'll decide to purchase the software if you are serious about working with Web graphics.

These templates work by filling in the colored areas on the pages with your own text, information, and images. Put all the images, HTML, and external files in the same folder and Netscape will be able to find them. Everything in magenta represents information to fill in your own information, such as an email address, or a title. Everything in cyan represented art-based files, such as images and movies. Sample artwork used in this document is available in the Chapter 18 folder on the *Designing Web Graphics* CD-ROM. Don't let that stop you from putting your own art and movies in here, though!

An HTML document always begins in some type of word processer. If you have the CD-ROM, these files can be opened in any word processer or text editor. Those of you who don't have CD-ROM drives, fire up your favorite word processer, and follow along. Be sure to save the documents in text mode (ASCII) and put an extension .html at the end. (Pre-Windows 95 users can put .htm at the end, because three letter extensions are what your operating system allows.)

The following files are supplied on the CD-ROM, should you choose to use them. You can also create your own files using these same file names, or change the file names within the template.

- jamie.gif
- pat.gif
- type.gif
- smiley.gif
- sample1.gif
- sample1.mov
- sample2.gif
- sample2.mov

The following templates will introduce you to many HTML commands and image and movie handling procedures for Web publishing, such as type treatments, alignment, tables, hexadecimal code, and working with background patterns. Try typing them yourself, or follow along with the electronic versions found on the CD-ROM.

Hexadecimal Template

The hexadecimal template allows you to put your own hexadecimal values into it, to experiment with changing background, text, links, borders, and visited link colors. For more information on hexadecimal HTML codes, see Chapter 5, "Fun with Hex."

```
<html>
<head>
<body bgcolor="ffffff" text ="ffffff" link ="ffffff" alink="ffffff"
vlink="ffffff">
</head>
<a href="http://www.domain.com"><img src="jamie.gif
"border="ffffff"></a>
</body>
</html>
```

Be sure to change these colors from white (ffffff)! Otherwise, you'll get white type on a white background. The <a href="http://www.domain.com"><img src="jamie.gif"border="ffffff"></a> is so you can test the colored border around a linked image. The color you choose for the image's border will be dictated by what value is put in the <body border=""> tag. Figure 18.4 is an example of what this screen would look like if you'd filled in the code this way, using the jamie.gif image:

```
<html>
<head>
<body bgcolor="ffffff" text ="009900" link ="cc00ff" alink="ff0000"
vlink="cc3333">
</head>
<a href="http://www.domain.com"><img src="jamie.gif"></a>
<p>
<a href="http://www.domain.com">Si meliora</a>
dies, ut vina, poemata reddit, scire velim, chartis pretium quotus arro-
get annus. scriptor abhinc annos centum qui decidit, inter perfectos
veteresque referri debet an inter vilis atque novos? Excludat iurgia
finis, "Est vetus atque probus, centum qui perficit annos." Quid, qui
deperiit minor uno mense vel anno, inter quos referendus erit? Veteresne
poetas, an quos et praesens et postera respuat aetas?
</body>
</html>
```

If I wanted the border around the image to be thicker (see fig. 18.5), I would choose to change that line of code from

```
<a href="http://www.domain.com"><img src="jamie.gif"></a>
```

to

```
<a href="http://www.domain.com"><img src="jamie.gif border=5></a>
```

I could also change it to <a href="http://www.domain.com"><img src="jamie.gif border=0></a> and get no border at all (see fig. 18.6).

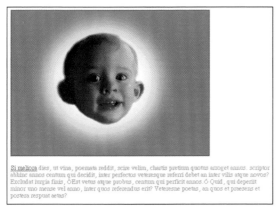

Figure 18.4
Jamie.gif with background, text, and visited link colors.

Si meliora dies, ut vina, poemata reddit, scire velim, chartis pretium quotus arroget annus. scriptor abhinc annos centum qui decidit, inter perfectos veteresque referri debet an inter vilis atque novos? Excludat iurgia finis, ÒEst vetus atque probus, centum qui perficit annos.Ó Quid, qui deperiit minor uno mense vel anno, inter quos referendus erit? Veteresne poetas, an quos et praesens et postera respuat aetas?

Figure 18.5

The jamie.gif image with a thicker border.

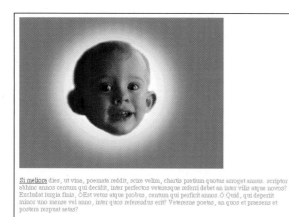

Si meliora dies, ut vina, poemata reddit, scire velim, chartis pretium quotus arroget annus. scriptor abhinc annos centum qui decidit, inter perfectos veteresque referri debet an inter vilis atque novos? Excludat iurgia finis, ÒEst vetus atque probus, centum qui perficit annos.Ó Quid, qui deperiit minor uno mense vel anno, inter quos referendus erit? Veteresne poetas, an quos et praesens et postera respuat aetas?

Figure 18.6

The jamie.gif image without a border.

Pattern Template

This template allows you to test your pattern tiles to see how they'll look. The file pat.gif is included on the CD-ROM, or use your own by studying techniques in Chapter 6, "Making Background Patterns." The HTML is very simple:

```
<html>
<body background="pat.gif">
</body>
<html>
```

Try using this code to test your own patterns. Either name your patterns pat.gif or change the HTML code to reflect the name of *your* jpeg or gif.

If you want to put text over the pattern background (see fig. 18.8) add this code:

```
<html>
<body background="pat.gif">
Some Text!
</body>
<html>
```

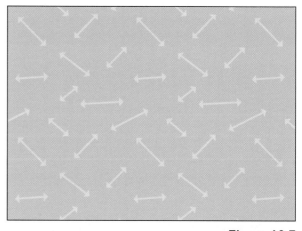

Figure 18.7

The page filled with a pattern.

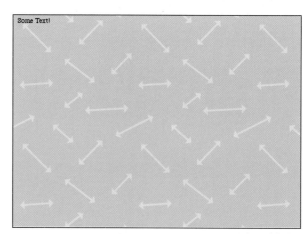

Figure 18.8

The results of adding text to the pattern HTML template.

Typography Template

This template allows you to test font sizes and headings. For more information on type for Web design, check out Chapter 9, "Typography for the Web-Impaired." Figure 18.9 shows the results of the following code.

```html
<html>
<head><H3> Here's a Headline of H3</H3></head>
<body>
<p>
Here's some regular body text. If I want to <font size=5> change font
sizes in the middle of my sentence, </font> it would look like this.
<p>
<pre>
I could     a   l   s   o       use pre-formatted text, like this.
</pre>
<p>
Then of course, I could always use an image of type instead:
<p>
<img src=type.gif>
</body>
</html>
```

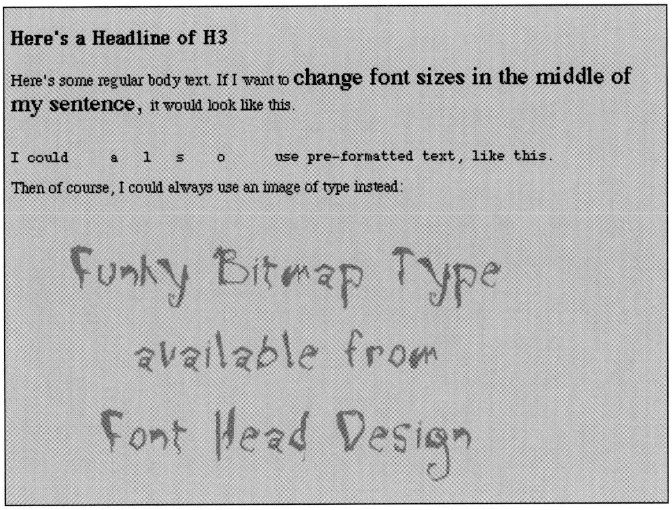

Figure 18.9

The results of the type HTML template.

Alignment Template

This template allows you to try some of the techniques we discussed in Chapter 10. The following code results in the screen shown in figure 18.10.

```
<html>
<body>
<center>Here is centered<br>text and image.<P>
<img src="smiley.gif"></center><p>
<img src="smiley.gif"> Here's text and an image with no alignment tags
<p>
<img src="smiley.gif" align=top> Here's text aligned to the top of the
image <p>
<img src="spacer.gif"><img src="smiley.gif"<p>
Here's an image next to an invisible spacer.
<body>
</html>
```

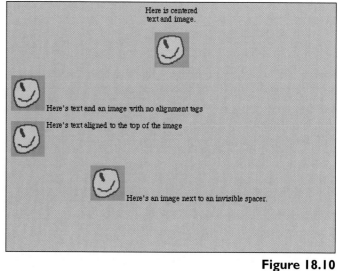

Figure 18.10
Different text and image alignments.

Table Template

This template allows you to try some tables. See the examples in figure 18.11.

```
<html>
<table border>
<tr><td>word </td><td>word </td><td>word </td><td>word </td></tr>
<tr><td>word </td><td>word </td><td>word </td><td>word </td></tr>
<tr><td>word </td><td>word </td><td>word </td><td>word </td></tr>
<tr><td>word </td><td>word </td><td>word </td><td>word </td></tr>
</table>
<p>
<table>
```

```
<tr><td><img src="smiley.gif"></td><td><img src="smiley.gif"></td><td><img
src="smiley.gif"></td><td><img src="smiley.gif"></td></tr>
<tr><td><img src="smiley.gif"></td><td><img src="smiley.gif"></td><td><img
src="smiley.gif"></td><td><img src="smiley.gif"></td></tr>
<tr><td><img src="smiley.gif"></td><td><img src="smiley.gif"></td><td><img
src="smiley.gif"></td><td><img src="smiley.gif"></td></tr>
<tr><td><img src="smiley.gif"></td><td><img src="smiley.gif"></td><td><img
src="smiley.gif"></td><td><img src="smiley.gif"></td></tr>
</table>
</html>
```

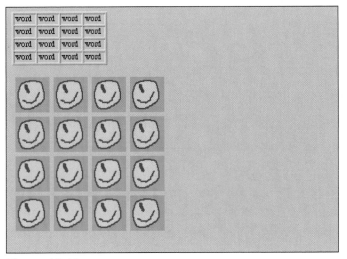

Figure 18.11
Examples of tables using the table template.

Step-by-Step—Motion Graphics Class Template

Here's a copy of the template my Motion Graphics students at Art Center worked with. These students made two movies over the course of one semester. The idea was to include their movies in small thumbnail form and a little information about themselves on each page. This template shows how to include a return email address, use centered and bold-faced type, and link a thumbnail image to a movie file.

```
<html>
<title>Student's Name</title>
<BODY background= "pat.gif">
<center>
<h3>C164-1 Motion Graphics</h3>
<p>
<p>
<body>
<strong>
Joe Student<br>
124 Your Street Name<br>
```

```
City, State zip<br>
818.555.5555<br>
<A HREF="mailto:emailname@provider.com">jstudent@artcenter.edu</a><p>
<p>
Advertising Major
Graduating Winter 1996</strong>
<P>
Say something here about your work, if you want to...
<P>
<P>
<a href="sample1.mov"><img src="sample1.gif"></a>
<P>
<hr size=8 width=8>
<P>
<a href="sample2.mov"><img src="sample2.gif"></a>
<P>
</center>
</body>
</html>
```

1. Fill in all the magenta text with your own information.

2. Prepare the art and media that's requested in cyan. It's *critical* that the art be named exactly as you see it in the template.

The pat.gif document should be a tiled background source image. Students were instructed to make the tile 100×100 pixels, though any size would work, as you know if you studied Chapter 6. Creating this pattern file was optional; if they chose not to have one, the screen would appear with the browser gray background, even though the tag was not removed from the HTML document. Feel free to use the file pat.gif supplied on the CD-ROM.

The sample1. mov and sample2.mov documents represent movie documents. Students were instructed to reduce their final projects to 160×120 movies, compress them in Cinepak to make flattened QuickTime format. For more information on this process, see Chapter 16. Feel free to use the files sample1.mov and sample2.mov on the CD-ROM.

The sample1.gif and sample2.gif are images that link to the movies. They were taken from frames of the QuickTime movie and saved as 160×120 pixel images in the Gif file format. This proceedure is documented in Chapter 16. Feel free to use the files sample1.gif and sample2.gif on the CD-ROM.

3. Make sure that the HTML document is saved in Text only format and has the extension .html or .htm at the end of it. Put all the art and media files in the same folder as the HTML document.

4. Open Netscape. Choose Open File and locate the folder with your .html text document. Provided you've named everything exactly as it appears in the template, and have saved the text file in ASCII mode, your page should preview just as it would appear on a Web site.

Refer to figures 18.1, 18.2, and 18.3 at the beginning of this chapter for the final results of the Art Center Student Web Templates.

Summary

Once you've worked with all these templates, you could try mixing them up, like using a patterned background with hexadecimal colored type. They can be cut and pasted into each other for interesting experiments and the launching pad for pages of your own design. Here are some rules to follow when working with these templates:

- Fill in the templates with your own information wherever you see magenta, and include artwork file names wherever you see cyan.

- Make sure the HTML documents are saved as text only files (ASCII) and reside in the same folder as the artwork the template uses.

- Use Netscape to test these templates from your hard drive.

- Experiment with your own artwork and mixing and matching templates. Refer to Appendix A, "HTML for Visual Designers" to study HTML structure and learn how to mix and match tags.

- If you like someone's Web page, study their source code, and treat it like the templates you see here. This is the best way to teach yourself HTML.

> **NOTE**
>
> If you include movies on a Web page template, you will not be able to download the files until they are posted on an actual Web server. This test cannot be done from a hard drive.

APPENDIX A HTML for Visual Designers

I always find myself fumbling through three different HTML books and several online sources to find the exact tag I'm looking for. This chapter was designed to save you (ok, me too) the time and hassle of searching through each chapter to find the code you know you read about somewhere.

Everything here is presented in summary form and reviews key tips that have been covered elsewhere in the book for creating, troubleshooting, and uploading Web pages. The HTML list is not meant to be definitive; it's intentionally tailored for Web graphic design needs. Look to this chapter when you need a quick reference guide, once you've finished reading the rest of the book.

Naming Protocols

Always use lowercase letters in file names and do not use spaces. If you have spaces between the title of your document—such as my document name.extension—either string it together, like: mydocumentname.extension, or use underscores, as in: my_document_name.extension.

If you are working with files that are going to be downloaded by your audience, such as audio and video files, remember to abbreviate names so they're under eight characters in the main title, and leave room for a period and three letter extension so Windows platform users' systems can access them, such as mydocunm.ext.

Common File Extensions

You must give images and media the proper file-name extensions so the browser reading your HTML can display them properly. The following is a list of the most common file types.

Name	Extension
HTML text document	.html
JPEG	.jpg
GIF	.gif
Quicktime movie	.mov, .qt
Video for Windows	.avi
MPEG Video	.mpg
MPEG Audio	.mp2
AU/μlaw	.au
AIFF/AIFC	.aiff
WAV	.wav

Checking Your Pages

You should always check your pages from your hard drive before you post them to your server. This way you will catch a lot of HTML and art-work mistakes before the rest of the world knows you made them. Be sure that all your artwork and HTML files are in one folder. Open your browser and then open your HTML ASCII (text only) document from there. All the images should load in properly and give a very accurate preview of what your page will look like once it's on the Web. For a step-by-step review of this process, check out Chapter 18, "HTML Templates for Designers."

Troubleshooting

If your page tested properly off your local hard drive, but not when you posted the files to the server, make sure the file names you requested in your HTML match the names of the actual document. Unix is case-sensitive, meaning if your file is saved JPG and your HTML calls for it as jpg, the code will not be able to read the file. Because you are most likely not on a Unix platform, this problem will not surface until you post your files and view them from a browser.

If your file is named jamie.gif and your HTML reads <img src="jamie.GIF"> it won't work! Redo the <img src> tag to read <img src="jamie.gif">.

Uploading Your Pages

Most likely, you'll need a password and authorization name to access either your, or your client's, Web server. This would be obtained from your online service provider or your client.

Whenever you transfer elements for a Web page to your server, remember these things:

■ Transfer the HTML document as Text Only (ASCII).

■ Transfer the image, sound, and movie files as Raw Data on Macs and as Image or Binary mode on PCs.

The Basic Structure of an HTML Document

```
<HTML>
  <HEAD>
    <title><meta>
  </HEAD>
  <BODY> or <Body bg color><body background><body text>
    Body of the document
    (all the text, images, links, etc.)
  </BODY>
</HTML>
```

■ HTML is not case sensitive (upper- and lowercase). The tag <HTML> will be just as effective as the tag <html>

■ Always save an HTML document in text only mode (ASCII) with the extension .html or .htm at the end.

Common HTML Tags

Table A.1 shows the various HTML tags and what they are used for. The table is divided into sections containing HTML tag information on the following:

Table A.1	HTML Tag Information
Tag	Description
Head Tags	
<head></head>	Enables you to use a headline or title tag within the document.
<H#></H#>	Enables you to set sizes inside header tags (H1, H2, H3).
<title></title>	Enables you to name the HTML document. Whatever you put inside this tag will show up in the title bar of your browser.
Body Tags	
<body bgcolor =# text=# link=#alink=#vlink=#> </body>	The following tags allow you to change the colors of your background, text, links and so on in browsers that support it. They belong inside the <body> tag. (Check the chart in Chapter 1.)

continues

Table A.1   Continued

Tag	Description
text=#	Sets text color.
link=#	Sets link colors for text and borders around images.
alink=#	Sets the link color when the mouse is clicked in the down position.
vlink=#	Sets the visited link color for text and borders around images.
<body background= "patterntile.gif"></body>	Using the <body background> tag allows you to load tiled background patterns to your Web pages.
<meta http-equiv=refresh content=#;URL=#>	Allows you to perform client pull effects, where you automatically send your viewers to another URL without their requesting it.

Text Tags

Tag	Description
<strong></strong>	Makes text bold.
<b></b>	Makes text bold.
<em></em>	Italicizes type.
<i></i>	Italicizes type.
<pre></pre>	Allows you to work with pre-formatted type.
<code></code>	Used for computer codes.
 	Denotes a line break.
<p>	Denotes a paragraph break.
<font size=#></font>	Enables you to change font sizes.
<tt></tt>	Denotes the typewriter style (monospaced font).
<font color=#></font>	Sets the color of type.

Horizontal Rule Tags

Tag	Description
<hr>	Creates a standard embossed horizontal rule.
<hr width=#>	Changes the length in pixels.
<hr size=#>	Changes the height in pixels.
<hr width=# align=left, right, center>	Aligns a horizontal rule that's shorter than the distance of your entire page.
<hr noshade>	Creates a plain black line.

Alignment Tags for Text

Tag	Description
<center></center>	Centers text or images inside this tag.

Tag	Description
Alignment Tags for Images	
<img src="#" align="top, middle, bottom, left, right">	Aligns text to the top, middle, bottom, left, or right of image inside this tag.
Image Tags	
<img src="#">	Contains an image.
<img src="#" alt="#">	Contains an image and a text description for viewers who don't have graphical Web browsers.
<img src="#"height=# width=#>	Allows for specifying image dimensions and causes the HTML text to load before large graphics.
<a href="#"><img src="#"></a>	Contains a linked image and automatically generates a border around the image in whatever link color has been specified.
<a href="#"><img src="#" border=0></a>	Insures that there's no border on browsers that support this feature.
<a href="#"><img src="#" border=#></a>	Depending on the value, puts a heavier or lighter border around the linked image.
List Tags	
<UL>	Unorganized list: Generates an indented list with bullets.
<OL>	Organized list: Generates numbers in front of list.
<LI>	Puts a bullet in front of each item, indents the text, and creates a line break at the end of each item.
<DL>	Definition list: Produces an indented list with no bullets.
<DD>	Produces items in a definition list.
Table Tags	
<table><table>	Put at the beginning and end of tables.
<th></th>	Makes bold text or numbers and accepts table attributes.
<td></td>	Includes text, numbers, or images and accepts table attributes.
Table Attributes	
align="left, right or center"	Aligns text or images in table.
valign="top middle, bottom, or baseline"	Vertically aligns text or images in table.
rowspan=#	Denotes the number of rows in a table.
colspan=#	Denotes the number of columns in a table.

continues

WWW.

Table A.1 Continued	
Tag	Description
width=#	Specifies the width of the table by pixels.
Linking Tags	
<a></a>	Anchors text.
<a href="URL"></a>	Links the image or text to an URL.
Comments Tag	
<!—...—>	Sets comments that appear as notes for the HTML document but won't show up on the actual Web page.

Glossary

8-bit graphics   A color or grayscale graphic or movie that has 256 colors or less.

8-bit sound   8-bit sounds have a dynamic range of 48 dB. Dynamic range is the measure of steps between the volume or amplitude of a sound.

16-bit graphics   A color image or movie that has 65.5 thousand colors.

16-bit sound   Standard CD-quality sound resolution. 16-bit sounds have a dynamic range of 96 dB.

24-bit graphics   A color image or movie that has 16.7 million colors.

32-bit graphics   A color image or movie that has 16.7 million colors, plus an 8-bit masking channel.

adaptive dithering   A form of dithering in which the program looks to the image to determine the best set of colors when creating an 8-bit or smaller palette. See *dithering*.

aliasing   In bitmapped graphics, the jagged boundary along the edges of different-colored shapes within an image. See *anti-aliasing*.

anti-aliasing   A technique for reducing the jagged appearance of aliased bitmapped images, usually by inserting pixels that blend at the boundaries between adjacent colors.

artifacts   Image imperfections caused by compression.

authoring tools   Creation tools for interactive media.

AVI   Audio-Video Interleaved. Microsoft's file format for desktop video movies.

bit depth   The number of bits used to represent the color of each pixel in a given movie or still image. Specifically: Bit depth of 2 = black and white pixels. Bit depth of 4 = 16 colors or grays. Bit depth of 8 = 256 colors or grays. Bit depth of 16 = 65,536 colors. Bit depth of 24 = (approximately) 16 million colors.

bitmapped graphics   Graphics that are pixel-based, as opposed to object oriented. Bitmapped graphics are what the computer can display, because it's a pixel-based medium, whereas object oriented graphics can be viewed in high resolution once they are sent to a printer. Graphics on the Web are bitmapped because they are in a computer screen-based delivery system. See *object-oriented graphics*.

browser   An application that enables you to access World Wide Web pages. Most browsers provide the capability to view Web pages, copy and print material from Web pages, download files over the Web, and navigate throughout the Web.

cache   A storage area that keeps frequently accessed data or program instructions readily available so that you do not have to retrieve them repeatedly.

CGI   Common Gateway Interface. A Web standard for the methods servers and external programs and scripts used to communicate.

client   A computer that requests information from a network's server. See *server*.

CLUT   Color LookUp Table. An 8-bit or lower image file uses a CLUT to define its palette.

codec   *C*ompressor/*dec*ompressor. A piece of software that encodes and decodes movie data.

color mapping   A color map refers to the color palette of an image. Color mapping means assigning colors to an image.

compression   Reduction of the amount of data required to re-create an original file, graphic, or movie. Compression is used to reduce the transmission time of media and application files across the Web.

data streaming   The capability to deliver time-based data as it's requested, much like a VCR, rather than having to download all the information before it can be played.

dithering   The positioning of different colored pixels within an image that uses a 256 color palette to simulate a color that does not exist in the palette. A dithered image often looks noisy, or composed of scattered pixels. See *adaptive dithering*.

dynamic   Information that changes over a period of time. Typically refers to time-based media, such as animation or interactive documents.

extension   Abbreviated code at the end of a file that tells the browser what kind of file it's looking at. Example: a JPEG file would have the extension .jpg.

external graphic   Graphics that must be downloaded from the Web, instead of being viewed directly from a Web page. See *inline graphic* and *links*.

fixed palette   An established palette that is fixed. When a fixed palette Web browser views images, it will convert images to its colors and not use the colors from the original.

FTP File transfer protocol. An Internet protocol that enables users to remotely access files on other computers. An FTP site houses files that can be downloaded to your computer.

gamma Gamma measures the contrast that affects the midtones of an image. Adjusting the gamma lets you change the brightness values of the middle range of gray tones without dramatically altering the shadows and highlights.

GIF A bitmapped color graphics file format. GIF is commonly used on the Web because it employs an efficient compression method. See *JPEG*.

HTML Hypertext Markup Language. The common language for interchange of hypertext between the World Wide Web client and server. Web pages must be written using HTML. See *hypertext*.

hypertext Text formatted with links that enable the reader to jump among related topics. See *HTML*.

image maps Portions of images that are hypertext links. Using a mouse-based Web client such as Netscape or Mosaic, the user clicks on different parts of a mapped image to activate different hypertext links. See *hypertext*.

inline graphic A graphic that can be displayed directly on a Web page. See *external graphic*.

interlaced GIFs The GIF file format allows for "interlacing," which causes the GIF to load quickly at low or chunky resolution and then come into full or crisp resolution.

ISP Acronym for Internet Service Provider.

JPEG Acronym for Joint Photographic Experts Group, but commonly used to refer to a lossy compression technique that can reduce the size of a graphics file by as much as 96 percent. See *GIF*.

links Emphasized words in a hypertext document that act as pointers to more information on that specific subject. Links are generally underlined and may appear in a different color. When you click on a link, you can be transported to a different Web site that contains information about the word or phrase used as the link. See *hypertext*.

live object Netscape's term for plug-ins that enable the browser to play image, movie, and sound files as an inline component of a Web page.

lossless compression A data compression technique that reduces the size of a file without sacrificing any of the original data. In lossless compression, the expanded or restored file is an exact replica of the original file before it was compressed. See *compression* and *lossy compression*.

lossy compression   A data compression technique in which some data is deliberately discarded in order to achieve massive reductions in the size of the compressed file.

MIME   Multipurpose Internet Mail Extensions. An Internet standard for transferring file non-text-based data such as sounds, movies, and images.

object-oriented graphics   A graphic image composed of autonomous objects such as lines, circles, ellipses, and boxes that can be moved independently. This type of graphic is used for print-based design because it can be printed at a higher resolution than a computer screen. See *bitmapped graphics*.

Postscript   A sophisticated page description language used for printing high-quality text and graphics on laser printers and other high-resolution printing devices.

provider   Provides Internet access. See *ISP*.

QuickTime   System software developed by Apple Computer for presentation of desktop video.

server   A computer that provides services for users of its network. The server receives requests for services and manages the requests so that they are answered in an orderly manner. See *client*.

splash screen   A main menu screen, or opening graphic to a Web page.

sprite   An individual component of an animation, such as a character or graphic that moves independently.

tag   ASCII text indicators with which you surround text and images to designate certain formats or styles.

transparent GIFs   A subset of the original GIF file format that adds header information to the GIF file, which signifies that a defined color will be masked out.

true color   The quality of color provided by 24-bit color depth. 24-bit color depth results in 16.7 million colors, which is usually more than adequate for the human eye.

URL   Uniform Resource Locator. The address for a Web site.

Video for Windows   A multimedia architecture and application suite that provides an outbound architecture that lets applications developers access audio, video, and animation from many different sources through one interface. As an application, Video for Windows primarily handles video capture and compression, and video and audio editing. See *AVI*.

WYSIWYG   Pronounced *wizzy-wig*. A design philosophy in which formatting commands directly affect the text displayed on-screen, so that the screen shows the appearance of the printed text.

Index

Adobe Systems Incorporated
End User License Agreement

NOTICE TO USER:

THIS IS A CONTRACT. BY OPENING THIS PACKAGE YOU ACCEPT ALL THE TERMS AND CONDITIONS OF THIS AGREEMENT. If you do not agree with the terms and conditions of this Agreement, return this media envelope, UNOPENED, along with the rest of the package, to Adobe Systems Incorporated ("Adobe") or the location where you obtained it.

This package contains software ("Software") and related explanatory written materials ("Documentation"). The term "Software" shall also include any upgrades, modified versions, updates, additions and copies of the Software licensed to you by Adobe. Adobe grants to you a nonexclusive license to use the Software and Documentation, provided that you agree to the following:

1. Use of the Software. You may—

- Install the Software in a single location on a hard disk or other storage device of up to the number of computers indicated in the "Permitted Number of Computers" section of this Agreement

- Provided the Software is configured for network use, install and use the Software on a single file server for use on a single local area network for either (but not both) of the following purposes:

    (1) permanent installation onto a hard disk or other storage device of up to the Permitted Number of Computers; or

    (2) use of the Software over such network, provided the number of different computers on which the Software is used does not exceed the Permitted Number of Computers. For example, if there are 100 computers connected to the server, with no more than 15 computers ever using the Software concurrently, but the Software will be used on 25 different computers at various times, the Permitted Number of Computers for which you need a license is 25.

- Make one backup copy of the Software, provided your backup copy is not installed or used on any computer.

Home Use. The primary user of each computer on which the Software is installed or used may also install the Software on one home or portable computer. However, the Software may not be used on the secondary computer by another person at the same time the Software on the primary computer is being used.

Font Software. If the Software includes font software, you may—

- Use the font software as described above on the Permitted Number of Computers and output such font software on any output devices connected to such computers.

- If the Number of Permitted Computers is five or fewer, download the font software to the memory (hard disk or RAM) of one output device connected to at least one of such computers for the purpose of having such font software remain resident in the output device, and of one additional such output device for every multiple of five represented by the Number of Permitted Computers.

- Take a copy of the font(s) you have used for a particular file to a commercial printer or other service bureau, and such service bureau may use the font(s) to process your file, provided such service bureau has informed you that it has purchased or been granted a license to use that particular font software.

- Convert and install the font software into another format for use in other environments, subject to the following conditions: A computer on which the converted font software is used or installed shall be considered as one of your Permitted Number of Computers. You agree that use of the font software you have converted shall be pursuant to all the terms and conditions of this Agreement, and that such font software may be used only for your own customary internal business or personal use and that such font software may not be distributed or transferred for any purpose, except in accordance with Paragraph 3 below.

2. Copyright. The Software is owned by Adobe and its suppliers, and its structure, organization and code are the valuable trade secrets of Adobe and its suppliers. The Software is also protected by United States Copyright Law and International Treaty provisions. You must treat the Software just as you would any other copyrighted material, such as a book. You may not copy the Software or the Documentation, except as set forth in the "Use of the Software" section. Any copies that you are permitted to make pursuant to this Agreement must contain the same copyright and other proprietary notices that appear on or in the Software. Except for font software converted to other formats as permitted in the "Use of the Software" section, you agree not to modify, adapt or translate the Software. You also agree not to reverse engineer, decompile, disassemble or otherwise attempt to discover the source code of the Software. Trademarks shall be used in accordance with accepted trademark practice, including identification of trademark owner's name. Trademarks can only be used to identify printed output produced by the Software. Such use of any trademark does not give you any rights of ownership in that trademark. Except as stated above, this Agreement does not grant you any intellectual property rights in the Software.

3. Transfer. You may not rent, lease, sublicense or lend the Software or Documentation. You may, however, transfer all your rights to use the Software to another person or legal entity provided that you transfer this Agreement, the Software, including all copies, updates and prior versions and all copies of font software converted into other formats, and all Documentation to such person or entity and that you retain no copies, including copies stored on a computer.

4. Multiple Environment Software/Multiple Language Software/Dual Media Software/ Multiple Copies/Upgrades. If this package contains, or, in connection with the acquisition of the Software contained in this package you receive, two or more operating environment versions of the Software (e.g., Macintosh® and Windows®), two or more language translation versions of the Software, the same Software on two or more media (e.g., diskettes and a CD-ROM), and/or you otherwise receive two or more copies of the Software, the total aggregate number of computers on which all versions of the Software are used may not exceed the Permitted Number of Computers. You may make one back-up copy, in accordance with the terms of this Agreement, for each version of the Software you use. You may not rent, lease, sublicense, lend or transfer versions or copies of the Software you do not use, or Software contained on any unused media, except as part of the permanent transfer of all Software and Documentation as described above. If you acquire an upgrade or update for Software, you may use the previous version for ninety (90) days after you receive the new version in order to assist you in the transition to the new version, after which time you no longer have a license to use the previous version, and all copies thereof, including copies installed on computers, must be destroyed.

5. Limited Warranty. Adobe warrants to you that the Software will perform substantially in accordance with the Documentation for the ninety (90) day period following your receipt of the Software. This warranty does not apply to font software converted into other formats. To make a warranty claim, you must return the Software to the location where you obtained it along with a copy of your sales receipt within such ninety (90) day period. If the Software does not perform substantially in accordance with the Documentation, the entire and exclusive liability and remedy shall be limited to either, at Adobe's option, the replacement of the Software or the refund of the license fee you paid for the Software. ADOBE AND ITS SUPPLIERS DO NOT AND CANNOT WARRANT THE PERFORMANCE OR RESULTS YOU MAY OBTAIN BY USING THE SOFTWARE OR DOCUMENTATION. THE FOREGOING STATES THE SOLE AND EXCLUSIVE REMEDIES FOR ADOBE'S OR ITS SUPPLIERS' BREACH OF WARRANTY. EXCEPT FOR THE FOREGOING LIMITED WARRANTY, ADOBE AND ITS SUPPLIERS MAKE NO WARRANTIES, EXPRESS OR IMPLIED, AS TO NON-INFRINGEMENT OF THIRD–PARTY RIGHTS, MERCHANTABILITY, OR FITNESS FOR ANY PARTICULAR PURPOSE. Some states or jurisdictions do not allow the exclusion of implied warranties or limitations on how long an implied warranty may last, so the above limitations may not apply to you. To the extent permissible, any implied warranties are limited to ninety (90) days. This warranty gives you specific legal rights. You may have other rights which vary from state to state or jurisdiction to jurisdiction. For further warranty information, please contact Adobe's Customer Support Department.

6. Limitation of Liability. IN NO EVENT WILL ADOBE OR ITS SUPPLIERS BE LIABLE TO YOU FOR ANY CONSEQUENTIAL, INCIDENTAL OR SPECIAL DAMAGES, INCLUDING ANY LOST PROFITS OR LOST SAVINGS, EVEN IF AN ADOBE REPRESENTATIVE HAS BEEN ADVISED OF THE POSSIBILITY OF SUCH DAMAGES, OR FOR ANY CLAIM BY ANY THIRD PARTY. Some states or jurisdictions do not allow the exclusion or limitation of incidental, consequential or special damages, so the above limitations may not apply to you.

7. Governing Law and General Provisions. This Agreement will be governed by the laws in force in the State of California excluding the application of its conflicts of law rules. This Agreement will not be governed by the United Nations Convention on Contracts for the International Sale of Goods, the application of which is expressly excluded. If any part of this Agreement is found void and unenforceable, it will not affect the validity of the balance of the Agreement, which shall remain valid and enforceable according to its terms. You agree that the Software will not be shipped, transferred or exported into any country or used in any manner prohibited by the United States Export Administration Act or any other export laws, restrictions or regulations. This Agreement shall automatically terminate upon failure by you to comply with its terms. This Agreement may only be modified in writing signed by an authorized officer of Adobe.

8. Notice to Government End Users. If this product is acquired under the terms of a: GSA contract- Use, reproduction or disclosure is subject to the restrictions set forth in the applicable ADP Schedule contract; DoD contract- Use, duplication or disclosure by the Government is subject to restrictions as set forth in subparagraph (c) (1) (ii) of 252.227-7013; Civilian agency contract- Use, reproduction or disclosure is subject to 52.227-19 (a) through (d) and restrictions set forth in the accompanying end user agreement. Unpublished rights reserved under the copyright laws of the United States. Adobe Systems Incorporated, 1585 Charleston Road, P.O. Box 7900, Mountain View, CA 94039-7900.

Adobe is a trademark of Adobe Systems Incorporated. Macintosh is a registered trademark of Apple Computer, Inc. Windows is a registered trademark of Microsoft Corporation.

Copyright ©1995. Adobe Systems Incorporated. Printed in the U.S.A. 0397 0986 7/95